The Learning Theory of Piaget and Inhelder

The Learning Theory of Piaget and Inhelder

Jeanette McCarthy Gallagher
TEMPLE UNIVERSITY

D. Kim Reid
THE UNIVERSITY OF TEXAS AT DALLAS

5341 Industrial Oaks Blvd.
Austin, Tx. 78735

Printed in the United States of America
10 9 8 7 6 5 4 3

Library of Congress Cataloging in Publication Data

Gallagher, Jeanette McCarthy, 1932–
    The learning theory of Piaget and Inhelder.

    Originally published: Monterey, Calif.: Brooks/Cole Pub. Co., c1981.
    Bibliography: p.
    Includes indexes.
    1. Learning, Psychology of. 2. Cognition. 3. Piaget,
Jean, 1896–   . 4. Inhelder, Bärbel. I. Reid, D. Kim.
II. Title.
BF318.G34   1983   153.1'5   83-24533
ISBN 0-936104-36-8

5341 Industrial Oaks Blvd.
Austin, Tx. 78735

In memory of Jean Piaget,
whose work will touch the lives of our children,
Beth Marie Gallagher
David Francis Gallagher
John Paul Reid-Hresko

Foreword

We would like, first of all, to give warm thanks to the authors of this fine book for having asked us to write the Foreword. It is not often that one has the pleasure of receiving such a request. In this particular case, our pleasure is great because the book has real qualities.

The first of these qualities is that it reflects the authors' willingness—we would even say the courage—to present our ideas to a wide audience, which may not always be sufficiently informed to easily grasp them. These ideas have resulted from a long process of collaboration between us that still continues today. In fact, our work is not complete even with regard to the most important points. One misunderstanding of some authors, who may agree with us or criticize us, is to present our work as a finished product, when our interpretations and even the facts on which such interpretations are based are still in a state of reelaboration, as are the analyses of the experimental results on which our theories are founded. Even in regard to the central phenomenon of conservation, we have recently found simpler explanations based on just two ideas. First, all change of form is due only to displacements. Second, in all displacements that which is added at the point of arrival is necessarily equivalent to that which is taken away at the point of departure.

Another merit—and, without doubt, the principal one—of the authors of this book is having understood the importance that the intimate connection between cognitive processes and their biological roots has had for us all along. The authors have, therefore, well understood the importance that the phenomenon of phenocopy actually has for us. That importance lies in the fact that exogenous acquisitions are replaced by endogenous reconstructions, which lead more and more to the subordination of the exterior acquisitions to inferential models.

Still another merit of this work is the authors' insistence on the revisions that the theory of equilibration requires every time progress occurs in any of the diciplines that make use of this notion. For example, we must today take into account the progress of physics in the direction of autoregulatory systems (the "dissipative structures" of Prigogine and others).

We are also pleased with the depth of the authors' understanding of our current view of the stages of cognitive development. Without putting them in question, we see the stages as dependent on their formative mechanisms (such as the evolution of the idea of the possible and the necessary), while retaining their role as necessary instruments of description and analysis.

The same is true of psychological structures, the analysis of which must be refined and rerefined—which is what we are trying to do when we study the mechanisms of correspondence (morphisms and categories) as well as the role of the connections between actions or operations and not just between "statements" (without mentioning the formalizations to which our structures of groupings and others have given rise on the part of pure logicians such as Wermus and Wittman).

The only reservation we have about this book—and a small one indeed—is that the reader may not always be able to distinguish, especially in the more difficult passages, what comes from us and what is contributed by the authors of this work.

Finally, we wish to say how happy we are that the authors have so well understood the essential role that our collaboration has played in the development of our ideas in the course of a cooperation that has never ceased to be very close and fruitful.

Jean Piaget
Bärbel Inhelder

Preface

This book differs from all other introductions to Piaget's theory because of its emphasis on the biological model and on regulatory mechanisms rather than on stages. In order to understand how a child moves from one stage of cognitive development to another—that is, in order to understand equilibration—it is essential to grasp the importance of regulatory mechanisms. It is only within the last few years that Piaget and the Genevan School have elaborated on the meaning of equilibration, or the self-regulation of how one comes to know. Research on causality clarified the importance of feedback from observables in modifying the actions of a person engaged in an activity and led Piaget to modify his model of equilibration. The notion of feedback, which is, of course, directly related to traditional learning-theory approaches in psychology, is a key concept in this book.

The Learning Theory of Piaget and Inhelder is an historic first in other ways, too. It is the first attempt to gather together concepts and research studies of Piaget's cognitive theory that directly relate to a learning theory. Since Bärbel Inhelder has in the past and continues in the present to play a key role in the design of studies of learning in the Genevan School, our book devotes much attention to her work, as the title of this volume indicates. Piaget often refers to Inhelder as his psychologist—in this case, the one who designs and implements empirical studies following from his theory. In significant areas, Inhelder has actually pioneered movements into new directions, and some of her recent training and strategy studies are essential to the formulation of a learning theory.

This book is also the first attempt to summarize, for both the student and the scholar, Piaget's new model of equilibration. We were aided in this endeavor by an excellent unpublished translation of Volume 33 of *Studies in Genetic Epistemology,* which we were able to use for three years before a published translation was available. Not only the model itself but also the training studies by Inhelder, Sinclair, and Bovet, as well as the Genevan studies in contradiction, awareness, reflexive abstraction, and correspondences, which we have included in our discussion, support aspects of equilibration relating directly or indirectly to learning.

Finally, this volume incorporates important concepts of Piaget's biological model, especially phenocopy, most of which were up to now presented only in untranslated works. Past introductions to Piaget's work emphasized the logical model to such a degree that, especially in the United States, Piaget's theory was misinterpreted as a theory of the development of logic. Our emphasis, like that of the Genevan School, is on the confluence of the logical and the biological models in the study of the development of natural thought—a confluence that represents the basis of Piaget's theory.

This book is designed for both students and scholars who want an up-to-date view of developmental epistemology from the perspective of learning. No attempt was made to incorporate all areas of research of the Genevan School. By emphasizing certain themes related to learning, we hope to encourage further research and applications in educational settings.

Sections of the book were used successfully in undergraduate and graduate courses in both psychology and education. Because instructors may wish to use single chapters or sections of the text, some basic concepts are repeated throughout the book, so that various chapters can stand on their own.

The four speeches by Piaget and Inhelder in Appendix B were included to encourage students to read *original* works and, eventually, the theoretical and research books of the Genevan School. New terms and difficult concepts are defined and clarified in the Glossary at the end of the book.

We were aided in our endeavor by the kind assistance of many scholars. Mr. Nicole and Mlle Monnier, Head Librarians at the Jean Piaget Archives, University of Geneva, were helpful in finding references and in making new manuscripts available to us. During the time we visited Geneva to study in the Archives, Bärbel Inhelder was generous with her interpretation of the new model of equilibration and the contemporary view of stages. Through her, helpful conferences were arranged with Willem Doise, Marianne Denis, and Elsa Schmid-Kitsikis at the University of Geneva.

Invaluable assistance was given to us by scholars who shared with us their prepublication and unpublished manuscripts. They are: Hans Furth, Constance Kamii, Juan Pascual-Leone, Rheta DeVries, Gilbert Voyat, Annette Perret-Clermont, Elsa Schmid-Kitsikis, Willem Doise, and Jack Easley. Our work in the Archives was greatly aided by the willing assistance of a group of translators—Nancy Reid Grahm, Laura Glass, Pamela Stevens, and the late Sarah Campbell—whom we sincerely thank. Todd Lueders and Fiorella Ljunggren, our editors at Brooks/Cole, proved to be invaluable scholars and critics, who encouraged the difficult task of pioneering a book on Piaget's learning theory.

The three reviewers engaged by Brooks/Cole also became helpful supporters of this project: Lorraine Nicolich of Rutgers University, George Forman of the University of Massachusetts, and Gilbert Voyat of the City University of New York. Special acknowledgment is due Professor Voyat for having alerted us to relevant publications and for having offered explanations that greatly clarified some aspects of Piagetian theory for us.

Our students at Temple and New York Universities were our best critics. It was they who, during our ten years of studying and teaching Piagetian theory, helped us search out those aspects relevant to learning. We would also like to thank our families, especially our respective husbands, Frank and Wayne, who took command of the domestic chores while we left our kitchens for quieter domains.

Finally, this book was a completely cooperative effort. Although it was necessary to list our names in some order, one cannot talk of a "senior" author. We have listed our names alphabetically, but they could just as well have appeared the other way around.

A Postscript. When our book was in the last stages of publication, we learned of the death of Jean Piaget in Geneva on September 16, 1980, at the age of 84. A central aspect of Piaget's theory is his emphasis on thinking as an extension of the environment: "The very nature of life is constantly to overtake itself" (Piaget, 1971a, p. 362). Through the careful study and application of Piaget's writings and those of the Genevan School, constructivist epistemology is and will continue to be a vital force for change in many areas—foremost, in the quality of education for children throughout the world. The theory, therefore, will continue to live.

Jeanette McCarthy Gallagher
D. Kim Reid

Contents

CHAPTER ONE

Genetic Epistemology as a Learning Theory

Seldom has the theory of Piaget and Inhelder been given much attention in discussions of **learning.**[1] Theirs is a theory of **development**—that is, a theory about how a variety of factors such as maturation, experience with people, objects, language, and culture, as well as internal **regulations,** interact to produce cognitive growth in children. Therefore, it has been argued that their work and the work of their colleagues throughout the world have little to teach us about how children learn. Perhaps this opinion is based on the Piagetians' lack of interest in how children learn to read, write, and do arithmetic—the very focus of most American theories of learning. Or, perhaps, their theory appears to many to be unrelated to learning because it does not stress the effects of environment or look for ways to accelerate the growth of knowledge by direct teaching and programming (Voyat, 1977). Finally, unlike most learning theorists, Piagetians do not explain learning as a recording of facts that are internalized through frequency and contiguity. Instead, they argue that a learner always makes inferences that go beyond the observable aspects of the world (Inhelder, Sinclair, & Bovet, 1974). In a sense, Piagetians are saying that what children are able to observe about the world is more dependent on what they already know— that is, on their own special system of thinking—than it is on what actually exists.

One vivid example of this approach is the experiment that Karmiloff-Smith and Inhelder (1975) conducted to study children's goal-oriented behavior in a block-balancing task. The strategies, or action sequences, the children used were dependent on their implicit theories about how the blocks would need to be positioned in order to balance. The theories, however, were in turn regulated by discoveries the children made as they organized and reorganized their actions to attain a workable solution.

[1]Terms in **boldface** are defined in the Glossary at the back of the book.

Hence, the importance of the role of experience. Although **genetic** (or developmental)[2] **epistemology**—the theory developed by Piaget and Inhelder—encompasses much more than a theory of learning, it does offer us a great deal of understanding about how children learn. *How it does so is the topic of this book.*

Principles of Learning

We begin with a little story that Piaget (1970a) himself is fond of telling. One of his friends, then 5 years old, was playing with some pebbles on the beach. After arranging his pebbles in a row, he proceeded to count them from left to right: ten. Next he counted them from right to left: again ten. What would happen if he put them in a circle? First, he marked his starting place and counted clockwise: ten! Next, he counted counterclockwise: still ten! Piaget's friend, now a noted mathematician, still remembers the joy and enthusiasm of that moment. He had discovered that sum is independent of order—what is called *commutativity.*

The little boy had played with pebbles before. He had already noticed that some were smooth and others rough, that some were gray and others shiny white, and that some were light and others heavy. The gradual learning of the properties of the pebbles (such as weight and the surface features of roughness and smoothness) is growth in knowledge. The type of knowledge we acquire when we abstract such properties from objects is called **physical knowledge,** and the process is called **empirical abstraction.** But, if the boy had abstracted only the characteristics of the pebbles he was playing with, he wouldn't have grasped any mathematical principle—in this case, the law of commutativity.

Learning as an Internal Process of Construction

Learning about things, such as laws, that we cannot observe in the environment requires a very different kind of learning. The boy's discovery that the sum remained constant no matter how he placed the pebbles or in what order he counted them was based on his reflecting on his own activities. One principle of learning that is clearly illustrated by this story is that *learning is an internal process of construction.* Nothing external imposed itself on this little boy. The pebbles summed to ten only by virtue of his counting them. Even after reordering and recounting the pebbles, the child couldn't have understood the law of commutativity without thinking about what he had done. He used the information

[2]Here and in later instances we have added *developmental* in parentheses to remind the reader that in this context the term *genetic* does not refer to genes or to maturation—that is, to changes in the brain. Such a misinterpretation often occurs in summaries of Piaget's theory. *Genetic* is an older term for *developmental* and does not imply greater emphasis on hereditary factors as compared with environmental factors.

he had gained from his actions to *construct* the idea that sum is independent of order. Knowledge deduced from activity is called **logico-mathematical knowledge.**

It is important to note that the activities of looking at the pebbles, touching them, moving them around, or even counting them were not enough to foster logico-mathematical knowledge. The boy had to reflect on (think about) the results of his actions: "No matter in what order or shape I place the pebbles, I still have the same number!" Learning by constructing rules from activities performed in interaction with objects is a form of **reflexive abstraction.** (Empirical and reflexive abstraction will be discussed again, and in greater detail, in Chapter Two.)

Now, let's see what we can learn about learning by watching Peter and Jane (Davis, 1971–1972). The two children have been asked to draw the water level inside a jar about one-third full of colored water as it is being rotated (Piaget & Inhelder, 1941). The jar is covered by an opaque bag, so that its outline can be seen but the position of the water cannot. First the jar is held in position 1, and the children are asked to draw the water level inside the already drawn outline of the jar in position 1 (see Figures 1-1–1-4, pp. 4, 5, 6, and 7). Then this same procedure is repeated with each of the remaining seven positions of rotation.

Peter (2 years, 10 months) always draws the water level parallel to the bottom of the jar, as if the water were stuck to it (Figure 1-1). Even when the cover is taken off the jar and Peter is asked to draw the water level while looking at it, he is simply unable to "see" what the water level looks like. He identifies rather well the water level when the jar is in the horizontal or vertical position (see positions 1, 3, 5, and 7 in Figure 1-2), but, surprisingly, his rendition of positions 2, 4, 6, and 8 is incorrect. We said "surprisingly" because infants learn very early to distinguish the horizontal and vertical positions in relation to their own bodies—that is, lying down or sitting up (Piaget, 1977f)—but not until much later do children learn to evaluate those positions when a reference other than their bodies is needed. Peter can, as indicated by Figure 1-1, relate the water to the jar—he always draws the water at the bottom of the jar—but he cannot relate it to a frame of reference outside the jar—that is, to the table or floor. He doesn't realize that the water line is *always* parallel to the table, no matter what position the jar is in. Peter simply hasn't come far enough in his development to understand this problem. To put it differently, he hasn't yet developed the tools he needs.

Now, let's look at what Jane (4 years, 1 month) does in the same situation. When the jar is covered, Jane is able to draw the water level correctly only if the jar is in any of the horizontal or vertical positions. (Remember: Peter could do that only when he could see the water.) But, like Peter, Jane is not able to draw the water correctly when the jar is rotated obliquely (see Figure 1-3).

When the jar is uncovered, however, we observe something very interesting. Jane draws position 1 correctly but not position 2, because she is still using the jar as the point of reference (see Figure 1-4). She draws the water level in position 3 correctly (as we would expect, because the

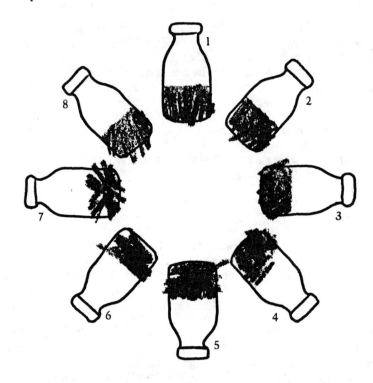

Figure 1-1. Drawing by Peter (2 years, 10 months) with jar covered by opaque bag. (From "The Structure of Mathematics and the Structure of Cognitive Development," by R. B. Davis, *Journal of Children's Mathematical Behavior,* 1971–1972, 1(1), 71–97. Reprinted by permission.)

jar is in the horizontal position). We see her make a predictable error at 4 and a predictable correct response at 5. Judging from her drawings up to this point, our prediction is that Jane will draw 6 incorrectly. She does— but then corrects herself. Jane is learning as she goes through the experiment! She corrects 6, draws 7 (which, as we have seen, is easy for her), then draws 8 correctly.

Learning as a Function of Development

Note that neither child was able to draw the water level correctly when the jar was covered. If observing were sufficient to explain learning, how could we account for this failure on the part of both children? After all, Jane and Peter have had experience with liquids in tipped containers every day of their lives, beginning with their bottles in their cribs. So, learning cannot stem from observation or experience alone (Piaget, 1957). Why?

Figure 1-2. Drawing by Peter with jar uncovered and plainly visible. (From "The Structure of Mathematics and the Structure of Cognitive Development," by R. B. Davis, *Journal of Children's Mathematical Behavior*, 1971-1972, 1(1), 71-97. Reprinted by permission.)

A second principle of learning, also derived from Piaget and Inhelder's work (Piaget, 1971a, 1977c), helps us understand why: *learning is subordinated to development.* From this perspective, experience is considered indispensable to learning but does not ensure it. We cannot expect that children will automatically improve in understanding or gain new skills by an accumulation of experiences alone. In order to be able to learn, children must have the capacity to respond to a new experience or concept; that is, they must be capable of **assimilation.** When Peter and Jane fail to draw the water level correctly, it is as if they were insensitive to the stimulus—in this case, the water in the container. Even when the jar is uncovered and the water is in plain view, they can't "see" where the water really is! Jane's drawings are somewhat more advanced than Peter's, but then she is more than a year older. When she gets to position 6, for example, Jane is able to notice that her drawing looks different from the water she is seeing in the jar. This observation leads her to make an **accommodation** and "see" what Peter cannot see. Piaget (1970b) explains that children are sensitive to stimuli only

Figure 1-3. Drawing by Jane (4 years, 1 month) with jar covered by bag. (From "The Structure of Mathematics and the Structure of Cognitive Development," by R. B. Davis, *Journal of Children's Mathematical Behavior*, 1971–1972, 1(1), 71–97. Reprinted by permission.)

when they have the competence to understand. Jane is able to assimilate what she is seeing to her prior knowledge and to modify her knowledge (*accommodate*) when what she draws doesn't fit with reality.

Peter, who is quite young, has not developed to the point at which he can learn during the experiment as Jane does. Learning in any specific situation is dependent on a broad range of prior experiences. Actually, research has shown that children cannot draw the water level accurately with the jar covered until they are about 9 or 10 years old. This means that at a younger age children are unable to put the water into a frame of reference outside the bottle. The stage of development, therefore, sets limitations on what can be assimilated.

Learning as a Higher-Level Reorganization

This example also clearly shows that Jane reorganized her knowledge—that is, that she regulated what she was "seeing" internally. Without any new evidence or reinforcement, Jane began to see in 6 what

Figure 1-4.   Drawing by Jane with jar uncovered and plainly visible. (From "The Structure of Mathematics and the Structure of Cognitive Development," by R. B. Davis, *Journal of Children's Mathematical Behavior*, 1971–1972, 1(1), 71–97. Reprinted by permission.)

she couldn't see in 2 and 4. This process of self-correction or self-regulation is called **equilibration** because it leads to increasingly advanced states of **equilibrium** of the cognitive system. Equilibration, which is the central concept of genetic epistemology, is a process that illustrates the reciprocal nature of the relationship between children and their environment. Children don't simply record what is in the external world; they act on it. Another principle of learning, therefore, is that children learn not only by observing objects but also by reorganizing on a higher mental level what they learn from coordinating their own activities in the construction of rules and principles.

Other Principles of Learning

More assumptions about learning can be made by watching children balance weights on a scale, as Piaget (1974b), in collaboration with Kamii and Parrat-Dayan, did in one of his studies. Two children, Pat and Rob, are

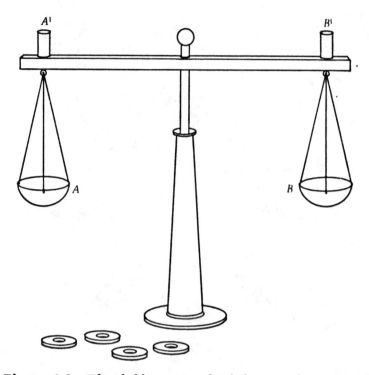

Figure 1-5. The children using this balance scale were given weights to be put in the pans, as well as rings, which could be placed on A' and B' or tied with a string to pans A and/or B. (Based on Piaget, 1974b.)

shown the balance scale illustrated in Figure 1-5. The scale has two platforms (A and B) suspended from the beam and two vertical columns (A' and B') just above the platforms.

Pat (4 years, 11 months) proudly remarks that he has a scale just like that at home. Then he predicts that, when a weight is put on B (but not on A), both A and B will go down (although not at the same time), so that the beam will be balanced. But after actually putting the weight on B and seeing it go down, Pat predicts that putting a weight on A (but not on B) will make A go down and B go up. If single weights are simultaneously placed on A and B, however, "they will both go lower . . . no, they will both go higher." When asked how he knows, Pat replies "Because I have a scale, and I've already seen it." He puts the weights on A and B and observes that they "stay like that." And if another weight were put on each? "They would stay like that." Why? "Because lots of scales are like that," and he verifies the equilibrium. Then, after having observed that, if one puts eight weights on A and eight on B, the platforms balance, he argues that, if one puts five weights on A and five on B, B will go lower.

Rob (6 years, 6 months) solves the initial problems correctly. When, however, he is confronted with the situation in which eight weights are on A and eight on B and is asked what he can do to make A go up, he says "Take some off [A]." Can it be done any other way? "Yes. If you want A to go down, you have to take some off [B]." And to make A go up? "No other way." Can you use the rings? "Yes" he says and puts a ring on B. A goes up. "Do you agree?" Rob agrees that, if rings are tied under platform A, the platform will go down, regardless of the length of the string to which the weights are attached. But, when asked what will happen if a weight is put on A', Rob suggests that "it will make it go down a little less than if you put it in there [A]." Why? "Because it isn't lower . . . that equals less weight." After seeing the weight on A', he changes his answer. He then predicts a difference for a weight on B and B', but corrects himself.

Pat, who has a scale at home, is confident throughout the session that he is accurate in his predictions. When he checks them and finds that the results he gets do not bear his predictions out, he simply changes his mind. He does not, however, attempt to understand why. "Lots of scales are like that" is reason enough for him. He is unable to anticipate that the scales will balance if five weights are put on each, because he has never understood either the reciprocal interaction between A and B or the equality of equal numbers of weights.

Rob, on the other hand, is able to profit from the errors he makes. He is aware that the results of his experiments contradict his predictions and is gradually able to use that information to predict that equal weights on B and B' will exert equal force.

These experiments suggest three more assumptions about learning. The first one is that *growth in knowledge is often sparked by a feedback process that results from questioning,* **contradictions,** *and consequent reorganization.* Note that the term *feedback* is not used here to refer to information, incentives, or disapproval offered by another person. Instead, feedback refers to an internal process of adjusting and readjusting expectations until one can anticipate the outcome of an action. Children learn through successive approximations. They anticipate what will happen if a certain action is carried out. They then perform the task and observe the results of their own actions on objects. Consequently, children are often able to revise their own expectations gradually until they are able to anticipate a correct solution from the outset. This process of self-correction derives from children's ability to observe contradictions between their initial expectations and the results of their actions.

Pat, who is happy with his answers and unquestioning in the face of contradictory evidence, makes little progress throughout the session. Like Peter in the earlier study, Pat doesn't have the competence to understand even that there is a contradiction. Rob, instead, recognizes the contradictions and grapples with them. Hence, he is able to reorganize his thinking in a way that will enable him to make correct predictions in the future.

Either child playing alone probably wouldn't have discovered the properties of the weights. Rob, who has reached a level of understanding that enables him to grasp the problem, benefits from his interaction with the teacher. As you have probably noticed, the teacher never gives Rob any answers, nor does she do any demonstrations or draw any conclusions. She simply continues to ask Rob questions that enable him to decide for himself what the effect of a certain action will be. Then she gives him the opportunity to carry out each activity to see whether the results match his prediction or contradict it. *Questions, contradictions, and the consequent process of thought reorganization are often stimulated by social interaction.* Pat's response, however, indicates that this is true only when the child has the competence to respond. It is the child's own activity rather than his or her reactions to environmental stimulation that is most important to the acquisition of knowledge (Inhelder, Sinclair, & Bovet, 1974).

Finally, we see that, when asked how to make *A* go up, Rob can think of only one possibility: take some weight off *A*. When he has an opportunity to manipulate the weights, however, he quite readily solves the problem in a second way—that is, by adding a weight to *B*. *Since awareness (conscious realization) is a process of reconstruction rather than sudden insight, understanding lags behind action* (Piaget, 1976b). Although Rob is able to perform an action whose effect is to raise *A*, he does not understand the equivalence of taking a weight off *A* and putting it on *B*. He is able to solve the problem on a practical level only. Piaget (1978d) has demonstrated that children are able to perform tasks successfully without *understanding* why what they are doing works.

For example, children can use one tiddlywink to snap another one into the air long before they understand the effects of the downward force exerted on one side (Piaget, 1976b). Piaget (Beth & Piaget, 1966) explains that the process of construction of knowledge, about which we have been speaking, is the result of two distinct but interrelated activities: discovery and invention. We discover laws, properties, effects, and characteristics that are **observable** in the world, and we invent those things that have never existed before. To grow in knowledge, children must both discover and invent.

Genetic Epistemology and Other Learning Theories

The six principles of learning we have just discussed (see Figure 1-6) express some of the most important ideas in genetic epistemology—the study of how people acquire knowledge. These and other principles will be discussed throughout the book. Note that genetic epistemology unquestionably seeks to explain permanent changes in behavior, as any learning theory does. It differs from the more traditional approaches to learning in that it does not postulate that growth in knowledge is only the "result of experience" (Cross, 1974, p. 7). Instead, genetic epistemology emphasizes the active role of the person.

The contribution of genetic epistemology to our understanding of learning has just begun to be recognized. Many texts dealing with

1. Learning is an internal process of construction; that is, children's own activities determine their reactions to environmental stimulation.
2. Learning is subordinated to development; that is, competence is a precondition for learning.
3. Children learn not only by observing objects but also by reorganizing on a higher mental level what they learn from coordinating their activities.
4. Growth in knowledge is often sparked by a feedback process that proceeds from questions, contradictions, and consequent mental reorganization.
5. Questions, contradictions, and the consequent reorganization of thought are often stimulated by social interaction.
6. Since awareness (or conscious realization) is a process of reconstruction rather than sudden insight, understanding lags behind action.

Figure 1-6. Six principles of learning derived from genetic epistemology.

learning include a discussion of genetic epistemology. The discussion, however, is often relegated to sections dealing specifically with thinking and/or problem solving (see, for example, Cross, 1974; Moursund, 1976). But more and more frequently, as learning theorists begin to investigate more complex behaviors, we find evidence that Piaget and Inhelder's influence has been more pervasive. When information-processing theorists, for example, began to create computer programs that would approximate the procedures humans employ to interpret, store, retrieve, and use information, they incorporated concepts traditionally associated with genetic epistemology. Most obvious is the inclusion of notions of **structure,** assimilation, and accommodation (see Tulving & Donaldson, 1972; Anderson, Spiro, & Montague, 1977).

Genetic epistemology is potentially useful to information-processing and learning theorists because it is the only comprehensive theory that defines the nature of intelligence per se (Duckworth, 1964). Although it would be inaccurate to suggest that learning theorists have adopted a typically Genevan approach to the study of learning, it would be equally misleading to overlook the relevance of the principles of learning uncovered by Piaget, Inhelder, and their many colleagues throughout the world. In fact, a number of authors (such as Flavell, 1977; Endler, Boulter, & Osser, 1976) have suggested that information-processing theory and genetic epistemology are quite compatible and that a new trend in cognitive research seems to be developing, which incorporates concepts from both.

CHAPTER TWO

The Meaning of Genetic Epistemology

Piaget's psychology cannot be separated from his epistemology. His epistemological theory may be called constructivist: ... knowledge is neither preformed in the object (empiricism) or in the subject (nativism) but results from progressive construction [Inhelder, 1977, p. 339].

In Chapter One the emphasis was on learning as an internal process of construction. In this chapter the meaning of this construction is explored in the wider context of the concepts that Piaget has borrowed from biology to enrich his approach to the study of knowledge—the discipline of genetic (developmental) epistemology. Our discussion will emphasize the contributions of Bärbel Inhelder, which strengthened and expanded this discipline, and will provide the necessary background for the detailed account in Chapter Three of one of Piaget's most important concepts—that of the models of equilibration.

Who Is Piaget? A Clarification

If one were to ask "Who is Piaget?" a variety of answers might be forthcoming. "A child psychologist," "A biologist," "An epistemologist," and perhaps even "A philosopher." It is because each of these answers is partially correct that it is difficult to understand Piaget, a genius of our century. It is evident from Chapter One that Piaget is interested in the study of children's thinking. One should keep in mind, however, that such a study is a means to a goal—to understand the development of knowledge. Inhelder, Sinclair, and Bovet (1974, p. 22) expressed this point clearly: "No adult is able to reconstruct his own cognitive development.

Development is an unknown territory that can only be charted by studying children, whose actions and ideas will continue to surprise us."*

The Method of Critical Exploration

In their studies, Piaget and his colleagues—now called the *Genevan School*[1]—use an adaptation of the scientific methods of psychology. Instead of studying large samples of subjects, the researchers in the Genevan School study small samples (approximately 30) in depth by the method of *critical exploration*. The method, characterized by great flexibility, consists essentially in letting the children's answers to the interviewer's probing questions govern the course of the procedure. It was this method (then known as the *clinical method*) that Piaget used in his famous studies on causality. For example, Piaget (1930) asked children, in a conversational manner, why the moon was both over their house and over the house of a friend. "Because it follows me" was not an uncommon reply.

Later Piaget (1952b) used the same method to study the cognitive development of his own three infants. Chapter Four will present in detail some of the simple problem situations that Piaget set up for that purpose. Among other things, he found that the infant's ability to understand that objects are permanent—that is, that they don't disappear just because they are hidden under a pillow—is a gradual acquisition.

In the traditional behavioristic approach to the study of learning and development, large groups of subjects are often studied in tightly controlled experiments. Therefore, according to an analysis by Voyat (1977), in the traditional approach the method *defines* the problems to be studied. For Piaget, instead, "the method to be followed is a function of the question being asked. . . . It is hard to find any common measure between, say, the data produced by administering a five-minute questionnaire to a hundred children and those obtained by conducting a one-hundred-minute experiment with just five children. Yet the differences between the results sought by the clinical or genetic [developmental] method . . . and [by] the classical behaviorist approach . . . are precisely of this order" (Voyat, 1977, p. 344).

The long and careful questioning characteristic of Piaget's method is emphasized here not only to highlight the uniqueness of Piaget's discipline but also to alert the reader to the unwarrantedness of regarding his work as "unscientific." It is interesting to note that in 1969 a prestigious group of scientists, the American Psychological Association, presented Jean Piaget with a citation for his distinguished contribution to psychology. In a defense of his discipline of genetic epistemology,

---

*From *Learning and the Development of Cognition*, by B. Inhelder, H. Sinclair, and M. Bovet. Copyright © 1974 by the President and Fellows of Harvard College. This and all other quotations from this source are reprinted by permission of Harvard University Press and Routledge & Kegan Paul Ltd.

[1]*Genevan* (rather than *Piagetian*) *School* is an appropriate term because it emphasizes the collaborative nature of the school and the contributions of Piaget's colleagues.

Piaget (1972b, p. 15) quoted what he considered a "significant passage" from the citation: "He has approached questions up to now exclusively philosophical in a resolutely empirical manner and has made epistemology into a science separate from philosophy but related to all the human sciences." He also warned, however, that his intent was not to ignore traditional epistemology but to focus on the development of knowledge.

As of this writing, Piaget has not attended a meeting of the American Psychological Association to accept his award publicly. (But, then, who would want to leave a pleasant mountain retreat in Switzerland to bustle around the hectic convention centers of Washington, New York, or Los Angeles?) However, if he did attend, Piaget would not be surprised that his discipline of genetic epistemology was receiving a mixed reception from the very psychologists who presented an award to him several years ago.

The Center for Genetic Epistemology

With the assistance of the Rockefeller Foundation of the United States, Piaget established in 1956 the Center for Genetic Epistemology at the University of Geneva. The Center quickly became, and still is, an idea exchange for research on the development of knowledge. Biologists, logicians, linguists, mathematicians, and specialists in developmental, experimental, and educational psychology actively puzzle over the problems of how children learn (Piaget, 1971b). The Center remains essentially interdisciplinary. In June of each year a final symposium is presented in order to probe the experimental findings relating to a topic selected the previous year by Piaget himself. These reports, edited by Piaget and including a lengthy theoretical conclusion by him, are then published as a monograph series (*Studies in Genetic Epistemology*) by Presses Universitaires de France. Unfortunately, not all of these valuable symposia have been translated into English. Other important material, especially relevant to a learning-theory approach to Piaget, is still unpublished. In writing this book, we have drawn on much of this unpublished or untranslated material to present a contemporary view of research at the Genevan School.

Piaget, the Genetic Epistemologist

Epistemology is a branch of philosophy dealing with the relationship between knowledge (what we know) and the different forms of reality (apparent, real, possible, and even impossible). A philosopher strictly interested in epistemological studies would ask such questions as "How do we know about objects in the external world?" "How valid or certain is our understanding of these objects?" and "By what methods are we able to study our interactions with the objects we encounter?"

Piaget (1971b) criticized the traditional philosophical view that questions of epistemology must be settled by philosophical methods.

These methods have traditionally been ones of reflection—that is, attempts to arrive at meaning and "truth" but not through the methods of science, which, by experimentation and calculation, lead to verification. This does not mean, however, that Piaget views the methods and subject matter of philosophy as useless: "Philosophy does not give us knowledge, as it lacks methods of verification. . . . On the other hand, by coordinating cognitive values with other human values it can give rise to a "wisdom" (Piaget, 1971b, p. 216)."* Thus, philosophy *is* important for the study of such questions as the meaning of life and the importance of values in our lives.

Epistemology, however, must be studied developmentally, Piaget says. "Genetic epistemology deals with both the formation and the meaning of knowledge. We can formulate our problem in the following terms: by what means does the human mind go from a state of less sufficient knowledge to a state of higher knowledge?" (Piaget, 1970a, pp. 12-13). It is clear that the study of children's thinking in all areas of reality would constitute the subject matter of this investigation of the transition from a lower level to a higher level of knowledge.

Piaget, the Psychological Epistemologist with Biological Roots

Piaget (1977a, p. 9) describes himself as "a psychological epistemologist who loves to return to his original biological interests." It is necessary to consider these biological interests carefully, for they provide the thrust of Piaget's theory, as well as the foundation for a learning-theory approach to genetic epistemology.

Let us start with a journey back through time, when Piaget's interest in biology had its beginning. In a treatise criticizing an exclusively philosophical approach to knowledge, Piaget (1971b) muses that adolescents accept philosophical reflections very readily, because they offer the opportunity to evaluate vital questions with which adolescents are often concerned. Piaget himself was about to pursue the study of philosophy as a young student, when an accidental turn of events made him change his mind.

> I decided to devote myself to philosophy as soon as I was introduced to the subject. But by an accident that influenced my subsequent development considerably, I already had at this time specific interests persistent enough to become permanent. Like many children I was fascinated by natural history, and at the age of eleven I had the good fortune to become the *famulus*, as he called me, of an old zoologist, Paul Godot, who directed the Museum of Neuchâtel solely on his own resources. In exchange for my small services, he introduced me to malacology and gave me a number of shells of land and freshwater molluscs with which I made my own collection at home.

---

*This and all other quotations from this source are from *Insights and Illusions of Philosophy*, by J. Piaget. Copyright 1965 by Presses Universitaires de France. Reprinted by permission of Presses Universitaires de France and The New American Library, Inc.

When he died in 1911, I published at the age of fifteen several notes by way of a supplement to his Catalogue of Neuchâtel Molluscs as well as on alpine molluscs, which much interested me in their variability of adaptation to altitude [Piaget, 1971b, p. 4].

It was at this time, at age 15, that Piaget set for himself a clear intellectual goal: to write an epistemology—that is, a theory of knowledge—based on biology. His two central ideas were (1) *knowledge as assimilation into structures* and (2) the *self-regulation of knowledge* (equilibration).[2] Both of these concepts were introduced in Chapter One and will be discussed again throughout the book. Recall that Peter's and Jane's understanding of the water line was assimilated—that is, filtered (modified) by the children's previous knowledge about water in tilted containers. If Peter and Jane changed their answers during the presentation of the various containers, it was because of self-regulation. Telling the children just where the water line should be (or asking them to look very carefully) wouldn't have helped. If growth in knowing was to occur, the growth had to be regulated by reorganizations, or reconstructions, of past understandings. Such reorganizations didn't destroy what was known before; structures of understanding, or present means of organizing thinking, are not eliminated by new knowledge.

This is how Piaget summarizes the two central ideas in relation to the water-line experiment:

> Why is the child unable to see that the line of water is horizontal? The reason for this is that he does not possess the necessary instruments of assimilation. . . . This seems to me a very striking example of the complexity of the act of assimilation, which always supposes instruments of integration. A well-developed structure within the subject is needed in order for him to take in the data that are outside. Assimilation is clearly not a matter of passively registering what is going on around us [Piaget 1977d, pp. 4–5].

What is remarkable about these two central ideas—assimilation into structures and self-regulation—is that their biological roots were summarized by Piaget over 60 years ago! Between the ages of 15 and 21 Piaget kept up his interest in the study of molluscs. After receiving a bachelor's degree in biology at the University of Neuchâtel at the age of 18, he continued his studies at that university, where three years later he presented and successfully defended his doctoral dissertation on the distribution and variability of land molluscs in the Valaisian Alps of Switzerland.

When he was a student at the Neuchâtel gymnasium,[3] Piaget grew to respect a philosophy teacher, Professor Arnold Reymond, who, paradoxically, led him both toward and away from philosophy. Over time Piaget became disappointed with his teacher's attitude toward objectivity and science. Reymond thought that it was sufficient to speculate about the central ideas of structure and self-regulation and that it was not necessary to put them to test. When, after receiving his doctorate, Piaget decided to study experimental psychology, one of his goals was to

[2]See Piaget's complete essay on equilibration in Appendix A.
[3]Secondary school for preparation toward university studies.

acquire the necessary tools to test his central ideas on a theory of knowledge based on biology. He studied psychology at La Sorbonne and, at the age of 23, had the opportunity to work in the laboratory of the late Alfred Binet, famous for his early testing of children's intelligence. The director of the laboratory was then Binet's co-worker, Dr. Theophile Simon, who assigned Piaget the task of standardizing one of these tests for Paris elementary school children. It is likely that Simon was unaware of Piaget's interest in the reasoning process behind the answers—especially wrong answers—that children of various age levels gave to the tests' questions. The following quotation commenting on this period is revealing, for it gives an inkling of the merging of the psychological, philosophical, and biological strains in what was to become Piaget's discipline of genetic (developmental) epistemology.

> At last I had found my field of research. First of all it became clear to me that the theory of the relations between the whole and the part can be studied experimentally through analysis of the psychological processes underlying logical operations. This marked the end of my "theoretical" period and the start of an inductive and experimental era in the psychological domain which I always had wanted to enter, but for which until then I had not found the suitable problems. ... Finally, my aim of discovering a sort of embryology of intelligence fit in with my biological training; from the start of my theoretical thinking I was certain that the problem of the relation between the organism and environment extended also into the realm of knowledge, appearing here as the problem of the relation between the acting or thinking subject and the objects of his experience [Piaget, 1952a, p. 245].

Piaget's Middle-Ground Position

We noted earlier that Piaget has pursued two central ideas over a period of more than 50 years: the assimilation of knowledge into structures and the necessity of equilibrium by self-regulation. Let us explore further what these concepts mean by investigating arguments drawn from Piaget's recent reformulations of his continuing interest in a biological approach to the study of cognitive development (Piaget, 1974a, 1977a, 1977c).[4]

Our exploration will start with examples drawn from Piaget's life-long study of snails *(Limnaea stagnalis)* common to the marshes and lakes of Switzerland and of a juicy plant called *Sedum* (Crassulaceae), two varieties of which are found in Savoy, France, and in the Mediterranean region. These collections and studies are more than "Piagetian hobbies." The careful analysis of habitat and of the variations in structural features in a wide range of altitudes and regions led Piaget to formulate a new viewpoint on evolution, a viewpoint that is crucial to understanding development of knowledge in humans.

[4]For a clear summary of Piaget's epistemology in relation to biological principles, see Inhelder et al., 1974, pp. 2-10.

Piaget versus Lamarck

The process of evolution—that is, the process of change that characterizes living organisms—has traditionally been explained in terms of one of two viewpoints: Lamarck's and Darwin's. Lamarck placed heavy emphasis on the role of the environment in an organism's adaptation and consequent structural changes. (According to a common joke, Lamarck thought that the giraffe's neck became elongated because of the animal's need to reach for the highest leaves!) While not calling himself a Lamarckian, Piaget (1971a, p. 105) gives due credit to the view that stresses the importance of environmental influences: "Now, even if Lamarck was wrong to leave almost everything out of consideration except [1] environment as a factor in transformism and [2] the organism's tendencies to choose a favorable environment, yet he was certainly right in attributing a necessary role to those factors, as is being increasingly realized nowadays" (numbers in brackets added to clarify translation).

Before continuing on the theme of why the Lamarckian emphasis on the role of the environment is not completely acceptable to Piaget, it is necessary to introduce the concepts of **genotype** and **phenotype.** The genotype is ordinarily defined as the inherited makeup, or gene structure, of an individual. The phenotype is often defined as the inherited observable characteristics.

Piaget, in line with the view of contemporary biology, does not make a sharp distinction between genotype and phenotype. To understand why, it is necessary to return to the concept of interaction. The genes—the units of heredity—always function as a whole. In other words, genes always interact with other genes and may never be considered as isolated units. To emphasize the wholeness and interacting aspects of hereditary material, Piaget often uses the term *genome* instead of genotype. *Genotype* seems to imply an aggregate of genes, whereas *genome* means a controlling system made up of interacting units.

The controlling-system notion permits us to place the role of the environment in proper perspective and contribute to our understanding of the phenotype. Another way of expressing the controlling system of the interacting genes is to use the term *reaction norm,* or range of reaction to environmental influences. An organism's range of reaction becomes expressed through the phenotype—that is, through the physical makeup of an organism that results from the interactions between the genotype and the environment. Therefore, the phenotype as an interacting concept places the emphasis on the organism's selecting into the environment rather than being controlled by that environment. We shall return to this point in the following sections. For now we need to point out that the concept of reaction norm is crucial to the understanding of Piagetian theory, because, by analogy, it helps fix the label of *interactionism* on key Piagetian principles of cognitive development.

To regard the environment as a controlling factor in the Lamarckian sense is to place the organism in a very passive role. If we move from the realm of biological evolution to the development of thinking, the analogy is clear. As was stressed in Chapter One, children actively assimilate the environment to their structures. As children are in the process of learning something new, they register some piece of information from the outside. However, this registering is always active and thus tied to assimilation structures; what has been learned before modifies (interacts with) what will be learned in the future. The reaction norm—the range of reaction—controls the learning experience.

Recall, however, that Piaget does give credit to Lamarck for his emphasis on environmental influences. Specifically, Piaget (1978a) notes that Lamarck assigns an important role to the animal's *behavior* in the environment. To repeat, the role is too one-way; that is, it implies passive control rather than active behavior that selects into the environment. Piaget agreed with Lamarck's observation that organisms regulate their adaptations to environmental stress. However, Piaget objected to Lamarck's explanation of adaptation because it did not sufficiently account for the interactive processes that occur when organismic structures are modified in response to environmental changes.

Piaget versus Classical Neo-Darwinism

Darwin's theory of evolution stressed natural selection: certain variations of a species are more likely to survive than others. Later in the history of the study of evolution, Mendel formulated the basic laws of inheritance. When the ideas of Darwin and Mendel were integrated, the resulting new view of evolution was labeled *neo-Darwinism* or *classical neo-Darwinism,*[5] as it is known today.

Piaget (1971a, 1978a) rejects classical neo-Darwinism, for it includes notions that are as passive as those of Lamarck. Classical neo-Darwinism emphasizes the role of chance mutations of the gene pool to explain evolutionary adaptation. Such an emphasis, according to Piaget, implies that the gene passively awaits a chance event or a mutation. But, as we have seen, the genes are never isolated units; they operate in a range of reaction to environmental influences through the phenotype—an operation that is always active and never passive. By analogy, the development of thinking is not a passive process: "Neo-Darwinism reasons as if the apple fallen by chance beside Newton was the source of the theories of this great man on gravitation" (Piaget, 1974a, p. 109; authors' translation). Newton, instead, "organized" this chance occurrence, because his mind was prepared by his previous work to assimilate the incident and actively structure a new idea.

Another way of expressing the same concept is to state that Newton *chose* the event and at the same time modified the environment through his choice. This is why the concept of phenotype and the related notion

---

[5]The reader should be aware that some summaries of Piaget's views on evolutionary adaptation use only the term *Darwinism* (not *neo-Darwinism*). The classical neo-Darwinian position is, however, implied (see, for example, Furth, 1969; Inhelder, 1976b; Inhelder et al., 1974).

of reaction norm are crucial in understanding the relation between evolution and the development of thinking. The organism's active role in choosing its environment is clearly stated by Piaget (1973a, p. 22).

> Above all, we know that the phenotype should be regarded as a response by the genome to environmental tensions and that selection does not directly involve the genes but the phenotypes as more or less adapted responses. Behavior, for its part, then no longer has anything secondary or negligible about it, since it represents the essential activity of the phenotype. Further, because of behavior, the relations between the organism and the environment become circular: the organism chooses its environment and modifies it just as much as it is dependent on it, and behavior thus becomes an important factor in evolution itself.

The notion that an organism chooses and modifies its environment stands midway between a view of evolution that emphasizes environmental control (Lamarck) and a view that emphasizes a passive organism open to chance events (classical neo-Darwin). Piaget's views on evolution were adapted, in part, from those of the biologist Waddington (Gallagher, 1977; Piaget, 1977a, 1978a). The key point in Waddington's theory of evolution—that the organism makes active choices into the environment—was the concept that had the greatest impact on Piaget's thinking. Although Piaget (1978a) does not agree completely with Waddington's views, the impact of this biologist's research and theory are clearly evident in many of Piaget's writings.

We turn now to Piaget's own biological research in relation to evolutionary adaptation and its connections with the development of thinking.

The Concept of Biological Phenocopy

Ever since his first work on the *Limnaea stagnalis*—research that coincided with his first observations of nascent intelligent behavior in his own children—Piaget (1952/1936) had regarded the adaptation of an organism to its environment from a point of view as far removed from Lamarckian empiricism as from Darwinism. He believes in a third possibility, intermediate between the theory of characteristics acquired under pressure of the environment and the theory of mutations. His observations and experiments concerning the morphogenesis of a type of snail, the *Limnaea stagnalis*, confirmed this possibility [Inhelder et al., 1974, pp. 2–3].

What observations of the behavior of snails could be so convincing as to lead Piaget to the identification of a third source of knowledge besides experience and heredity? Figure 2-1 illustrates the pond snails that were responsible for Piaget's interest in adaptation. Note that the figure—based on Piaget's descriptions (1971a, 1974a, 1977a, 1977c)—shows three separate groups of *Limnaea stagnalis*, each characteristic of a particular environment: those that live in still, tranquil waters (habitat A), those that live in mildly disturbed waters agitated by waves (habitat B), and those that live in severely disturbed waters agitated by high winds and waves (habitat C). As you can see in Figure 2-1, the shape of those that

Habitat *A:* Still waters
↓
Phenotype = Elongated form

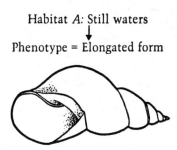

Habitats *B* and *C:* Disturbed waters
↓   ↓
B: Mildly disturbed   *C:* Severely disturbed by wind
↓   ↓
Phenotype = Globular form   Globular form

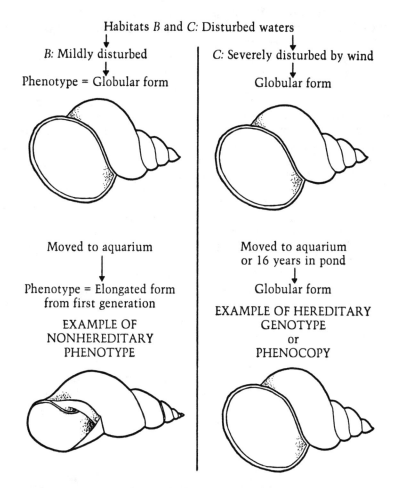

Moved to aquarium   Moved to aquarium
                                   or 16 years in pond
↓   ↓
Phenotype = Elongated form   Globular form
from first generation

                                   EXAMPLE OF HEREDITARY
EXAMPLE OF   GENOTYPE
NONHEREDITARY   or
PHENOTYPE   PHENOCOPY

Figure 2-1. Pond snail *(Limnaea stagnalis)* as an example of phenocopy. (Based on Piaget, 1971a, 1974a, 1977a, 1977c.)

live in mildly disturbed waters is globular—wider and shorter than that of the snails living in tranquil waters. Piaget (1977c, pp. 809–810) explains the adaptation as follows: "At the time of each agitation by the waves the animal in the course of its growth attaches itself to its solid support, which dilates the opening. At the same time and even because of this, it draws on the muscle that attaches it to its shell, and this tends to shorten the spine (i.e., the upper part of the spiral shell)." The offspring of pond snails in habitat *B* (mildly disturbed waters and pebbly shores) have globular shells as long as they live in this habitat. But when these snails are moved to an aquarium (habitat *A*), as diagrammed in Figure 2-1, the phenotype of the offspring becomes elongated. Thus, what may have seemed to be a change in genetic makeup is only a temporary change.

The truly different snails are those that live in the stormy habitat of high winds and waves. Their shape is very globular, which, in view of Piaget's explanation above, is not surprising. What is surprising is that the globular shape is passed on to the offspring even when the habitat is an aquarium or a pond. "We have verified this for six generations in aquarium (in numerous lines) and for 16 years in a small pond at quite a distance from the lake" (Piaget, 1977c, p. 810). Piaget sees this phenomenon as an example of a progressive reorganization, or gradual change, in the "response" of the genome. It is as if there had been a genetic assimilation whereby the genome entered into an interaction with the environment and selected the best response. The final result is the process of biological **phenocopy:** the replacement of an initial phenotype by a genotype presenting the same distinctive characteristics.

The middle-ground position of phenocopy is essentially an emphasis on regulations from within the organism. These regulations, in turn, are modified through interaction with the environment. For the snails of habitat *C*, there was a regulated reconstruction of the original genetic material so that the change in their shape was observed in offspring no matter where the new habitat was located.

Piaget (1974a, 1977c) cites another important example of phenocopy. One of the herbs that Piaget studied, *Sedum album*, is commonly found at lower altitudes. When the herb is found at higher altitudes, its phenotype is of a smaller size. However, when the herb is transplanted to a lower altitude, it recovers its normal size (a phenomenon analogous to that of the snails in habitat *B*). But, like the snails of habitat *C*, a certain variety by the name of *micranthum*, found at high altitudes in Savoy, retains its characteristics from one generation to the next, no matter what the habitat is. Thus, when *micranthum* is planted in Geneva, the small size is retained. This indicates that an internal control is manifesting itself by means of the "small-size" genotype.

Piaget (1977c) gives another example of sedum to clarify the meaning of phenocopy:

> We studied particularly a not-yet-known variety (that we have named *var. parvulum*) of the *Sedum sediforme*, very widespread around the Mediterranean. This type of species is of great size and its color is generally glaucous. The *var. parvulum* that one finds at heights or in places north of the usual habitat of the species are of very small size, with thicker leaves and

generally of a dark green color, due (as one of our colleagues, a professional botanist, has confirmed) to an increase in chlorophyll and in photosynthetic power. In this case, as in preceding ones, we find numerous *parvulum* phenotypes, but also we find in some places a genotype the stability of which we have verified over thousands of descendants at 400, 1000 and 1600 meter altitudes. Here again the genotype, rarer than the phenotype, has replaced them under certain conditions, and this again constitutes a case of *phenocopy* [p. 810].

Why are these observations on snails and herbs examples of Piaget's middle-ground position? Because Piaget doesn't recognize a direct action of the environment on the organism, as the Lamarckians would. And he rejects the neo-Darwinian hypothesis of adaptation to the environment by chance and *not* by direction. Instead, Piaget stresses the importance of internal and directive factors of assimilation, which are not passively received or built in by hereditary givens (Piaget, 1978a).

The Concept of Cognitive Phenocopy

The important question is: are Piaget's excursions into the lakes and mountains of Switzerland and France to study snails and herbs related to his theory of cognitive development? The resounding yes to this question is based on the fact that these excursions were designed to probe Piaget's key to his theory, the concept of equilibration. In Chapter One equilibration was defined as the self-regulatory process by which the child moves from one state of equilibrium to increasingly advanced states of equilibrium. Equilibration is the third element in development, besides environment and heredity, and it embodies Piaget's middle-ground position, or third possibility.[6]

All these factors will be explained in detail in Chapter Three. Still, a brief investigation of the concept of equilibration will be helpful in understanding the links between the biological and the cognitive meanings of phenocopy (the latter relates to the development of human knowledge). The key to understanding these links is the notion of equilibration as *regulation*. The following experiment by Piaget and Inhelder (Greco, Inhelder, Matalon, & Piaget, 1963; Piaget, 1977c), illustrated in Figure 2-2, may serve to clarify this notion.

Children were asked to place a red marble into a container with their right hand and a blue marble into a partly concealed container with their left hand. They were asked two questions: (1) "As we put one in here and one in here, do we have the same amount in both containers?" (2) "If we were to continue for a very long time, would we still have the same amount in both containers?" The children, as young as 4 and 5, had no difficulty with the first question. A typical response was "Yes, both the same." However, the same children, confronted with the second question, couldn't predict the results of continuing the process; that is, they failed to understand that if $n = n$, then $n + 1 = n + 1$ (always). They couldn't anticipate that equality would be maintained.

[6]Piaget's middle-ground position, or third possibility, is frequently called *tertium quid*.

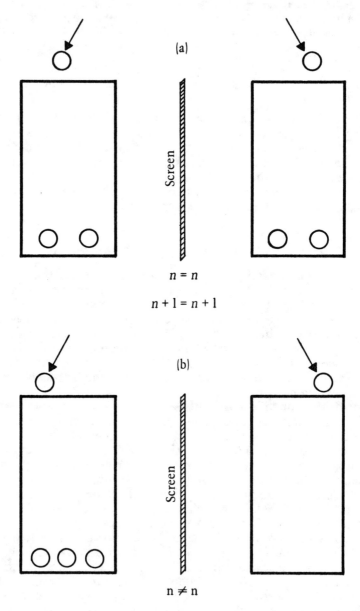

$n = n$

$n + 1 = n + 1$

(b)

$n \neq n$

Younger children: $n + 1 = n + 1$
Older children: $n + 1 \neq n + 1$ (conserve inequality)

Figure 2-2.   Example of cognitive phenocopy.

An interesting variation of this experiment emphasized even more strongly the change in understanding that results from experience. The children were given a visible inequality: three marbles in the first jar and none in the second (before screening). Young children thought that equality eventually would be achieved $(n = n)$ and that somehow the initial inequality could be canceled by succeeding equal additions. Older children understood that inequality would be maintained.

What would lead the child to a higher level of understanding? More specifically, why would a child begin to realize that, if there was equality (two marbles in each container) or inequality (three in one container, none in the other) at the beginning, that equality or inequality would have to be maintained? It is obvious that simply observing the placing of marbles into each container is not enough. In order to achieve a higher level of understanding, children need to reorganize their own thinking. This reorganization is what we call regulation and represents the basic meaning of equilibration.

What sparks this reorganization? Perhaps the children notice the contradiction: how can there be more marbles in one container if we started out with the same number in both? Or how can there be equal numbers of marbles when we started out with unequal numbers? Such a contradiction, when noticed, acts like a *disturbance* that places the child in a temporary state of puzzlement. Also, the children may be disturbed because they realize that there is a gap in their understanding, something they don't know. Again, they are puzzled. So the disturbance may be due to a contradiction or to a gap in understanding (these topics will be discussed in detail in Chapters Three, Four, and Five.) In either case, children need to reorganize their thinking and move to a new level of understanding to resolve the contradiction. This reorganization, controlled by the child, is the self-regulatory process that is the essential meaning of equilibration.

Now back to snails and herbs. The basic theme of Piaget's recent expansion of his biological model (Piaget, 1971a, 1974a, 1977c, 1978a) is that biological and cognitive regulations are *related*. However, the student of Piaget cannot be cautioned enough to avoid the notion that human thinking is regulated in the *same* manner as biological growth. We are not snails or herbs. But there are analogous aspects in the development of all living things. One such aspect is equilibration. Neither the environment nor built-in maturational tendencies can explain how living organisms make complex adaptations to their surroundings. The shells of the snails in habitat C didn't change just because of the winds and waves. Nor did they change because of heredity. Similarly, the children didn't begin to understand the need to maintain equality in the number of marbles by just observing. Nor was the change that occurred in their thinking built into their developing brain structures.

The analogy between biological phenocopy and cognitive phenocopy rests on the notion of the need for regulation: an orderly reorganization that leads to a new way of functioning. This reorganization is not imposed from the outside, nor is it "given"; it is self-regulated.

All other Piagetian concepts and all other sections of this book build on equilibration: children grow in knowledge by constructing their own understandings, which are not imposed from the outside but are reached through an internal process of reorganization.

Summary

The Piagetian position sees cognitive development as a process parallel to that of biological development. It is a middle-ground, interacting position. On the one hand, such a position doesn't see the organism as too easily affected by environmental stresses. On the other hand, it avoids the view that one waits for a natural unfolding process—that is, maturation "built into the genes." The environment is not ignored. Children have many experiences in their day-to-day living and the importance of such experiences is not underrated. However, the Piagetian position sees the information children gain from these learning experiences as actively filtered and modified by assimilation structures. For now it is sufficient to think of these assimilation structures as the level of understanding that the child brings to the learning experience. What has been learned in the past modifies what will be learned in the future. The reaction norm—that is, the range of reactions according to the level of understanding—controls the learning experience. Stated differently, the perceptual experiences, as an aspect of the learning experiences, are controlled by the level of development. Recall that experience with the marbles didn't lead to a new level of understanding. Progress in the children's cognitive growth was tied to the construction of the rule that, given original equality, $n + 1 = n + 1$ holds forever.

We return to the basic Piagetian principle: growth in knowledge is not a simple registering of experience—perceptual givens that pass from eye to mind—but a process of construction controlled by equilibration. It is this control, or regulation, that represents the central theme of this book.

Reflexive Abstraction and Equilibration

The crux of the notion of phenocopy is that development is not a phenomenon instigated by stimuli from the environment. Neither is it a phenomenon due to an unfolding of maturational tendencies—that is, growth. In traditional psychological terms, it is not due to nurture (environment) or to nature (maturation, or biological givens). What the notion emphasizes is the interaction between the person and the objects in the environment. This interaction is controlled by the self-regulations (equilibration) of the person encountering the objects.

What we are saying is that people construct understandings for themselves. But how do they do that? For example, how did the children in the earlier example construct the understanding that an initial inequality in the number of marbles could not be erased by subsequent equal additions? Or, to put it more simply, how did these children grow in knowledge?

A partial answer is, of course, environmental experience. Children bring to the experimental situation many previous experiences of counting objects such as marbles. As the years go by, children grow and mature. In the above example, we noted that experience wasn't enough and that just observing didn't lead to an understanding of the relationship between inequality and infinity. But maturation is not sufficient either. From clinical as well as biological studies we know that, without stimulation through environmental experiences, a person does not develop properly.

Another element is needed. That element is the interactional factor of equilibration, or self-regulation. However, unless one finds a way of spelling out the meaning of this factor by explaining how knowledge develops, a discussion of equilibration has little usefulness. In the pages that follow, we will try to offer a detailed explanation of the development of knowledge.

The Two Types of Abstraction

We begin by probing the meaning of the following quotation: "All new knowledge presumes an abstraction, because, in spite of the part of reorganization that it requires, it never constitutes an absolute beginning and it draws its elements from some earlier reality" (Piaget, 1974a, p. 81; translation by P. Stevens and authors).

As we mentioned in Chapter One, Piaget (Beth & Piaget, 1966; Piaget, 1974a, 1976b, 1977e) lists two types of abstraction: empirical and reflexive (Figure 2-3). To clarify this distinction, let's return to the little boy playing on the beach (see Chapter One). The little boy notices that the pebbles are smooth, that they are light, and that they can be moved. All these learning experiences are what Piaget calls *empirical abstraction*. In this type of abstraction, information is drawn from objects—that is, from exogenous (external) sources—and is, of necessity, based on observation. Therefore, the knowledge that results is called **exogenous knowledge.** The essential characteristic of the first type of abstraction is that it is based on observables and on the subject's actions on those observables. By observables we mean the characteristics of the object that the child is capable of noticing—in this case, smoothness, lightness, and movability. Much of what we know comes from empirical abstraction.

However, for further growth it is necessary sometimes to go beyond the observables, or, as Bruner (1973) would say, "beyond the information given." And this is where the second type of abstraction comes into the picture. This type of abstraction, which was introduced in Chapter One in the discussion of logico-mathematical knowledge, is *reflexive*

A.   *Empirical abstraction:* Draws its information from objects; is based on observables (exogenous source).

Important: Empirical abstraction does not intervene by itself at any level of knowing; it is made possible by previous reflexive abstractions through activities of the person.

B₁.   *Reflexive (réfléchissante) abstraction:* Is based on coordination of actions or operations (endogenous source) and is, therefore, constructive.
      Two fundamental characteristics:
         1. *Projection:* the raising (or projecting) to a higher level of what is borrowed from a lower level of understanding.
         2. *Reflection,* or mental *reorganization:* need to reconstruct what was abstracted from the lower level.

B₂.   *Pseudoempirical abstraction* (a form of reflexive abstraction): the object is modified by the person's actions and enriched by properties drawn from the coordination of the actions.

Figure 2-3. Two types of abstractions that children use to construct their understandings. (Based on Piaget, 1974a, 1976b, 1977e.)

abstraction.[7] Unlike empirical abstraction, reflexive abstraction is based not on what is observed (exogenous source) but on interior (intrinsic) structuring (**endogenous knowledge**). In other words, reflexive abstraction always involves **coordination,** defined as the unifying form of the elements of an action. Empirical abstraction does not involve coordination (Furth, 1969; Piaget, 1977e).

Recall that the children didn't learn that $n + 1 = n + 1$ to infinity by merely observing the marbles being placed into the containers. As we said earlier, experience was not enough. At some point a reorganization—that is, an intrinsic restructuring—was needed: if we start with an equal number of marbles and we keep adding equal numbers of marbles, equality will be conserved even if the number of marbles we add is infinite and the containers are infinitely huge.

Reflexive abstraction includes *pseudoempirical abstraction,* which is a process whose importance should not be underrated. Piaget clarifies:

> When the object is modified by the subject's actions and enriched by properties drawn from the coordinations of the actions (for example, ordering the elements of a group), the abstraction relating to these properties is said to be 'pseudoempirical,' even though it proceeds by means of the object and by means of the object's characteristics, as in the empirical abstraction. . . . Thus, it [pseudoempirical abstraction] is a question of a particular case of reflexive abstraction and not at all of one derived from empirical abstraction [Piaget, 1977e, p. 303; translation by the authors].

What Piaget is stressing here is that, even though the child's manipulations and observations of the object may be interpreted as empirical activity, these manipulations may lead to higher levels of understanding. A clear example of pseudoempirical abstraction is the case of a child *seriating* sticks *A-H.* At some point the child grasps that, if there are seven sticks longer than *A,* there must be seven sticks shorter than *H.* This understanding is not constructed by mere manipulation of the sticks but is drawn from the coordinations—that is, the mental understanding of the interrelationships among the seriated sticks, which the child grasps as asymmetric.

As we said earlier, reflexive abstraction is actually another term for logico-mathematical knowing, which is of necessity *constructive* and *endogenous* (intrinsic). It should be stressed, however, that empirical abstraction doesn't cease to exist once reflexive abstraction takes place. "Reflexive abstraction does not 'replace' empirical abstraction but frames it from the start and then goes infinitely beyond it (in the correct sense of the term); and the universe of logico-mathematical possibilities does not replace the real world but plunges it there in order to better explain it, reflexive abstraction thus being a source but not the seat of phenocopies" (Piaget, 1974a, p. 88; translation by the authors).

Thus, the "tools of assimilation," or the previously built-up structures, are used when information is drawn from an object, as in

---

[7]In some English translations, the French term *réfléchissante* was expressed as *reflective.* The preferred term is *reflexive* to avoid confusion with *reflected,* which refers to the level of abstraction characteristic of adolescent thinking (see Chapter Six).

empirical abstraction. These tools make empirical abstraction possible. However, these tools are not taken from the object but "are due to the subject's activities and, as such, are derived from earlier reflexive abstractions even though, let us repeat, the empirical abstractions that make them possible draw products only from the object" (Piaget, 1974a, p. 82; translation by S. Campbell).

This interplay between empirical abstraction and reflexive abstraction is of crucial importance, for it is at the heart of the meaning of activity for a learning theory (Gallagher, 1978b). To clarify this point, consider the two fundamental characteristics of a reflexive abstraction. First, reflexive abstraction is characterized by a *projection* in a physical sense. It is a transposing to a higher level of what is borrowed from a lower level. Such a characteristic may be found even at the sensorimotor stage, when simple movements are coordinated and transposed to more complex movements to attain a goal.

Second, reflexive abstraction is characterized by a reflection in the sense of mental *reorganization*—that is, a need to reconstruct that which was abstracted from the lower level. This reconstruction is necessary because there must be an adjustment (accommodation) to the higher-level structure. Growth in knowledge at all levels, then, is a constant spiral of projection and reorganization, then another projection and another reorganization, and so forth.

Phenocopy and the Meanings of Structure and Operation

In Chapter One and in the preceding portion of this chapter we offered examples of children constructing their own understandings. The little boy on the beach constructed the understanding that sum was independent of order. The children who placed marbles into containers constructed the understanding that, if one begins with unequal numbers, successive equal additions do not cancel the initial inequality. In order to understand more fully the discipline of genetic (developmental) epistemology illustrated by such examples, it is necessary to introduce some basic concepts and definitions that thread their way through that discipline.

The Meaning of Structure

The concept of **structure** is no doubt one of the most basic in genetic epistemology (Inhelder, 1977; Piaget, 1971a, 1974a; Voyat, 1973). One of the clearest examples is the structure of seriation, which was the research topic in several major works of the Genevan School (Inhelder & Piaget, 1964; Piaget, 1976b; Piaget & Inhelder, 1973; Piaget & Szeminska, 1952; Sinclair, 1967a). The simplicity and the strength of the seriation experiments are the reasons for their inclusion in several sections of this book.

In the basic seriation investigations, children are given ten sticks ranging in size from 9 to 16.2 cm. The children's task is to order the ten sticks from shortest to longest or the reverse. A successful strategy is to keep the bottom ends of the sticks even so that the "stair steps" of the top ends can be graduated correctly.

Piaget (1971d, pp. 3-4) effectively related the problem of **seriation** to the meaning of structure:

> Bärbel Inhelder, Mimi Sinclair and I have once again returned to this problem of seriation in our recent studies on memory, and our findings confirm the stages discovered in our earlier work. For instance, we found that during the initial stage, which we may call stage A, the youngest subjects maintain that all the sticks are of equal length. During the next stage (stage B), the subjects divide the sticks into two categories, large and small, with no ordering of the elements. At stage C, the children talk of the large ones, the middle-sized ones and the small ones. At stage D, the child constructs a series in an empirical fashion, by trial and error, but he is not able to produce immediately a faultless construction. And finally, at stage E, the child discovers a method: he chooses the largest of all the sticks and he sets this on the table, then he takes the largest of all the remaining sticks and places this beside the first stick, then the largest of the remaining ones, until he has placed all the sticks on the table. At this stage, he constructs a correct ordering without any hesitation, and this construction presupposes a reversible relation. That is to say, an element *a* is both smaller than the ones which have gone before it and larger than the ones to follow. This is a good example of what I mean by a structure.*

Piaget doesn't mean here that the structure is the configuration "out on the table"—that is, the seriated sticks. Neither does the term *construction* in the quotation, as a manipulated or physical phenomenon, have the same meaning as construction in relation to a mental phenomenon. The thinking ability guides the construction. However, the thinking ability is not to be *identified with* the construction. We will return to this point after a more formal definition of structure.

Structure is a concept that Piaget borrowed from mathematics. "A structure is a system with a set of laws that apply to the system as a whole and not only to its elements" (Piaget, 1972c, p. 15).† The nonmathematician can return to the seriation problem in order to understand this definition. What is a structure in relation to the problem of seriation? It is a set of asymmetric relationships—that is, relationships lacking symmetry. Stick A is smaller than (<) B, < C, < D, and so forth or the reverse: stick D is larger than (>) C, > B, > A.

The set of asymmetric relationships in the problem of seriation, as a structure, needs laws. If stick A is shorter than stick B, it follows that stick B cannot be shorter than stick A. Once the children solve the seriation problem, they may show surprise if asked "If stick A is shorter than stick B, could stick B be shorter than stick A?" These children would

*From "The Theory of Stages in Cognitive Development," by J. Piaget. In. D. R. Green, M. P. Ford, and G. B. Flamer (Eds.), *Measurement and Piaget.* Copyright 1971 by McGraw-Hill, Inc. Reprinted by permission.

†From *Play and Development,* by M. W. Piers (Ed.). Copyright © 1972 by Norton Publishers, Inc., New York. This and all other quotes from the same source are reprinted by permission.

think it logically *necessary* that the asymmetric relationships be retained. Thus, the structure is self-regulating, or equilibrating. Once the child has understood this point, it would be unlikely for him or her to make a mistake when asked the above question.

It may be said, then, that a basic characteristic of structures is that they are self-regulating, or governed from within (Piaget, 1970d). Here is the notion of *construction*,[8] the building up of understandings by the child. If the child cannot comprehend that, if *A* is smaller than *B*, of necessity *B* must be larger than *A* (an asymmetric relationship), it will be of little use to tell the child, force memorization, or give demonstrations. Thus, another way of understanding that learning is subordinated to development is to view learning as a self-regulatory process.

A structure is not observable. This is why constructivist epistemology is not well accepted by empiricists, who place heavy emphasis on observed behavior. Furthermore, children, as well as adults, may be not aware of the mental structures that underlie their thinking. Through questions and careful analysis of both behavior and verbal answers as the child interacts with the environment, we are able to infer structure. However, we would be amazed if a child who said that the sticks in a seriation problem were in the right order told us "I know because I've grasped the principle of asymmetric relationships!" In sum, a technical explanation is not a prerequisite for the presence of a structure. Another method of determining whether a structure is present is to give additional problems that are logically related to the first one.

Return to the seriation problem. An essential aspect of seriation is *transitivity*: if stick *A* is shorter than stick *B*, and stick *B* is shorter than stick *C*, it follows that stick *A* is also shorter than stick *C*. (Commonly, this transitive relationship is written: if $A < B$ and $B < C$, then $A < C$ (see Figure 2-4.) If this ability to order systematically the transitive

Figure 2-4. The relationship of transitivity.

relationships—that is, the seriation ability—is inferred from observing a child, can one expect that same child to be able to carry out other relationships of transitivity? In other words, is it possible to put the "realness" of a structure to a test? To answer this question, the Genevan School devised the following investigation (Piaget, 1972c, p. 18):

[8]The Genevan School often uses the term *constructivist epistemology* in place of *genetic epistemology* to emphasize the necessity of interactions between subject and objects. The term *constructivist* is used to reinforce the basic hypothesis of developmental constructivism: "No human knowledge is preformed in the structures of either the subject or the object" (Inhelder, Sinclair, & Bovet, 1974, p. 8).

We . . . presented a child with two sticks, stick *A* being longer than stick *B*. The child noted which one was longer. Then we hid *A*, the longer one, under the table and gave the child a third stick, *C*, which was shorter than the middle-sized one, *B*, which at this point was clearly visible. We then asked him to compare the two visible sticks with the third hidden one. Young children at the stage where they are making couples (pairings) in the seriation would say that they couldn't tell whether this one was shorter or longer than the other one, because they hadn't seen them together. But a group of seven- or eight-year old youngsters, the age when children are able to build seriation systematically, will say, "Well, of course, stick *C* is shorter than stick *A*; it just goes without saying."

Note that the older children express that it is *necessary* (as commonly stated, "it necessarily follows" or "is of **logical necessity**") that, if *A* is larger than *B* and *B* is larger than *C*, *C* must be shorter than *A*. As we said earlier, for Piaget such statements help to verify the psychological existence of a structure even though such structures are not directly observable. When seriation is understood as a system of asymmetrical transitive relationships—that is, the ordering of sticks of various lengths—then that understanding assists the child in solving other problems based on transitivity.

The problem of testing the reality of structures is not always so easily solved, however. Sometimes children (and, yes, even adults!) fail to apply a given structure in a variety of situations or under a variety of circumstances. As Duckworth (1979, p. 304) so succinctly put it, we have to "think of thinking about it in that way" before we can demonstrate the consistent use of a structure. A similar phenomenon has been described by Piaget as a time lag *(décalage)* and will be described later in this book.

Structure as Organization: Schemes and Operation

In Chapter One and in the preceding section on phenocopy, we stressed the basic notion that the growth of knowledge is always linked to action. Knowledge does not originate in the child or in the objects with which the child plays; it originates in the interactions between the child and those objects. A simple way to express the meaning of a structure is to say that it is an organization of these interactions. For example, when a little girl stacks blocks in seriated fashion, she is demonstrating a mental structure of seriation at a very action-oriented level.

This small child playing with blocks is capable of many actions connected with the blocks: looking, grasping, stacking, and—alas!—throwing. Such actions are really simple structures labeled **schemes** (or action schemes) in Piagetian theory. Schemes, however, are really broader than the simple actions, for the term is used to emphasize what in an action can be repeated and generalized. Thus, if an infant grasps its bottle, the action of grasping may be extended to other objects in the crib and, later, to more complex actions such as grasping and stacking blocks. Here the grasping and the stacking are examples of the coordination of actions and consequent growth in knowledge.

When children see blocks and if the scheme of "stacking" is available, then the sight of the blocks is filtered through this structure, which consists of the scheme of stacking (Piaget, 1970d). The filtering process, or modification of the input of what was seen (the blocks), is the same mechanism of *assimilation* that was defined in Chapter One.

Around the age of 6 or 7 (age is not so important, as we shall see), the child's internalized actions, represented in thought, become reversible. The child's structures may then be called **operations.** Recall the task of seriating sticks. When children (1) are able to represent *in thought* what must be accomplished in order to seriate the sticks correctly, *and* (2) can understand that the order is reversible (*C* is longer than *A* and *B* but shorter than the rest of the sticks in the series), then there is evidence of an operational structure or operation of seriation. Such operational structures are never isolated but always coordinated into overall systems of understandings. Thus, the ability to seriate paves the way for carrying out other problems based on the notion of transitivity, because the latter is essential for the solution of problems requiring seriations.

In this chapter we have sketched a very brief outline of the meaning of terms such as *scheme* and *operations*. In Chapters Four and Five these and other basic concepts will be elaborated in detail.

Stages of Cognitive Development and the Spiral of Knowing

Stages of Cognitive Development

Genetic epistemology divides cognitive development into four stages. The following summary lists the currently used terms for the stages, the approximate ages for each stage, and some general characteristics of the four stages.

1. **Sensorimotor stage** (0–1½ years): Emphasis on coordination of *action*; gradual connecting of means to reach goals.
2. **Preoperational (representational) stage** (2–6 years): Internalization of actions (representation in thought); use of symbols in play, language, and mental imagery; use of elementary functions of one-way relationships.
3. **Concrete-operational stage** (6–11 years): First use of reversible operations signified by conservation; thought structures connected to the concrete—concerned with relations among objects (seriation) and classes of objects (class inclusion).
4. **Formal-operational stage** (beginning around 11 or 12 and expanding during adulthood): Ability to deal with the possible; understanding of relations between relations; ability to verbalize rules used in solving problems.

In Chapters Four and Five we shall discuss in detail those aspects of the developmental stages that are especially meaningful for a learning-theory orientation. Here we simply point out that, from the very beginning of cognitive development, the stages must be viewed within the concept of interaction—the tertium quid described at the beginning of this chapter. At each stage there is interaction between the endogenous processes, which are continually being expanded by the constructive effect of reflexive abstractions, and the exogenous processes—that is, the effects of experience (learning in the narrow sense). Progress within each stage and between stages is achieved by projection and reorganization, the characteristics of reflexive abstraction.

In sum, from a dynamic perspective, the developmental stages are the products of the interaction between the properties of the object discovered through experience (empirical abstraction) and the endogenous activities of the subject (reflexive abstraction). Each stage opens up possibilities for the next. Even at the final stage—that of formal thought during adolescence and adulthood—the dynamic equilibration through the mechanism of reflexive abstraction ensures "limitless elaborations and particular applications" (Furth, 1969, p. 219).

The Spiral of Knowing

Having touched upon the basic concepts of cognitive phenocopy—reflexive abstraction and structure—we can now summarize the essential aspects of the constructivist epistemology of the Genevan School by means of a diagram of the **Spiral of Knowing** (Figure 2-5). We shall also discuss how the stages of cognitive development can be related to the dynamics of the spiral.

Note that the diagram is an inverted cone, with a peripheral "envelope" surrounding spiral A. The envelope represents interactions with the environment, with E and E' symbolizing empirical abstraction and the reflexive "frames" that operate as recording instruments. Spiral A is the endogenous process of reflexive abstraction, or logico-mathematical knowing. Vector a represents the successive, hierarchical levels of the cognitive structures. Vector b represents the changes due to the effect of the environment and the resulting **disequilibriums.** Note that, although in the figure the direction of vector b is horizontal, it could be inclined slightly toward the base or toward the top. Such direction indicates that the environmental events may interact with the endogenous processes (spiral A) of the same level or possibly with those of a slightly lower or higher level (those in the process of construction). Following the traditional Piagetian maxim that learning is subordinated to development, we wouldn't expect that these environmental events would destroy previous constructions or that learning experiences would be functional well beyond a certain structural level.

Vector C represents explorations, which may be of a trial-and-error nature, leading to partial reorganization or to a complete endogenous synthesis. The latter is analogous to the phenomenon we observed in the snails that lived in an environment of high winds and waves:

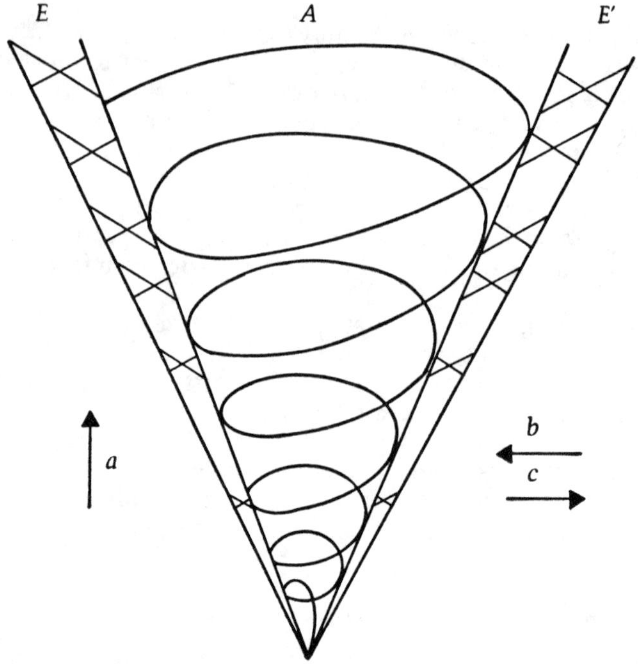

Figure 2-5. The Spiral of Knowing. (From *Adaptation Vitale et Psychologie de l'Intelligence: Selection Organique et Phénocopie*, by J. Piaget. Copyright 1974 by Hermann, Paris. Reprinted by permission of Hermann, Paris.)

replacements of exogenous characteristics by an endogenous reconstruction.

Note that the spiral is open and ever widening. These characteristics represent the more and more complex set of endogenous syntheses previously explained by the alternation of "reflecting" and "reflection," which are the two characteristics of projection and reorganization of reflexive abstraction. Piaget (1977b, p. 30) summarizes the meaning of the ever-widening spiral as follows: "Any knowledge raises new problems as it solves preceding ones."

The raising of new problems upon solution of previous ones provides a link with the notion of stages in developmental epistemology. Inhelder (1977, p. 333) clearly summarizes how the concept of stages has changed from a structurally oriented to a more dynamically and functionally oriented concept: "At first, the concept of stages was used by Piaget as a useful heuristic with which to account for the successive, qualitatively different forms of a construction process; later, the developmental stages define equilibrium states in a continuous process of cognitive structurations whose formation is ordered so that each construction having attained a state of relative equilibrium opens up new possibilities, each step in the process necessary for the subsequent one."

The key phrase in this description of developmental stages is "opens up new possibilities." The Spiral of Knowing expresses the openness and dynamics of the concept of stages—a continuous line that is ever expanding. There are no rigid breaking points; that is, one does not search for the task that neatly separates one stage from another. Also, the spiral, as an "opening up of possibilities," cannot fit within a theory that reduces development to bits of learning (Piaget, 1977a). At any one point in the spiral, what the child learns is dependent on the child's developmental level, on his or her competence in the sense in which the biologist Waddington used the term (Gallagher, 1977; Waddington, 1961). Neither Piaget nor Waddington views competence as prewired or as a set of innate structural states that permit organisms to respond in specific ways. Rather, they define biological competence as a range of adaptative potentials that cause adaptive behaviors to emerge in response to the range of possible environmental stresses.

Constructivist Epistemology: Inhelder's Contribution

It is in the area of constructivist epistemology that Bärbel Inhelder, one of Piaget's closest collaborators, has made her most valuable contributions. Thus, it is only appropriate that we pay tribute to Inhelder in the section of this overview chapter that deals with that topic. Too often Inhelder is classified as an "assistant" to Piaget. However, in much of her work she has been an initiator as well as an innovator and has made significant contributions to constructivist epistemology in her own right. This is especially true of the research on learning in which she is engaged at the present time.

Before turning to the importance of Inhelder's research, the following section of an interview is presented to summarize her first collaboration with Piaget. In answer to the question as to whether she had always planned to become a psychologist, Inhelder replied:

> It is mostly a matter of chance. I was born in Saint Gall, in the German part of Switzerland. Originally I came to Geneva for a summer course at the University. I wanted to learn some French. I had some background in biology and in education, and then I discovered psychology and Edouard Claparède and Piaget here at the University [Geneva]. Originally I thought I would study psychology for a few years. Then I liked it so much that I stayed on to take my doctorate.
> After I had been at the University for a few weeks, first Claparède and then Piaget asked me to do some research. . . . My first publication was on conservation [Piaget & Inhelder, 1974/1942]. I still remember the day when Piaget said: "Now look, I have some ideas on this. Let's write a book together." So I wrote my first with Piaget before I delivered my thesis [Hall, 1970].

Inhelder's interest in research on learning within a Piagetian framework falls into three periods (the last two being very closely connected). In the early period of her doctoral studies and thesis, in 1943 (see Inhelder, 1968), she was the first to be concerned with the application of Piagetian stage concepts to the problem of individual differences. Her research on the diagnosis of reasoning in the retarded found that severely retarded subjects remained at the sensorimotor stage, that trainable children functioned at the representational (preoperational) stage, whereas the educable retarded reached concrete operations. No retardates were able to complete tasks associated with the formal-operational stage. This research set the stage for a number of studies dealing with development in exceptional children and will be discussed again in Chapter Nine.

The second period, which had its beginnings in 1966 and continues into the present, centers specifically around the topic of learning (in the traditional sense) in relation to the developmental stages. Piaget, in referring to this work, continually emphasizes Inhelder's role in the design of the studies: "Research on learning, directed by B. Inhelder, M. Bovet, and H. Sinclair, in which I had no part, originated in the work of the Center of Epistemology on the learning of logical structures and especially studies by B. Inhelder in some cases which were followed longitudinally. One of the essential problems was to find out how a child passes from one operational stage to the next" (Piaget, 1976a, p. 146).

The most important aspect of the research on learning at the Center (Inhelder, 1977; Inhelder et al., 1974) is that, according to Inhelder, it expands the model of the Spiral of Knowing:

> Development can no longer be an accumulation of pieces of learning, and learning must depend on the laws of development and the competence of the subject, according to his cognitive level, as has been shown in our research on learning and the development of cognition. In other words, knowledge is never a simple copy of reality but always results from a construction of reality through the activities of the subject [Inhelder, 1977, p. 339].

The third period is in a sense an extension of the second one. At the present time, Inhelder is engaged in research on the strategies that children demonstrate when they solve problems. These studies (Inhelder, 1976a; Karmiloff-Smith & Inhelder, 1975) are directly related to learning, in that children pick up cues in their interactions with objects, cues that help them modify their further actions.

Thus, when we included Inhelder's name in the title of this volume, our intent was not only to stress her collaboration with Piaget on important works related to learning (Piaget & Inhelder, 1971, 1973, 1975), but, more importantly, to spotlight her creative contributions to those aspects of the theory related to the process of learning. It is her work that provided the major research foundation for Chapters Three and Seven of this book.

CHAPTER THREE
Learning
and Development

Most learning theories emphasize learning as a source of development. More specifically, they propose that development is a result of a series of discrete learning experiences. Children learn to grasp, to walk, to talk, and to read and write; because of these accomplishments, they develop. Genevan theory focuses on development as the essential process of growth and postulates that what children are capable of learning depends on the level of development they have attained. For example, babies simply have not developed to the point at which they can do arithmetic, no matter how much instruction they receive. Learning and development, therefore, are considered to be interrelated but distinct. By *development* the Genevans refer to a spontaneous process that is linked to the child's total growth. This process is biological as well as psychological, in that it concerns changes in the body, in the nervous system, and in intellectual functions.

In genetic (developmental) epistemology, learning differs from development in two ways. First, learning is not spontaneous but must be provoked by situations or events in the environment. Second, it is limited to a specific situation or problem. Learning, for example, that a comma directs the reader to pause is dependent on very specific instructions. A child's ability to walk and talk results instead from the child's total growth, not from specific environmental events.

To put it in other words, Piaget (1959) distinguishes two types of learning. *Learning in the strict sense* is defined as the acquisition of information (for example, the notion that Albany is the capital of New York State) and skills (for example, riding a bicycle) through experience and exercise. *Learning in the broad sense* includes both learning in the strict sense and equilibration. Thus, it embraces all of development (Inhelder, Sinclair, & Bovet, 1974) and is dependent on the four factors discussed in the pages to come.

Like other theorists, the Genevans emphasize the roles played in children's growth by physiological maturation and by learning. Learning is defined as the information and abilities children derive from experience. There are two types of learning experiences: those in which children learn from objects in the environment (physical experiences) and those in which they learn from other people (social experiences).

Traditionally, learning theorists have thought of maturation and learning as two completely separate processes; what is not maturation is learning. But many now recognize that maturation involves environmental experience and vice versa. Even though children don't need instruction to learn to walk, they do need exercise. Conversely, without an adequate level of maturation, all the exercise in the world will not cause a baby to walk. Piaget argues that there is another factor to be considered, one that balances and integrates the effects of maturation and learning. That factor is equilibration. The child can learn from specific experiences only when his or her cognitive structures are mature enough to be able to assimilate the experience.

In sum, the Genevans see cognitive development as the result of the interplay of four factors: physiological maturation, physical experience, social experience, and equilibration. All four are necessary for development to take place.

The First Factor of Development: Maturation

Piaget tells us that, although children progress through the stages of development in the same order (first, sensorimotor stage; then, preoperations, and concrete operations; finally, formal operations), the average ages at which they achieve the specific stages vary a great deal.[1] In their studies the Genevans have found, for example, that children in Geneva and in Teheran progress at approximately the same rate but that children in the Iranian countryside lag behind by about two years (Mohseni, 1966). Mentally retarded children also progress through the same stages, but they are systematically late in reaching them (Inhelder, 1968).[2] Extremely bright children, on the other hand, tend to be at approximately the same stage as their agemates but solve problems within a given level with greater facility and skill (Webb, 1974). This evidence indicates that physiological maturation plays an important role in development but that development is also the result of other factors such as the child's level of intelligence and his or her culture. In other words, maturation is important, but it doesn't explain everything.

[1]These stages are described at length in Chapters Four, Five, and Six.

[2]The ultimate level these children are likely to attain is dependent on the severity of their retardation. Children who are in the IQ range of 30 to 50, for example, are likely to become fixated at the level of preoperations, while those with a somewhat higher IQ (50 to 75) will eventually attain concrete operations.

The Second Factor of Development: Physical Experience

Another factor that underlies development is experience—that is, contact with the environment. Piaget (1970b) distinguishes three types of physical experience: exercise, physical experience proper, and logico-mathematical experience.

Exercise

Exercise refers to activities children perform with objects in the environment that don't lead to new knowledge. Children who have already learned to throw objects, for example, may improve their throwing ability by repeated practice, but they won't necessarily learn anything new about the objects they are throwing. This is true not only of physical activity but also of intellectual operations. A child may keep grouping the same objects according to some physical properties— perhaps their color—over and over again. Here, too, the child may become increasingly skilled at grouping, but he or she won't acquire new knowledge.

Physical Experience Proper

Piaget uses the term *physical experience* to refer to those activities children perform with objects that lead to new knowledge—that is, the object manipulation that allows the child to discover the properties inherent in the object. It is through their actions that children learn that blankets are warm, that blocks are heavy, or that long, thin metal rods can be bent. Piaget (1974c) calls these positive characteristics of objects **affirmations.** He refers to the process of noticing specific attributes, or affirmations, as *empirical abstraction.* This term, which we have already encountered in the preceding chapters, helps us understand how children gain knowledge about their world, because it emphasizes that they are active. The term draws our attention to the fact that the properties of objects do not impose themselves on passive minds and that children *abstract* the attributes from the objects..

Logico-Mathematical Experience

The third kind of experience, which is almost never mentioned by other learning theorists, is what Piaget calls *logico-mathematical experience.* In this kind of experience, knowledge is gained *indirectly* from one's activities with objects by reflecting on such activities. Recall that, when the child on the beach acquired new knowledge about the pebbles he was lining up and counting, such knowledge was not inherent in the pebbles themselves but, rather, in the boy's thoughts. Only because he thought about what he did was he able to learn that the sum of the pebbles didn't change when he reordered them. He could not see, feel, hear, smell, or otherwise sense that concept. In other words, the boy's learning was the result of his use of *reflexive abstraction* (discussed in Chapter Two).

A very important aspect of logico-mathematical knowledge is that it involves logical rules that can be applied to any objects. Sum is independent of order, whether the objects to be counted are pebbles, apples, dimes, or people. Even if children were not thinking of any particular objects, it would be possible for them to state that sum is independent of order. Logico-mathematical knowledge gradually becomes "content free." At first, the acquisition of logico-mathematical knowledge is inseparable from the learning of content—for example, learning that the sum of pebbles doesn't change when the pebbles are aligned in different ways or that a quarter cup of sugar is still a quarter cup when melted, even though it looks different and takes up a differently shaped space. Only gradually, through experience with many objects, will a child learn that sum is independent of order or that quantities remain invariant when solids are melted. Physical experience (in Piaget's sense of the term) provides the foundation on which logico-mathematical knowledge is built.

Physical experience, however, is also the *product* of logico-mathematical thinking. As was indicated earlier, children are actively engaged in abstracting physical knowledge from objects. What they abstract is dependent on the knowledge they bring with them. Children may recognize that objects are round, heavy, and blue as early as 2 or 3, but it usually takes them another nine or ten years to develop the notion that objects have density[3] (Inhelder & Piaget, 1964).

In logico-mathematical experience, knowledge is gained not through simple observation of properties (affirmations) but through the construction of **negations** (Piaget, 1974c). Negations are the nonproperties of objects, such as the property of *nonredness* of a green object. If we take a ball, for example, the affirmation (the physical property) is that the ball is round; the negation is that the ball is not square. The child needs not only to discover the affirmation that the ball is round but also to construct simultaneously the negation that the ball is not square.

When children argue that there are more counters in a set that is spread out than in one in which the counters are set close together, they are looking only at the affirmations—the clearly visible evidence that one row extends further in space than the other. To understand that the sets are equivalent, children must become aware of the not-so-visible empty spaces between the counters; that is, they must construct the negation. In reflexive abstraction, it is not enough to affirm the positive characteristics of something, as we do in empirical abstraction; we must also exclude and therefore deny the properties that don't exist in the

---

[3]*Density* refers to the mass of a substance per unit of volume.

object. Thus, there is always collaboration between
reflexive abstraction (Piaget, 1977e).

Logico-Mathematical Experience versus

though the acquisition of logico-mathematical knowledg
formulation of logical rules, genetic epistemology sl̲ ̲ ̲ ̲ ̲ ̲ot ve
understood as the study of logic. Piaget (1953, 1957; Beth & Piaget, 1966)
makes a clear distinction between the development of logic and the
development of natural thought. He argues that logic does not explain
natural thought but, rather, is a result of it.

In logic, for example, a negation denies the truth of a postulate. In
genetic epistemology a negation enriches the affirmation. Piaget does,
however, draw analogies between systems of logic and cognitive
development. He even goes so far as to record thought in logical symbols.
But he does not equate logico-mathematical reasoning with logic. He
postulates neither that logic is the cause of development nor that the
development of natural thought is logical. Instead, he sees logic as a
vehicle that enables us to describe and understand logico-mathematical
experience, thereby making clearer the structures of thought.

The Figurative/Operative Distinction

Everything in the world can be described in one of two forms: states
or transformations. In the example of children drawing water levels
illustrated in Figures 1-1 through 1-4 (Chapter One), we saw the water in
several different states. Those states were the results of
transformations—in that case, the changes in the position of the jar.
Children cannot understand the static state until they understand the
transformations from which the static state results or to which it gives
rise. Conversely, the understanding of the transformations is dependent
on an understanding of states, because a transformation always begins in
one state and ends in another.

Piaget (1977f) suggests that, to understand the world, children
develop two kinds of cognitive functions: the ability to *describe* states
(physical knowledge) and the ability to *reproduce* states (logico-
mathematical knowledge). In order to comprehend, we must be able to
describe. Description, however, is not enough to ensure comprehension.
Take, for example, the experiment of the rotation of the falling rod used
by Piaget and Inhelder (1971). A rod with red and blue ends, with the blue
end extending over the edge of a box, was allowed to fall onto a table.
Children were asked to draw the rod before and after the fall and to show
the movement of the rod's ends. Some children who were able to
recognize the initial and final static states (as evidenced by their
correctly drawing the end colors both before and after the fall) were
unable to reproduce the intermediary movements—that is, the
transformations. They had seen the change, but they had not understood
how the rod had fallen. States, therefore, are said to be subordinated to

transformations, because we really understand them only when we understand the transformations that created them. Piaget refers to the knowledge of the states of reality (configurations) as *figurative knowledge*.[4] The cognitive functions that enable the child to understand reality's figurative aspects are perception, imitation, and mental images. Since empirical abstraction is the process of acquiring knowledge about the features of objects, its close relation to figurative knowledge is evident.

Operations are the cognitive functions needed to understand transformations. At the three levels of development these are sensorimotor schemes, internalized preoperations, and operations themselves (see Chapters Four and Five). To review briefly, operations are mental actions that are internalized, reversible, and coordinated into systems of structures. By *internalized* we mean that they are carried out in thought. They are reversible in the sense that the child understands simultaneously the two states and their relation. A clay ball, for example, is still understood to be a clay ball even when it is rolled into a sausage, although the action of rolling it back into a ball is never carried out. Operations never exist in isolation. The understanding of a class, for example, presupposes a classificatory system (Piaget, 1957).

The operative aspects of cognitive functions are indispensable to the reproduction of a transformation and, therefore, to its understanding. Without acting on an object and transforming it, the child will not comprehend the nature of the transformation and will remain at the level of description.[5] Take, for example, something so simple as the child's knowledge of eggs. He sees eggs in their shell, fried, scrambled, and hard boiled. In each of these various states, eggs look and taste quite different. How is the child to know that the object of all these different visual and gustatory experiences is the same, unless he is aware of the process of the object's transformations? He must understand that the various states were produced by heating the eggs after breaking their shells open and mixing the eggs up with a fork or just by dropping them unshelled into boiling water.

Behaviorists have argued that this knowledge accrues from perception. They believe that children perceive eggs in their various forms and, because eggs are always called eggs, they learn to generalize. Piaget argues against this view. Perhaps children can use the word *egg* in all of these situations, but we must question whether they truly understand.

Piaget has even shown that perceptions often develop differently from the concepts to which they correspond. At the end of the first year of life, a little girl knows that shapes and many spatial arrangements are

---

[4]Figurative knowledge can also refer to the description of a transformation but only when that description translates the transformation into a series of states—for example, perception of movement in slow motion.

[5]It should be noted that not all cognitive functions that relate to transformations are operations. Cognitive functioning entails various kinds of information processing. Some are potential operations; others involve transformations. It is possible to have operations without transformations, since operations are broader than transformations (Voyat, personal communication).

constant; that is, she expects her ball to be round and her mother's face to have two eyes above the nose. Although children are able to perceive these shapes and spatial arrangements, it is not until they are approximately 7 years old that they understand that a spatial arrangement often looks different because of the position of the object in relation to the observer. It is not until they are 10 or 11 that children can *anticipate* what these different arrangements will be. Given a model of three mountains, for example, with a doll on the side opposite her, the child will not be able to imagine what the mountains look like from the opposite side and draw what the doll sees.

Why? When the child looks at the model of the mountains, she can see them from only one viewing point at a time. But when she understands transformations, she is able to imagine different viewpoints simultaneously. Thus she understands why the object looks different when its position is changed. The understanding of transformations also provides the basis for deductive reasoning, which allows children to *anticipate* how something will look when it is in a given position. It is very important to understand that both comprehension and deductive reasoning result from the child's actions. Before children can understand changes in the appearance of an object, they must have moved themselves in relation to the object. And these are *actions*, not perceptions (Piaget, 1977f).

Although it is clear that the development of concepts depends on information from perception, concepts are not merely "extracted" from perceptions by empirical abstractions. They always involve a system of transformations and the construction of negations. This is particularly clear in the development of the notion of size constancy, which is so strong in adults that they nearly lose their ability to judge apparent size. We will also see in the description of how children acquire **conservation** of substance in Chapter Five that their focusing on the states—that is, the ball shape and the elongated shape into which the ball is deformed—impedes their ability to understand that the quantity of the substance has not been changed. Children's conquest of conservation awaits their understanding of the transformation. It is, therefore, impossible to develop operative structures from perceptions. It is the child's *activity* that provides the basis for both perceptions and concepts. Knowledge is not a copy of reality. To know an object is to act on it, to change it, and to think about the results of one's activity.

The Third Factor of Development: Social Experience

The third factor of development is social experience, which is gained by interaction with people and includes social relationships, education, language, and culture. Our earlier discussion indicating that children's rates of progress vary from culture to culture suggests that acculturation can accelerate or retard a child's development. However, the fact that the sequence of stages remains unchanged among children of different cultures gives evidence that, like maturation, culture alone cannot explain everything.

Interactions with others have a profound effect on development. As an example, let's consider how children form classes. A young child asked to group the collection of objects illustrated in Figure 3-1 might do so by matching objects *A* and *B* on the basis of one property—in this case, shape—and objects *B* and *C* on the basis of a different property—in this case, color. Here the child proceeds by noticing similarities but ignoring differences. The work of Doise and his colleagues (see Chapter Seven) has

A   B   C   D

Figure 3-1. Sample items to be grouped.

shown that social interaction forces children to notice more attributes. When children work together, some children may notice one property while others may notice different properties. It is not so likely for a child to continue to ignore the properties with which his or her peers are concerned.

Social interaction also makes it possible for children to understand other persons' points of view and thus become flexible in their reasoning. They learn that people have different ideas about what is honest or beautiful. They also learn that people may literally see things differently, depending on where they are in a room.

As we said at the beginning of this chapter, the Genevans believe that development is spontaneous.[6] Studies comparing children from various cultures have shown that children progress through the same stages of cognitive development and in the same order, whether they have had formal schooling or not. Formal education, however, can influence the rate at which children learn, and it determines the particular content of knowledge. Consider, for example, two high school students. If one studies languages and the other mathematics and science, the knowledge that they have at graduation will be quite different from the point of view of content, even though they may be at the same level of cognitive development.

Many authors have argued that language (a specific kind of social factor) is at the origin of logical operations. Piaget agrees that language is essential to thought. What he argues is that it is not *the* essential, critical factor. It is necessary, he says, but not sufficient. He believes that the knowledge children are exposed to through language can be received— and thus can influence their development—*only* if they can assimilate it to what they already know.

_____

[6]Genevans use the term *spontaneous* to describe learning that is not acquired through direct teaching.

Sinclair (1967a) compared the language of children who could conserve substance with the language of children who could not. She noticed that the conservers said that one ball of clay was "longer but thinner" or "shorter but wider," while the nonconservers didn't coordinate the two dimensions in their speech. They simply said "This one is longer" or "This one is fatter." Sinclair then taught the nonconservers to describe the clay balls using the language of the conservers. The children became quite proficient at using the language, but they still were unable to conserve! Piaget insists that children understand only through their own activities. Learning a particular phrase didn't help Sinclair's children to conserve, because they were not given the opportunity to construct their own knowledge.

What we are saying doesn't imply that Piaget thinks that language is unimportant to development and learning. That is not true. Piaget argues that language is very important in helping children to represent actions in images and thoughts. He reminds us, however, that children evidence intelligent behaviors before they begin to speak. A good case in point is the baby who turns her rattle to allow it to fit through the bars of her crib. Language is only one vehicle for thought.

At about 1½ to 2 years of age, children begin to play symbolic games. A stick might be used as a baton, a gun, a cone, or a comb. A young child will put on his father's hat and pretend he is daddy. The beginnings of deferred imitation, mental imagery, and drawing are also seen at this time. All of these activities constitute forms of imitation. It is this active imitation that provides the basis for interiorizing action—that is, representing actions internally in images and language (see Chapter Four). Language is only one aspect of the ability to function symbolically. However, the older a child gets the more important language becomes as a tool in the child's thinking. This is particularly true of late adolescence. Language, like all social experience, is a necessary but not sufficient condition for learning.

The Fourth and Central Factor of Development: Equilibration

Experience, both physical and social, cannot account for the sequential character of development, and maturation cannot account for the variations in children's rates of development. There must, then, be a fourth factor that coordinates all the others. As we have indicated earlier in our discussion, this factor is equilibration.[7] It is through the process of equilibration that the child organizes the other three factors into a coherent whole (Piaget, 1970b).

All living things have two innate tendencies, or functions: organization and adaptation. Plants, for example, readily adapt to variations in the amount of light and water they receive. They also take

---

[7]For an in-depth discussion of the relation between equilibration and learning, see Reid (1979).

in hydrogen and give off oxygen in a systematic, well-organized manner. They interact with the environment in a way that makes the two functions inseparable. We never seem to ask ourselves why plants behave this way. We are satisfied that they do so simply because they have the competence to do so. A similar situation exists for the human organism, both at the physical and at the psychological level. It, too, tends toward organization and adaptation. There are two mechanisms of adaptation in the human organism, and they operate simultaneously. Humans *assimilate*—that is, incorporate elements of the environment into their current physical or psychological structures—while at the same time they adapt, or *accommodate,* to the demands of the environment. Through the mechanisms of assimilation and accommodation each person regulates his or her own growth. Comparisons are often made between the self-regulatory functions of assimilation and accommodation and a thermostat regulating the temperature of a room. Although these processes are indeed quite similar, it should be noted that the thermostat in a room always brings the temperature back to the original, set temperature.

Like physical adaptation, cognitive adaptation takes place through the processes of assimilation and accommodation. The person assimilates elements of the environment into his or her framework of understanding and, at the same time, accommodates (that is, modifies) his or her framework to meet the demands of the environment. This active process of self-regulation results in ever-new and increasingly advanced states of equilibrium and thus in developmental growth. It never leads to a return to the original (that is, lower) state of equilibrium (Piaget, 1978a).

More specifically, a person faced with a particular problem will first try to solve it by assimilation—by attempting to use whatever knowledge or strategies he or she has available. If the strategies work and the problem is readily solved, there will be no modification in the person's current system of knowledge. Suppose, for example, that a child is asked to group red, purple, blue, orange, and yellow circles and squares. The child makes two groups, one of circles and one of squares, regardless of their color. Then the child is given another piece and asked to add that piece to one of the two groups already sorted. If the block is, say, a purple square, the child can add it to her collection with no difficulty. The previous strategy will work quite well in solving this new problem, and the child's current state of equilibrium (the balance between the mechanisms of assimilation and accommodation) will remain unchanged.

The Effects of Contradiction

What happens, however, if the child is given a purple triangle? The previous classification scheme has no place for a purple triangle! The child is faced with a contradiction.[8] Her present schemes of assimilation

---

[8]The other two terms used interchangeably with *contradiction* to denote an inability to apply already acquired strategies to a situation at hand are *disturbance* and *perturbation*.

are no longer adequate, and a state of disequilibrium results (Piaget, 1974c, 1976b, 1977b). The child may react in one of a variety of ways.

1. She may simply ignore the problem and put the purple triangle into the group of squares. In this case the child may be vaguely aware of the contradiction, but her current strategies and system of knowledge won't be modified to any extent; that is, she won't change (or accommodate) her assimilative scheme. On the other hand, the child may be sure that the purple triangle doesn't really belong with either of the previously established groups. Then she may compensate by creating a third group of objects consisting of only one piece—the purple triangle. Both of these forms of **compensation** (activity aimed at neutralizing a contradiction) change the original strategy of grouping as little as possible. Piaget (1977b) refers to these two forms as **alpha behavior.** We may say that the assimilatory scheme has been maintained, or conserved, rather than accommodated. The compensation in both these cases is only partial; consequently, the resulting equilibrium is very unstable.

2. Instead of ignoring the problem or trying to cancel out the purple triangle, the child may attempt to integrate the new object into her previous scheme of classification. In this case she may change her classification completely and adopt a new one, perhaps color. This change constitutes a clear accommodation of the assimilation scheme. The purple triangle can then be appropriately placed among the purple circles and squares. What was at first a contradiction is now a variation of the child's grouping strategy. By compensating for the disturbance, the child has extended the possibilities for responding. Here the compensation was not aimed at canceling the contradiction; instead, it modified the assimilation itself in order to accommodate the object. This modification, which applies only to specific instances, is called **beta behavior** (Piaget, 1977b).

3. There is a third possibility. As the child makes her groups of circles and squares, she may be aware that the blocks could be grouped also by color. When presented with a purple triangle, she experiences no contradiction, because she has already anticipated the possibility of grouping by color. The compensation in this case doesn't involve any cancellation of contradiction. It involves, instead, an anticipation of a possible transformation (for example, that the blocks may be grouped also by size, thickness, texture, and so forth) and leads to an easy accommodation of the assimilation schemes to a variety of objects. Anticipation of all possibilities is referred to as **gamma behavior** (Piaget, 1977b).

In very young children the balance between assimilations and accommodations is very unstable, and children use the simple kinds of partial compensation we described first. This instability of equilibrium results from children's focusing on affirmations (the properties of objects) and their inability to construct negations. They have difficulty replacing (and therefore enriching) exogenous knowledge with their own endogenous constructions.

Later, children become aware of negations—for example, of the fact that a purple triangle is a nonsquare. It is the contradiction that provokes becoming aware of the negative aspects of objects and therefore leads to a state of disequilibrium. Remember: contradiction always refers to the child's own subjective perception. Even when a child says "You have five buttons and I have five buttons. But you have more than I do, because yours take up more room," there is no contradiction unless the child himself considers one to exist. If the child is happy with his answer, he is operating at alpha level, that of no or partial compensation. As children begin to construct negations and to compensate for the difference between affirmations and negations, they accommodate and, therefore, reequilibrate (counterbalance the effects of affirmations and negations).[9] As a result of this reequilibration, children add new assimilatory strategies to their repertoires and thereby enrich their possibilities for responding. They replace exogenous with endogenous knowledge. It is in this way that the process of equilibration leads to more accurate, more stable, and more complete knowledge systems.

In summary, if the child's initial attempt at assimilation is not effective, a contradiction occurs, and the child is put in a state of disequilibrium. In the effort to compensate for the contradiction, the child reequilibrates, thereby enriching his or her system of knowledge. Piaget (1977b) calls this movement toward higher and higher levels of equilibrium *équilibration majorante*. (For further discussion of this topic, see the section on the Spiral of Knowing in Chapter Two.)

The Five Models of Equilibration

As we have indicated, the process of equilibration fosters successive states, which may be stable or unstable, depending on the interactions of observables and coordinations. By observables Piaget means the understanding of the "facts."[10] These "facts" result from the immediate reading of the data and from the child's observation of the results of his or her own actions. By *coordinations* Piaget means the inferences that the child may derive from his or her own actions or from the actions of objects on each other to unify the elements of such actions. Equilibration can occur in five ways, to which we shall refer as "models," each reflecting one type of interaction between observables and coordinations (Piaget, 1977b).[11]

IA. The first model (observable-causal) refers to the equilibration that occurs when children observe the results of their actions on objects. For example, a child pushes a ball and observes that, the harder she pushes, the further the ball goes. This child has observed a covariation—

---

[9] When children who make collections based only on similarities (see Figure 3-1 and related discussion) begin to take the differences between objects into account, their groupings take on a higher-level, more logical form, such as grouping of circles and squares.

[10] It is important to emphasize that Piaget is referring to the "facts" in terms of the child's subjective understanding, which may vary considerably from the actual reality.

[11] For those familiar with Piaget's previous description of equilibration, a comparison between the new (Piaget, 1977b) and old (Piaget, 1957) models, as well as a formal description of the new model, are presented in Appendix A.

that is, she has noticed that the distance the ball travels is related to the force of her thrust—but has limited her observations to that relation. She makes no inferences about why or how the observed phenomenon occurs. The child certainly makes use of "tools of assimilation" (the preexisting cognitive structures); that is, what she sees is dependent on her level of cognitive development. But she uses her logico-mathematical knowledge only as a framework for reading the physical facts.

IB. In the second model (observable-operative), children apply their logico-mathematical knowledge to objects. They may, for example, order the objects, group them, or put them in correspondence. There is no resistance from the objects themselves in the sense that energy is expended. Of course, the objects may "resist" in the sense that three objects of the same height cannot be ordered or that a fork cannot be included in a group of "objects to write with." What happens in model IB, however, is that children view the objects as part of a single set. They see them as a group. Both level-I (observable) models are artificial. They don't really exist, because they always depend on previous experience. They constitute only a special case of the level-II (inferential) models.

IIA. In the third model (inferential-causal), children not only observe the results of their actions but also conceptualize them. They reconstruct on a conscious level what they had observed before only at the practical level (see discussion of the observable-causal model). An example will help to clarify.

The Genevans (Piaget, 1976b) asked children to spin a sling containing a ball and to release the ball into a box. With a little practice, even children who were quite young could accomplish the task. When the box was moved, the children were again able to accomplish the task, this time either by adjusting their throws or by moving themselves so that they could maintain their original relation to the box. This adjustment by covariation corresponds to the IA interaction (observable-causal model). If, however, the Genevans asked the younger children to describe how they performed the task—that is, to indicate where they had released the ball in order to ensure its landing in the box—the children couldn't explain it. They had learned only at a practical level. The older children, instead, by making hypotheses, checking them, modifying those that were incorrect, and rechecking them, were able to deduce the interrelations between the trajectory of the released ball and their own position in relation to the box. This reconstruction on a conceptual level, based on making and checking inferences that united elements of the problem, constitutes the IIA interaction.

IIB. The fourth model (inferential-operative) has the same characteristics as the IB (observable-operative) model but includes coordinations of inferences. Children become conscious of their operative intentions by projecting them onto objects (that is, by applying them to objects) and thereby verifying them. In a game called the Hanoi Tower, children are required to move discs of different sizes from one peg to another. A third peg, situated between the two, is also available to be used as a storage place. There is a rule, however, that a larger disc may never be placed on a smaller one. This rule sufficiently complicates the game so that the children must develop a strategy, or overall plan, for moving the discs. They learn about how effective the plan is by moving the discs and observing what happens. Each trial enables the children to gain information that can be used to modify and improve the plan. Children will recognize, for example, that an old system is inadequate and will construct a new system by reflecting on the activities they have performed. Actual strategies children use in playing this game are described in Chapter Six.

IIC. In the fifth model of interaction (again, inferential-operative) objects act on each other, and children intervene only insofar as they examine or vary certain factors. In this model the objects act on each other in such a way that no intervention on the child's part is necessary. Piaget illustrates the interaction by comparing it to the "interaction" between an astronomer and the celestial movements he observes. The child, however, infers explanations that are consistent with his or her level of cognitive development. Young children, for example, think that the moon follows them at night (Piaget, 1930). Later, children acquire knowledge about the rotation of the earth and the effects of distance on what they see and are able to understand why they can see the moon wherever they happen to be.

What is especially important about these models is that the level-I models are subsumed into the level-II models. Level-I interactions are never lost but, rather, modified and enriched. Equally important is that these interactions are always in a state of flux. A true equilibrium is never attained. Instead, one interaction—let's call it N,—is modified and enriched through the compensation of affirmations and negations and becomes a new state, $N + 1$. $N + 1$, in turn, may be modified and enriched, leading to $N + 2$, and so forth. Finally, it is important to note that in every model empirical and reflexive abstractions interact. The process is a spiraling one, in which the reading of the observables (observing the variations and covariations without making any inferences about why or how those covariations are occurring) precedes their coordination.

Children first read the observables with whatever "tools of assimilation" they have available. After they have read the observables— what for them constitute the "facts"—they make inferences about how and why the facts occur. These observations then become enriched by the children's newly achieved understandings, and the new coordinations can be used as the basis for later readings. The process of conservation of substance is again a case in point. Very early the child observes a covariation: when the clay ball is rolled out, it becomes longer (N). The child argues that the longer sausage has more clay. When he is able to construct the negation that the clay ball has been reduced in diameter as it was extended in length, he is able to read the conservation experiment differently (N + 1). Since he understands the transformation, he now sees that the sausage has no more clay in it than it had when it was in the shape of a ball. The newly acquired information becomes the basis for the more sophisticated reading of the "facts," or observables. It is this continual enrichment that Piaget calls *équilibration majorante.* Cognitive equilibration never leads back to the original state. The construction of negations enriches the affirmations and changes their nature. Once, for example, the child understands that the clay sausage is both longer and narrower than the clay ball, he understands that the two have the same amount of clay, and, as one of Piaget's young subjects once told him, once you know, you know forever!

Structure. Before we continue with our discussion of equilibration, we need to reexamine the notion of structure. Structuralists observe people (or societies or languages) in order to discover regularities in behavior across individual occurrences. Gardner (1973, pp. 165–166) suggests that this process of discovery is similar to the process of discovery on the part of a being from outer space observing a baseball game. Probably our visitor from outer space would first notice that the members of each team remain alternatively in place on the field and take their turns at bat. It would take a considerably longer time for the visitor from outer space to tease out the more subtle rules of the game and to determine which features are merely incidental (for example, the color of the uniforms) and which are essential (for example, the number of men on a team).

It is exactly this kind of observation that Piaget carried out initially with his own children and later with thousands of others. He was looking for evidence of structures (regularities) in their behavior. As we noted in Chapter Two, structures have three important characteristics: wholeness, transformation, and self-regulation (Piaget, 1970d). Children learning arithmetic, for instance, soon realize that numbers do not exist in isolation. They don't discover numbers one by one or in some accidental sequence. To be understood, numbers must be ordered into a system—3 is one less than 4 but one more than 2. Children also learn quite readily that numbers can be transformed. They can put 1 and 1 together to make a new group of 2. Or they can begin with a group of 2 and take 1 away and have two groups of 1 again. The laws they use to organize the system—in this case numbers—allow them to regroup without changing the system as a whole.

Finally, transformations depend on the interplay of anticipation and correction—that is, self-regulation. Psychological structures are also characterized by wholeness, transformations, and self-regulations. Throughout our earlier discussion on the process of equilibration, we observed how self-regulation occurs. Human abilities are always organized into systems, and these systems can be transformed through self-regulation.

The Three Types of Equilibration

There are three types of equilibration: (1) equilibration between assimilation and accommodation, (2) equilibration between subsystems, and (3) equilibration between the parts and the whole.

Equilibration between Assimilation and Accommodation.   Many of the examples of equilibration given in this chapter are examples of equilibration between assimilations and accommodations. One more example is given here, because it enables us to observe the process of equilibration quite clearly.

Inhelder et al. (1974) asked children to predict what would happen when they poured liquid into the apparatus illustrated in Figure 3-2 and

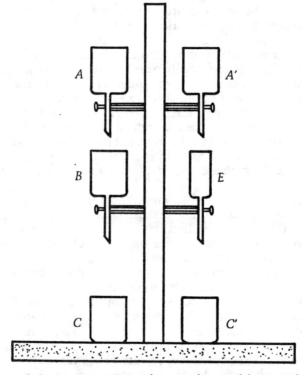

Figure 3-2.   Apparatus used to study equilibration between assimilation and accommodation. (From *Learning and the Development of Cognition*, by B. Inhelder, H. Sinclair, and M. Bovet. Copyright 1974 by the President and Fellows of Harvard College. Reprinted by permission of Harvard University Press and Routledge and Kegan Paul Ltd.)

opened and closed the taps to let the liquid flow through. The experimenters asked the children whether the amount of liquid would be the same in jars B and E, since they had agreed that it was the same in jars

A and *A'*. The expectation was that children would predict that the quantities would remain equal. The use of a narrower glass at *E* was meant to induce contradiction; that is, the water levels in *B* and *E* would not be the same. The children were then asked to predict whether the quantities would be the same when the water was allowed to flow into *C* and *C'*.

The observable features of the situation seemed to play different roles, depending on the children's initial levels of organization of action schemes, or, to put it another way, their ability to assimilate new information. Children who made no progress were able to apprehend all the features but were unable to put the features to use. These children did notice that the water level was higher in one jar and lower in the other, but they were unable to coordinate the height of the liquid with the width of the jar; that is, they were unable to make inferences linking the two observations. Inhelder et al. (1974) report that "as long as the child does not incorporate the observable features of the situation into a system of inferences allowing him to link the various observations made in the successive phases of the experiment, he cannot make any progress. The observable features themselves cannot alone lead to change in the thought processes" (p. 54). What is needed, of course, is an internal regulation—that is, equilibration between assimilation and accommodation.

Some children, exhibiting alpha behavior, tended to change their minds about whether there was more, less, or the same amount of liquid in the jars. They didn't grasp the crux of the problem and didn't attempt to overcome the contradictions.

Children at a higher level, who could link their predictions, were aware of contradictions and tried to resolve them. They were able to use the observable information to compare their successive judgments and to become aware of the contradictions between such judgments. This ability to accommodate an existing assimilation scheme is what we earlier referred to as beta behavior.

Finally, some children who, at the beginning of the task, were able to conserve substance but not liquid appeared to be able to extend their structures to a different content and therefore did not have to construct new structures—the gamma behavior previously described.

Equilibration among Subsystems. Subsystems refer to structures related to different domains of knowledge—for example, number, length, distance, or time. An example of equilibration among subsystems also comes from the work of Inhelder et al. (1974). Children who conserved number but not length were presented with two straight lines of sticks (all the same length) with tiny toy houses glued onto them (see Figure 3-3a). The top row of sticks was then rearranged into various patterns such as the one illustrated at the top of Figure 3-3b.

The children were asked whether the two rows (which the experimenter called "roads") contained the same number of houses. After they had answered, the children were asked whether one road was as long as the other. Would a person walking one road have just as far to walk as a

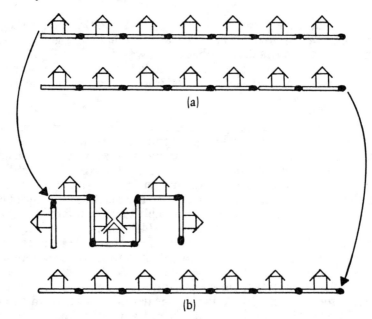

Figure 3-3. Matchstick roads used to contrast knowledge of length and knowledge of number. (From *Learning and the Development of Cognition*, by B. Inhelder, H. Sinclair, and M. Bovet. Copyright 1974 by Harvard University Press. Reprinted by permission.)

person walking on the other road? The experimenter went back and forth asking questions about number and length in an effort to provoke the children into bringing the two subsystems into conflict.

When asked about the number of houses, the children could count to make sure that there was the same number in each row. But when they were asked whether the two roads were equal in length, many became confused, because the end points of the roads didn't match. Children who became increasingly confused during the training session made clear progress when a posttest was given, using two pieces of wire, one straight and the other bent. Children who had relied on counting to solve the problem and, therefore, avoided the conflict between the subsystems of length and number made no progress on the posttest.

Equilibration between the Parts and the Whole. Equilibration between the parts and the whole explains how subsystems are united into a totality. It differs from equilibration of subsystems because here the whole always dominates; that is, this type of equilibration involves a hierarchy. The integration of a subsystem (a part) into a whole is a process of assimilation into a larger and more powerful entity. In Chapter Six, which deals with formal thought, we will see how the understanding of the totality of a problem may lead to the construction of new contents to which that problem may be applied.

Summary

In this chapter we have seen that learning in the strict sense is specific and results from experience. In the broad sense, however, learning depends on the interaction of four factors: physical maturation, physical experience, social experience, and equilibration.

Piaget has described four models of equilibration that can be applied to activity during all three types of equilibration—equilibration between assimilation and accommodation, equilibration between subsystems, and equilibration among the parts as they are organized into a whole. Nearly all theories of cognitive development recognize the roles played by maturation and experience. What is unique about genetic epistemology is that equilibration is seen as the major factor in development. Therefore, genetic epistemology sees knowledge as stemming not from maturation or experience alone but as a new construction arising from the interaction between the child and his or her environment.

Learning is neither a product of language nor a product of perception. It grows instead from activity and the consequent process of self-regulation, or equilibration, that integrates both assimilation and accommodation and the various subsystems of the organism. Learning (in its broad sense) results from contradictions that lead to states of disequilibrium. By overcoming the contradictions, children progress to higher and higher levels of equilibrium. Children's incorrect hypotheses about their world are not, therefore, simply errors that adults need to help them correct. Errors in thinking are crucial to learning, because only through the resolution of the conflict between their predictions and reality or between their operational subsystems do children progress.

What learning a child achieves is dependent on his or her initial level of development. Through practice, for example, we may be able to teach a child that several clay balls are equal in weight regardless of their shape, but this knowledge will be quickly lost unless it is understood—that is, unless the child is able to assimilate it to his or her own logical structures. This assimilation can occur only when the child is active. "The more active a subject is, the more successful his learning is likely to be. However, being cognitively active does not mean that the child merely manipulates a given type of material; he can be mentally active without physical manipulation, just as he can be mentally passive while actually manipulating objects" (Inhelder et al., 1974, p. 25).

CHAPTER FOUR

The Concept of Stages; Sensorimotor and Representational Stages

The Concept of Stages

> It is one thing to recognize the necessary sequence of the stages, but another thing altogether to explain them by invoking an innate "programme." Piaget's explanation, which is best presented in constructivist terms, deals with the sequence of stages by a process of equilibration or autoregulation. This regulatory activity enables the subject truly to construct knowledge—something which simple maturation does not do [Inhelder, 1976a, pp. 7–8].

As we saw in Chapter Two, Piaget divides development into four broad periods: (1) the sensorimotor stage, (2) the preoperational stage, (3) the concrete-operational stage, and (4) the formal-operational stage. A simple definition of stages is "broad periods in development" (Piaget, 1971d). The question that has guided investigations about stages by Piaget and Inhelder is as follows: "Is it possible to detect broad periods in development with characteristics that can be applied in a general manner to all the events of these periods?" (Piaget, 1971d, p. 2). The search, then, has been for characteristics or common elements that may be used to describe the special capabilities that appear at different times in development.

Special emphasis must be placed on the word *describe*, for the stages were never meant to be used for prediction. In other words, it is correct to consider the stages as classifying or describing different behaviors. It is not correct, however, to ask questions centered upon the prediction of certain behaviors, just because a child is old enough to be in a certain stage (Gallagher, 1979).

Another special emphasis, in line with recent research by Piaget and Inhelder, is the emphasis on mechanisms rather than on individual stages. Mechanisms, or processes, involve the reasons for the transitions

58

from one stage to another—the very focus of this book. A good grasp of mechanisms can be gained by studying actions and verbal explanations of children who have been given the same problem to solve. Some of the new volumes on Genevan research (see, for example, Piaget, 1976b, 1978d) are excellent sources for grasping the concept of mechanisms in relation to stages. However, to understand the organization of these volumes and research summaries, it is essential that the reader be aware of the variations in the use of the terms *levels* and *stages.* Levels may be thought of as substages. However, the substages are not necessarily subdivisions of the traditional four stages we mentioned above. In addition, when the term *stage* is used, it does not have to refer to one of the traditional four stages. An example will clarify these points and will help the reader develop a flexible approach to the Piagetian notion of stage.

Each time the Genevan School plunges into a new research area related to the construction of knowledge, the search begins for the common processes or methods that children use in approaching a problem that seems to distinguish one stage of functioning from another. Suppose, for example, that the research topic for the year is the relationship between success in a task and understanding of the task (Piaget, 1978d). The task in this case is to line up some dominoes spaced so that a push on the first domino will result in the chain reaction of all the dominoes falling. Children between the ages of 4 and 12 are asked to predict what will happen if one pushes the first domino.

Three broad levels of development emerge when the children's answers are analyzed using the method of critical exploration (see Chapter Two). At stage 1 (approximately ages 5 to 7), children gradually discover the link between a push on a domino and the fall of the adjoining dominoes, when the elements of the domino chain have been correctly spaced. An important characteristic of this level is the inability to extend the discovery to more than two dominoes. With a series of eight dominoes, for example, the children will say that, if the first is pushed, the following three will fall (domino D in Figure 4-1) but that the

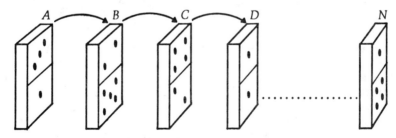

Figure 4-1. The chain of aligned dominoes. (Based on Piaget, 1978d.)

others are just "too far" to be affected. In other words, children at this stage cannot grasp the concept of chain reaction. Even after having watched the chain reaction in progress, not all the children agree that the chain reaction must, by physical necessity, occur again every time the first domino is being pushed.

At stage 2 (approximately ages 7 to 11), the children understand the *necessity* of a chain of events—in our example, the fall of aligned dominoes when the first acts as an initial cause. Thus, children at this stage understand that, if the dominoes have been spaced correctly, the reaction must, and will, continue to the end of the chain, no matter how long the chain is. Children at stage 3 (approximately 11 years and older) are able to articulate the principle behind the chain reaction and explain that it is the weight of the first domino that sets the reaction in motion. Thus, older children can grasp the notion of a recurring series extended into the infinite world of the possible, if one could actually line up thousands and thousands of dominoes. In other words, older children can formulate a principle that goes beyond the immediate action before them.

What structure (general understanding) is evident when the behavior of stage-2 children is analyzed? If A causes B to fall and B causes C to fall (see Figure 4-1), then by logical necessity there must be a causative link between A and C, the effects of which have repercussions all the way to the last domino. Such a relationship (A related to B, B related to C, therefore A related to C) is a relationship of transitivity—an operation we described in Chapter Two and that we shall discuss again in Chapter Five when we deal with the stage of concrete operations.

Before we proceed further with our discussion of the concept of stages, we need to clarify and to emphasize some points relating to the meaning and characteristics of these stages. Each of these points applies equally to stages in the more traditional sense and to stages in the individual sense of special tasks (example of the dominoes). This is in keeping with the definition of stages as periods of development in which one finds common elements.

Think back to the example of the chain of dominoes. Stage 1, as illustrated by the example, was certainly not the traditional sensorimotor stage ordinarily designated as the first stage. Stage 1 in the dominoes example, and in all studies in which performance in experimental tasks is analyzed, usually describes performance of the youngest children. Obviously, the ages selected for study will depend on both the topic and the difficulty of the task. Although we did not discuss these details, each of the stages in the dominoes example was divided into level IA and level IB—that is, two substages. Performance at these two sub-stages was essentially the same except for a slight advancement at level IB. Stage 2 (or level IIA, if so designated) always signals an important change in performance. For example, in the dominoes experiment, we noted the use of transitivity at stage 2. Often, but not always, there will be a stage 3, which, again, means a significant advance in understanding.[1]

[1]Some of the new research summaries (see, for example, Piaget, 1976b; 1978d) are not too difficult and thus provide an excellent introduction to the methods used in genetic epistemology. However, unless readers are alerted to the various uses of the terms *stages* and *levels*, they may be confused. For example, it is not uncommon to find these divisions in the descriptions of children's protocols: level IA, level IB, stage II, and stage III. The reader

Sequence of Stages   ·

First, it is absolutely essential to understand that the sequence of stages is vastly more important than the age at which children reach a particular stage. This point is made unmistakably by Piaget (1971d):

> Each stage is necessary for the following one. If this were not the case, one would be in no position to talk of stages. Naturally, the ages at which different children reach the stages may vary. In some social environments the stages are accelerated, whereas in others they are more or less systematically retarded. This differential development shows that stages are not purely a question of the maturation of the nervous system but are dependent upon interaction with the social environment and with experience in general. The order, however, remains constant [p. 7].

Therefore, it is not surprising that some 7-year-old children are able to give a transitive explanation for the fall of the dominoes while others are not. And this is why in the protocols of the Genevan School we find a mixture of ages (within limits, of course) for the various levels of tasks. The researchers of the Genevan School are not rigid about age; instead, they probe for general characteristics, which, in the end, may fall within a particular age range.

This is how Piaget (1971a, p. 16) defines the sequence of stages (thus the term *sequential*): "We call sequential a series of stages, each of which is a necessary part of the whole and a necessary result of all the stages that precede it (except for the first one), as well as naturally leading on to the next stage (except for the last one)." We saw in the example of the dominoes that, before a a child can verbalize the principle of a recurring series, he or she must understand the transitive relationships involved in that principle. This does not mean, however, that the stages are linear and based on an accumulation of information from one stage to the next.

> In fact, if the development of behavior only obeyed the law of cumulative succession, the levels as well as the stages would express only an arbitrary division in the midst of a continuous or purely additive process. On the contrary, the fundamental fact is that the structures acquired at a previous level are not simply brought forward to the later levels, but must be reconstructed before they can be integrated into the new structures elaborated at these later levels [Piaget, in Beth & Piaget, 1966, p. 159].

Thus, before the relationship of transitivity is understood at the concrete-operational stage, a reorganization (reconstruction) is necessary. The notion of phenocopy emerges again. In the example of the marbles we presented in Chapter Two, an understanding of the effect of initial equality or inequality on further additions was necessary before the child could make accurate predictions. There, too, such an

---

needs to supply stage I by combining levels IA and IB. Levels IA and IB, levels IIA and IIB, and stage III refer to levels of performance within a research task. However, *levels, stages,* and *substages* have been used interchangeably. Piaget himself uses *stade* and *niveau* to refer to "stage of development" and "level," respectively; but, in his usage, both French terms are often extended to include any plateau or level of understanding occurring within the major stages of development.

understanding resulted from a reorganization process—the reconstruction of the understanding that initial inequality cannot be erased.

Stages and the Concept of Construction

A second general point in understanding the Piagetian stages is closely connected to the ideas presented in the section above and in Chapters Two and Three on the mechanism of reflexive abstraction. Recall that empirical abstractions draw their information from the observables (watching domino A push over domino B). The sequence of stages, however, is a continuous result of the interaction of empirical and reflexive abstractions. Recall that reflexive abstractions are characterized by two inseparable aspects: (1) projection onto a higher level of coordinations formed at a lower level (the observation of the successive fall of the dominoes) and (2) a mental act of reconstruction and reorganization at the higher level of that which was transferred from the lower one (the transformation, through the operation of transitivity, of the observed chain of dominoes from the level of "action out there" to the higher mental level of the understanding of a recurring chain with infinite possibilities). To observe is not enough. The understanding of the recurring chain is a construction—that is, something new that was not present in thinking before. This construction/novelty concept permeates each of the stages of cognitive development.

Stages and the Logical and Biological Models

Another point we need to make with regard to the concept of stages is the necessity of viewing the stages from the perspective of both the logical and the biological models. Here, too, the example of the dominoes is of help. Our concern is not so much with the completely formed presence of the logical principle of transitivity (A related to B; B related to C; thus, A related to C). In the dominoes example, the grasp of the internal logic of the problem centered on and emerged from the activities of the child. As we stressed in Chapter Three, logic does not cause development. Rather, genetic epistemology focuses on the interactions between the child and the object of the subject's activity. Thus, the question becomes "Given a certain level of understanding of transitivity, how will this level affect the child's interactions with the objective nature of a problem?"

As Piaget (1972b) states, transitivity does not just "fall from the sky." And logic is not the focus of our study or its end point. Our concern is the development of "natural" thought, in which we may observe some logical substructures. Thus, if transitivity is a characteristic of concrete operations, how does this level of understanding (that is, transitivity) control learning experiences such as the observation of the fall of aligned dominoes? In sum, how is the notion of transitivity constructed and not "given"?

In the concept of stages, the biological model is intertwined with the logical model. The necessity for regulation in all areas of life processes affects our view of the acquisition of knowledge. For example, when children realize that the spacing between the dominoes is an important factor in the chain reaction, they balance this information with the observation of the effect of the push of the first domino on the second. Here is the self-regulatory aspect of the process, an aspect analogous to biological functioning and operating by compensation, which is a dominant mechanism in each of the stages.

The notion of the biological model helps us understand that each of the stages is really an open and not a closed system (Gallagher, 1977). It is not as if certain structures were acquired at certain stages, perfected, and then left to stagnate in a static state. Even the simple example of the dominoes contains elements of advanced mathematical thought in the notion of a possible alignment extending to infinity.

In sum, Piaget (Beth & Piaget, 1966, p. 161) states: "From the genetic [developmental] viewpoint, mental constructions are never complete, and the fact that they remain 'open' leads us to consider any construction as capable of extending into later constructions." Thus, genetic epistemology examines the relationship existing between the formation of logical structures and biological influences.

As stressed in previous chapters, Piaget explored the thoughts of children that occur naturally in informal activities. Logico-mathematical structures, like that of transitivity, appear to act as mechanisms of informal problem solving in the infralogical[2] area at all stages of development. Piaget believes that all children view problems according to their current modes of constructing the objective world. Therefore, changes in children's logical activity reflect developmental shifts in their epistemological view of the problems. Moreover, the reorganization of logical activity occurs in important ways as lower levels of logical organization are modified and then projected to higher levels. The beginning of infralogical activity, such as the measurement of the length of a line, occurs precisely because the biological influences of regulation and organization permit a learner to structure external problems in increasingly robust ways. Finally the child understands how logical necessity is implied in object relationships.

Keeping these general points in mind, we will now highlight those aspects of the four traditional stages that are most relevant to our learning-theory approach.

The Sensorimotor Stage

Introduction

Even if Piaget had stressed only the sensorimotor stage of development, his theory would still be revolutionary. The first revolutionary idea is that the growth of intelligence begins long before language is used. Language, according to Piaget, is based on the

---

[2]Infralogical refers to operations that are based on space and time. Infralogical operations are parallel to logico-mathematical operations; they don't occur earlier than and are not inferior to logico-mathematical operations (Piaget & Inhelder, 1969).

symbolic function, which, as we shall see, enables the infant to represent (bring to mind) absent persons or objects. When discussing the period of sensorimotor development, it is necessary to stress that, even though language is not present, it is during this time (from birth to approximately 18 months) that infants construct all the cognitive substructures that represent the foundation for later perceptual and intellectual development. By 18 months, the Spiral of Knowing is already well on its way toward wider and wider possibilities.

The second revolutionary idea is that knowledge is based on activity and not on what is perceived or observed. A related idea is that growth in knowledge is not just a simple associative process of linking one observed object to another. According to Piaget, what the infant observes (feels, touches, sees, hears, and so on) is filtered through structures—that is, action schemes. Such action schemes are simple practical structures of knowing.

These action schemes—or just *schemes,* as we will call them here—increase in complexity through the six substages of the sensorimotor stage. This development may seem slow and too centered on detail. What must be kept in mind is that infants at first don't differentiate themselves from objects. For example, when an infant looks at her hands, she perceives them as foreign objects crossing the field of vision and not as part of her own body. The movements of the hands may actually startle the infant. Actions, then, have to be decentered, or separated from the infant's body. The infant gradually becomes aware that he or she is one object among many other objects in the world and that he or she is the initiator of actions.

During these important learning experiences involving decentration and the initiation of actions, many disturbances arise, for, of necessity, there are many contacts with objects. It is the aim of our overview of the sensorimotor stage to point out the regulations necessary to compensate for disturbances. In the following example we shall focus on some concepts introduced in Chapter Three, which will aid in understanding compensations throughout the six substages. Piaget (1952b) observed Jacqueline (18 months) trying to reach a watch by pulling the chain to which the watch was attached. Jacqueline's movement changed as she noticed the resistance of the weight of the watch. The amount of pull covaried with the resistance of the weight of the watch. Jacqueline overcame the resistance through an assimilation of the casual relationship between the strength of her movement and the strength of the pull necessary to retrieve the watch.

Another way of understanding the interaction of pull and weight is to use the term *compensation* for accommodation. Jacqueline had to compensate (balance) for the force of the pull in relation to the weight of the watch. This regulation of the pull did not rest just in Jacqueline's ability to pull (that is, within the subject) or in the resistance of the watch (that is, within the object). The *compensatory regulation* here was in the interaction between the object and the action scheme of pulling. This action scheme was modified by Jacqueline's understanding that more weight meant more pull. She constructed (assimilated) the change through an interaction process that followed the simple disturbance created by "more weight than expected."

In the pages that follow, we present an explanation of the traditional six substages of the sensorimotor stage that incorporates the notions of constructivism—that is, the role of compensation following a disturbance. Piaget's (1977b) revised explanation of the role of equilibration is based in part on his earlier observations of his own children, Jacqueline, Laurent, and Lucienne, during their infancy. The cartoonist of Figure 4-2

"KEEP AN EYE ON THE KIDS FOR A WHILE, WILL YOU JEAN?"

Figure 4-2. (From *APA Monitor*, Fall 1974. Reprinted by permission of the American Psychological Association.)

has caught the spirit of the situation rather nicely. What better way to discover how small children construct their own understandings than by directly observing and carefully recording their activities in the natural and intimate surroundings of their homes? In the following sections we shall outline each substage according to the increasing complexity of the equilibration model. We shall also complement our exposition with quotations from Piaget's (1952b; 1954) classic works *The Origins of Intelligence in Children* and *The Construction of Reality in the Child.*

Piaget sometimes calls these substages "six sensorimotor stages" and other times "six levels." We are using the label *substage* to maintain clarity throughout the discussion of sensorimotor thought.

Substage 1 (0 to 1 Month): Reflexes and Spontaneous Movements

The reflex of sucking is central to this stage, because it brings the infant very early in contact with disturbance. When the infant is only a few days old, one can observe a very simple type of compensation or adjustment during the feeding process (Piaget, 1977b). If the infant accidentally loses the nipple by moving her head to the right, she learns to turn her head to the left to find the nipple again. Also, the head movements gradually cover a shorter and shorter distance. The loss of the nipple—that is, the space between nipple and mouth—creates a disturbance. The movements necessary to orient the head back toward the nipple represent the compensation. Note, however, that the disturbance is of a weak type and that it is compensated by cancellation—moving the head back toward the nipple. Attempts to compensate for such weak disturbances are called *alpha behavior* (see our discussion of contradiction in Chapter Three).

The self-regulation observed in early sucking is a dramatic example of the organization necessary to all forms of life. Piaget (1952b, p. 39) says:

> That organization exists is substantiated by the fact that there is directed search. The precocious searching of the child in contact with the breast, in spite of being commonplace, is a remarkable thing. Such searching, which is the beginning of accommodation and assimilation, must be conceived, from the point of view of organization, as the first manifestation of a duality of desire and satisfaction, consequently of value and reality.

The searching behavior described above may be linked to the traditional learning concept of generalization. For Piaget, such a concept is always tied to that of assimilation and becomes **assimilation by generalization,** or generalizing assimilation. Such a generalization describes the situation in which a scheme is extended to an ever-increasing number of objects. Of course, in sucking such extensions may include many objects that have nothing to do with nourishment. The sucking behavior found at this substage is a searching into the environment to extend that environment. Each searching and consequent regulations may be thought of as an advance due to the enlarging of the application of schemes. Schemes are often referred to as action patterns that the infant can demonstrate and enlarge.

Repetition is another important aspect of learning at this substage. The searching we emphasized above implies a need for repetition as if the reflex of sucking tended to reproduce itself. But such a repetition is not necessary for survival. This early form of learning by repetition is another way by which infants expand their contacts with the environment or select their modes of interacting with the environment (Piaget, 1978a; see also our discussion of phenocopy in Chapter Two).

In the following observation, Laurent demonstrates "generalized" searching when he assimilates his thumb to the basic reflex of sucking:

> Laurent (age 21 days) is lying on his right side, his arms tight against his body, his hands clasped, and he sucks his right thumb at length while remaining completely immobile. The nurse made the same observation on the previous day. I take his right hand away, and he at once begins to search for it, turning his head from left to right. As his hands remained immobile due to his position, Laurent found his thumb after three attempts: prolonged sucking begins each time. But, once he has been placed on his back, he does not know how to coordinate the movement of the arms with that of the mouth, and his hands draw back even when his lips are seeking them [Piaget, 1952b, p. 27].

The adjustments by means of movements of the hand to find the thumb highlight again the process of compensation that takes place when there has been a disturbance—in this case, the loss of the satisfaction of sucking the thumb.

Another simple form of learning can be observed as the scheme of sucking becomes more and more regulated. As early as 2 weeks of age, an infant is able to be selective in what he or she will suck. Consider the example of Laurent exploring his father's finger. As the following episode illustrates, Laurent becomes aware that the finger is not the nipple he was searching for:

> He immediately sucks it [his father's finger] but rejects it after a few seconds and begins to cry. Second attempt: same reaction. Third attempt: he sucks it, this time for a long time and thoroughly, and it is I who retract it after a few minutes [Piaget, 1952b, p. 27].

The element of disturbance is present when Laurent recognizes that his father's finger is not what he expected, and it is manifested by crying. Compensation follows when the infant adjusts to the finger. His awareness, or recognition, is an example of **recognitory assimilation,** or assimilation by recognition. Such recognition is a form of discrimination (awareness of differences) and is not as productive in extending children's knowledge of their world as generalization is.

In these examples, although no coordination between schemes is noted, some simple forms of learning through adaptive sucking are certainly taking place. Piaget (1977b) emphasized that these disturbances and adjustments are all of a primitive type. However, these examples indicate that three aspects of assimilation—repetition, recognition, and generalization—have their roots in this stage. Each of these aspects is, in turn, tied to the traditional notion of learning.

Why so much emphasis on sucking—or on any reflex, for that matter? Reflexes, as primitive forms of behavior, help us to understand the continuity of the learning process. Very early in life, the infant manifests elementary yet complex adjustments to environmental disturbances. These earliest behaviors clarify the relationship between reaction norms and phenocopy discussed in Chapter Two. Reaction norms or normative ranges of reaction to specific irritation, are not completely predictable responses linked to environmental stimuli. Rather, reaction norms specify possible responses to external irritations, and those responses have potentially adaptive value for the learner if they are retained as purposive behavior at later stages. Thus, the above examples of sucking behavior must be understood not so much as innate abilities but as seeking-out processes interacting with the environment. "Explaining" behavior by saying that it results from innate abilities hardly clarifies the processes involved in the emergence of new structures of behavior. Piaget (1972b) summarizes this point as follows:

> It should be pointed out, moreover, that using heredity as an explanation only serves to exchange one problem for another, because if we postulate an innate nucleus, we then have to explain its biological formation. Neither chance mutation nor biological selection could give us the answer to this mystery. The generality of regulatory mechanisms, on the other hand, renders them much more apt to account for cognitive developments [p. 397].

Thus, the constructive process starts in the first days of life and in the first searchings for food. The adjustments to disturbances, although primitive at this time, are adaptive, and they are manifestations of the rapidly evolving subject/object distinctions of infancy.[3]

Substage 2 (1 to 4 Months): First Habits and Primary Circular Reactions

Let us search now for regulations and compensations in the acquired constructions that prolong the sucking and looking of the first substage. Here are some observations that Piaget (1952b) made when Laurent was approximately 1 to 1½ months old:

> He is lying down, his head resting on his right cheek; I show him my fingers 20 cm away, and he follows them so that he turns all the way to the left. . . . Same experiment with a handkerchief: I make his head describe an angle of 180° moving backward and forward, so attentively does he follow the object. . . . Laurent stops crying when I put my handkerchief 10 cm away from his eyes. He looks at it attentively, then follows it; but when he loses sight of it, he does not succeed in catching sight of it again [p. 64].

At first, Laurent's looking is purely a reflex (just as sucking was in the previous example). Then it becomes an acquired construction, or **primary circular reaction,** defined as the active reproduction of interesting results that were first produced by chance. For Laurent looking becomes interesting and is worth the extra effort of pursuing the

---

[3]It cannot be stressed too often that the *extension* of reflexes is not considered an innate event, and neither is the sequence of stages. Piaget has consistently disavowed a central contribution to a view of the growth of knowledge that attributes it to innate or hereditary structures. His reasoning points out that, if the growth of knowledge could be accounted for through the unfolding of innate structures, intelligent activity that extends beyond the immediate potential of a learner would never be realized. Something must account for the extension of schemes and the expansion of earlier structures in response to disturbances from the environment. The innate structures and the press of the environment are necessary but insufficient to explain intellectual growth or change itself. Change, according to Piaget, requires a regulatory mediator between biology and experience—that is, equilibration.

moving handkerchief, at least until it is out of sight and Laurent's interest is lost. The slight disturbance is represented by the moving object. Compensation follows in the form of turning the head to keep the moving object in view.

This observation of Lucienne at 4 months of age offers a striking example of disturbance and compensation:

> Lucienne looks at her rattle with the same reactions of buccal desire. She opens her mouth, makes sucking-like movements, raises her head slightly, etc. But she does not stretch out her hands although they make grasping-like movements. A moment later, her right hand being outstretched, I place a rattle next to her. Lucienne looks alternately at her hand and the rattle, her fingers constantly moving, but she does not move her hand closer. However, when the rattle touches her hand, she grasps it immediately [Piaget, 1952b, p. 103].

The difficulty of coordinating vision and grasping is evident in this example. By looking alternately at her hand and at the rattle, Lucienne attempts to compensate for the disturbance[4]—the thwarting of her desire to hold the rattle. By prolonging the reflex motion of moving her fingers, Lucienne is compensating for her failure to make the coordination.

Something else is evident in this example: this substage witnesses the beginning of true coordination—that is, a construction involving new relations going beyond what is observed.

> The hand tends to conserve and repeat the movements that the eye looks at, just as the eye tends to look at everything the hand does. In other words, the hand tends to assimilate to its schemata the visual realm just as the eye assimilates to its schemata the manual realm [Piaget, 1952b, p. 106].

What is important here—and was not present in substage 1—is the visual regulation of behavior. But the coordination , or construction, is only between vision and hand movements; it is not the advanced coordination of vision and grasping characteristic of substage 3. The back-and-forth activity, or circular reaction of looking at hand movements and hand movements initiating eye movements, however, is providing the structural foundation for the important coordinations to follow. Piaget calls this back-and-forth activity **reciprocal assimilation**—a term that emphasizes that the infant is able to assimilate the "seeing" and "moving" aspects of the event. The process of reciprocal assimilation, which only just begins during this substage, plays a major role in the construction of more complex schemes at the next levels.

Substage 3 (4 to 8 Months): Secondary Circular Reactions

With the coordination of vision and grasping (eye/hand coordination) at this substage, the learning phenomenon of **secondary circular reaction** is manifested. In this type of circular reaction, the

---

[4]See our discussion of compensation in relation to disturbance in Chapter Three.

infant goes beyond the mere continuation of a result. Note how Lucienne at 5 months discovers a result and then continues it:

> Lucienne tries to grasp the rattle when it is attached to the bassinet hood and hangs in front of her face. During an unlucky attempt she strikes it violently: fright, then a vague smile. She brings her hand back with a doubtless intentional suddenness: a new blow. The phenomenon then becomes systematic: Lucienne hits the rattle with regularity a very great number of times [Piaget, 1952b, p. 167].

It is by means of secondary circular reactions (prolongation of results) that new schemes are multiplied and repeated. Piaget (1977b, pp. 90–91) describes this construction process with symbols: x = seeing an object, and y = grasping an object. If there is a distance between the object and the hand, such a distance may serve as a disturbance. The infant may attempt to compensate for the disturbance, as in Lucienne's case, by reaching for the object. However, in the reaching process an interesting result, such as striking an object, may occur by chance. A new scheme, striking, which has characteristics of both x (seeing) and y (grasping), is formed. The new scheme may be labeled xy, because it shares some of the characteristics of both x and y. As Figure 4-3 shows, the secondary circular reaction of continuing to strike is structurally related to the previous schemes of seeing and grasping. There is no environmental

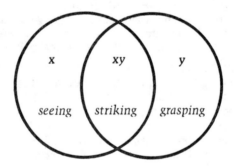

Figure 4-3.   A schematic representation of secondary circular reactions.

pressure to continue to strike. The activity continues because the infant is able to construct a new relationship linked to previous schemes.

We already noted the regulatory mechanism involved in compensating for the distance between the hand and the object to be grasped. One would expect Lucienne to compensate for the startled reaction (fright) when the rattle starts to swing. However, the slight disturbance at this point is ignored, and the child smiles vaguely. Therefore, such a momentary disturbance would be classified as alpha behavior.

As we saw earlier, primary circular reactions pertain to activities associated with bodily movements but that do not involve the continuation of a result. The essential aspect of secondary circular reactions is repetition, which we see in Lucienne's behavior when she continues to hit the rattle although at first that was not her goal. Piaget (1952b, p. 154) ties such repetition to a prelogical understanding of conservation: "After reproducing the interesting results discovered by chance on his own body, the child tries sooner or later to conserve also those which he obtains when his action bears on the external environment." Another early sign of prelogic can be detected at this substage. The operation of classification has its roots here, in that the infant begins to perceive objects as belonging to the simple categories of "something to shake," "something to rub," or "something to hit."

Although early signs of logic through very practical action-oriented examples of conservation and classification may be found in these early months of infancy, it must be emphasized that the secondary circular reactions of this substage are not true acts of intelligence. The first reason for this claim is that the relations discovered by the child—Lucienne's continuing to strike the rattle with her hand, for example—are discovered by accident. It is unlikely that Lucienne set out to solve a problem or satisfy a need. Piaget (1952b, p. 182) explains: "The need arises from the discovery and not the discovery from the need. On the contrary, in the true act of intelligence there is pursuit of an end and only subsequently discovery of means."

The second reason for the claim that secondary circular reactions are not true signs of intelligence is that the only need involved is the need for repetition. According to Piaget, a true act of intelligence is motivated by a need to adapt to the results of one's discoveries and does not merely lead to repetition of a scheme. Repetition implies a concentration on some observable features of an environmental event. However, in Chapter Three we emphasized the importance of going beyond the observable. Going beyond the immediately observable dimensions of an event *is* construction. In sum, to understand is to construct, and that is more than repetition. True construction—thus, true acts of intelligence—is finally found in the last three substages of infancy.

Substage 4 (8 to 12 Months): Coordination of Means and Ends

This substage sees the emergence of true acts of intelligence. In examining them, we should not forget that their foundations lie in the first three substages. The action schemes we saw in substage 3 were "detached," for no preplanning of the relationship between means and goals was apparent. In Piaget's (1974a, 1976b, 1977b) recent writings, which reflect his new thinking about the centrality of equilibration, the expression *mise en relation* is repeated again and again. What Piaget wants to emphasize is that at the heart of construction is the process of "bringing into relationship." Here again we encounter the internal reordering—or control from within—of phenocopy: the infant relates means and goals more and more independently of environmental stimulation.

The process of *bringing into relationship* represents the individual's attempts to extend the environment beyond its concrete and observable nature. This extension of the environment makes the external world richer, by virtue of what can be inferred about its imperceptible aspects, than its immediate offerings to the learner. Intelligent acts depend on construction of relationships that are essentially imperceptible and on enrichment of the objective world through inferences that do not have observable dimensions. Thus, intellectual growth could never be explained only in terms of the effects of environmental inputs and experiences. The process of bringing into relationship contributes to the environment and makes it richer than the experiences it offers (Piaget, 1971a, 1978a).

Here are two observations of Jacqueline's means/end behavior at 8 and at 11 months (with the interesting twist that Mrs. Piaget gets into the act!).

> Jacqueline looks at her mother, who is swinging a flounce of material with her hand. When this spectacle is over, Jacqueline, instead of imitating this movement, which she will do shortly thereafter, begins by searching for her mother's hand, places it in front of the flounce, and pushes it to make it resume its activity. . . . Jacqueline grasps my hand, places it against a swinging doll which she was not able to set going herself, and exerts pressure on my index finger to make me do the [what is] necessary [Piaget, 1952b, p. 223].

Jacqueline uses the hand of her parent to compensate, through the movements the hand will make, for a spatiotemporal distance that prevents grasping and thus "disturbs." The "bringing into relationship" *(mise en relation)* of the hand to compensate for distance becomes the regulatory mechanism for achieving a higher level of cognitive development (Piaget, 1977b).

In other observations of this stage, Piaget sets up situations in which the infant must remove a pillow that has been preventing free movement of the hand when reaching for an object. In such observations the "disturbance" is the pillow and the "compensation" is the pushing aside of the pillow. The latter is also an indication that the infant is beginning to construct negations.

An important area of study in substage 4 is the child's difficulty with the permanence of objects. Such a difficulty is demonstrated in the following observations of Jacqueline at 12 months:

> Jacqueline is seated between two cushions, A and B. I hide a brush under A. Jacqueline raises the cushion, finds the brush and grasps it. I take it from her and hide it under B, but quite far down. Jacqueline searches for it in B, but indolently, and then returns to A where she pursues her investigations with much more energy.
>
> Jacqueline holds a trumpet which I take from her in order to put it under an eiderdown quilt on her left, in A. She finds it, then I hide it in B, that is to say, on her right under the same quilt. Jacqueline searches for it in B, but does not find it. She then returns to A and searches for a moment. Then she goes back to B and after a few seconds abandons all attempts. . . .
>
> *Third attempt:* The trumpet is first put in A; Jacqueline searches for it and takes it. Then I place it in B; Jacqueline begins by searching in A, and

only after this tries in B. She finally returns to A and gives up [Piaget, 1954, p. 56].

What is striking in these observations is the infant's return to the first hiding place even though she has observed the *real* hiding place. It is as if the infant's world were a continual slow-motion film with the smooth connections missing. In all three observations, the disturbance is a simple one: a desired object is hidden. However, because the events are not connected, there is no compensation (movement of object from *A* to *B*, thus the necessity to look under *B*). Later, compensation, such as pushing the cushion aside, will take place.

At first, infants give up quite quickly when they cannot find the hidden object. The infant at substage 4 has very few schemes. Not knowing what to compensate for, he or she gives up the search, because the disturbance (the cushion) is too great. However, there are regulations that will help in retrieving the hidden object. As schemes multiply in number—that is, as cognitive development advances—the infant treats the cushion as only a slight disturbance. In other words, the act of removing the cushion implies that the child has constructed, at the level of action, a negation of a disturbance. He has, in effect, reversed the original disturbance which led him to compensate for the frustrating circumstances in the first place (Piaget, 1977b; see also Chapter Three). We will see how the *construction of negations* plays a major role in many aspects of cognitive development in older children.

Substage 5 (12 to 18 Months): Tertiary Circular Reactions

A clear distinction between secondary and **tertiary circular reactions** is apparent in an observation of Laurent at 10 months. He is playing with a slippery metal container of shaving soap. As the baby continues to play, Piaget notes that what interests Laurent is the "letting go" of the container in successive repetitions:

> It is this characteristic of Laurent's behavior which permits us still to class it among the secondary circular reactions and not among the tertiary reactions. The "tertiary" reaction will begin, in effect, at the time when Laurent will study the trajectory of the object and to do this organize a true "experiment in order to see." He will vary the conditions, relinquish the object in different situations, watch it, try to recapture it, etc. For the time being, on the contrary, he limits himself to repeating the same gestures and is only interested in his own action which certainly constitutes a "secondary" reaction [Piaget, 1952b, p. 257].

It is the variations, the inventions of new means, that are the focus of this stage. A simple observation of Jacqueline at age 1 year highlights the experimental attitude of this stage:

> Jacqueline places her red ball on the ground and waits to see it roll. She repeats the attempt five or six times and reveals a lively interest in the object's lightest movement. Then she puts it down and gives it a slight push

with her fingers: the ball rolls better. She then repeats the experiment while pushing harder and harder [Piaget, 1952b, p. 271].

Let us analyze this simple observation from a constructivist viewpoint (Piaget, 1977b). By pushing harder and harder, Jacqueline is accommodating—that is, adapting—to the ball. At this level the child is not disturbed by the fact that the ball rolls faster because she has made a compensatory accommodation. The "push" on the ball is increased so that the ball will move faster (discovery of new means to speed up the movement of the ball).

Why is Jacqueline able to grasp the connection between a harder push and greater speed? The infant is now acting more from a totality of reciprocal assimilations. The experimental situation of pushing the ball to gain speed is assimilated into the already existing scheme of pushing. Gradual equilibration (self-regulation) is demonstrated by a refinement of the pushing with each experimentation. Thus, to every accommodation there corresponds an assimilation that links it to coordinations. Jacqueline accommodates to the new event of the ball moving, because she assimilates this event into her consciousness of the effects of pushing other objects. Only at substage 5 is it possible to note beta behavior exemplified in the tertiary circular reactions. At this level, compensations for disturbances finally consist of integrating disturbances into a child's level of understanding (Jacqueline's pushing harder and harder on the ball).

Substage 6 (18 Months to 2 Years): Inventions through Sudden Comprehension

Claparède, the famous Swiss educator, describes this stage as characterized by an awareness of relationships rather than by trial-and-error groping. An essential feature of substage 6 is that children produce reasoned predictions; that is, they operate on their environment in a premeditated way, mentally combining important environmental clues. Children now begin to grasp the important features of a situation and appear to construct the means to a problem's solution. However, the inventions[5] of this stage are very simple and are no doubt missed by many parents if they are unable to make step-by-step observations. Here is an example of invention on the part of Jacqueline when she was 1 year and 8 months old:

> Jacqueline . . . arrives at a closed door—with a blade of grass in each hand. She stretches out her right hand toward the knob but sees that she cannot turn it without letting go of the grass. She puts the grass on the floor, opens the door, picks up the grass again and enters. But when she wants to leave the room, things become complicated. She puts the grass on the floor

---

[5]Recall from Chapter Three that, for Piaget, both *discovery* (substage 5) and *invention* (substage 6) are constructed (Beth & Piaget, 1966). Piaget speaks of invention here to stress that at this level growth in knowledge is due to *mental* combinations that are original and novel. These mental combinations presuppose, of course, already acquired schemes.

and grasps the doorknob. But then she perceives that in pulling the door toward her she will simultaneously chase away the grass which she placed between the door and the threshold. She therefore picks it up in order to put it outside the door's zone of movement.

This ensemble of operations, which in no way comprises remarkable invention, is nevertheless very characteristic of the intelligent acts founded upon representation of awareness of relationships [Piaget, 1952b, p. 339].

Note the absence of trial-and-error groping. It is as if reflection on the relationships involved lead to a sudden understanding of what must be done to solve the simple problem. Several events need to be related: the door swings through a certain arc; the grass will be dropped if the doorknob is turned while holding the grass; the grass may be lost if the swinging door brushes against it; and so forth. All of these events may be predicted by the child. So Jacqueline needs to construct a new solution and is aided in this task by a newly emerging capacity for imagery. She now begins to imagine the results of her actions and can represent them mentally. We will see how such a capacity for imagery ties to the development of language.

What may be noted here is that in a very short time Jacqueline balances the positive and negative aspects of the situation and regulates her behavior by selecting a new solution. The solution is constructed, however, on the basis of previous compensatory regulations. What is novel and creative in the situation is the new combination of actions never practiced before. This is the meaning of creativity in the Piagetian sense (see Piaget's essay on creativity in Appendix B).

The Preoperational Stage (Stage of Representation)

Inhelder, Sinclair, and Bovet (1974) note that earlier research on the child between the ages of 2 and 7 tended to focus mainly on the negative features of this stage. Textbooks, too, were likely to deal with this stage by offering a list of all the abilities the preoperational child did *not* have, usually centering around the failure to demonstrate various forms of conservation.

Two factors have offset this negative image of the preoperational child. One is Piaget's (1977b, 1978b, 1978c, in press) emphasis on the importance of **correspondences** as paths to the understanding of transformations. In Chapters Two and Three we discussed a basic notion of genetic epistemology: to know is to transform—that is, to make something assimilable into past structures of understanding. Small children, however, are very often able to work with correspondences, which provide the learning foundation for the grasp of transformation. Correspondences are essentially comparisons that link similar features of objects or analogous objects having a mutual basis for comparison. Thus, correspondences show how an individual object can also be understood as an analog of another, without obscuring the inherently unique characteristics of either item being compared. In this section we give several examples of how children begin to grasp the notion of correspondences.

The other factor that has contributed to a more positive view of the preoperational child is the attention being paid to **constituent functions.** Such functions, as we shall see, provide children with a semilogical ability to solve problems requiring a notion of **qualitative identity.**

In sum, the preoperational stage (between 2 and 7 years of age) is both an extension of the sensorimotor stage and the basis for the stage of concrete operations (Inhelder, 1977). Much is happening at this stage, and to underplay its importance is to distort the meaning of the Spiral of Knowing.

To highlight the importance of the preoperational stage, we will focus on two tools of assimilation: the symbolic function and the constituent function.

The Symbolic Function

We have seen in the preceding section that the infant compensates for disturbances, begins to coordinate activity, and moves to "intelligent" behavior by "bringing into relationship" goals and means. It is a period of rapid learning. For the Genevan School the most important aspect of the preoperational stage is the emergence of the *symbolic function,* which makes the use of language possible. In this section we highlight some of the views of the Genevan School on language learning in order to clarify the relationship between the symbolic function and language.

The symbolic function refers to the child's ability to use mental images and words to represent something that is not present. The broadness of the skills required by the use of symbols is aptly expressed by Furth (1970):

> You may have noticed that for Piaget "symbol" is a very broad term that covers any event (including verbal language) which represents something a person knows. Since we are no longer dealing merely with practical knowing, symbols are a necessary guide to evaluating the status of intellectual development. If you wanted to investigate a three-year-old child's comprehension of the social family structure, how would you go about it? Even if the linguistic competence of the child were excellent, you would hardly expect the child to come up with adequate verbal definitions. A better way would be to observe the symbolic activity of the child playing family [p. 34].

Furth's quotation indicates that the symbolic function relates to several areas: mental imagery (past images of how mother, father, and children interact), imitation (which can be observed by watching the child play house), symbolic play, and, of course, language. This section emphasizes language and symbolic play in relation to language. Our goal is to highlight the importance of language in learning and not to belittle the importance of such areas as imitation and mental imagery.

We have stressed repeatedly that each of the Piagetian stages involves a reordering of intellectual structures leading to demonstrations of newly learned behaviors (novelties). Furthermore, each stage is a realization of the possibilities opened by the constructions of preceding levels. The constructions of the earlier stages are not lost; they are modified and enriched in the successive stages (refer to the Spiral of Knowing in Chapter Two). Of course, since equilibration is the cause of the movement through the stages, modification and enrichment must proceed through the levels of equilibration (see Chapter Three).

Language, then, as well as other areas of the symbolic function, has its roots in the constructions of the sensorimotor stage. New possibilities open up for children when they start communicating by means of language. However, before they use words, children communicate through imitation and symbolic gestures. The intention of the Genevan School is not to downplay the role of language in learning but to place it in proper perspective with regard to cognitive development.

At this stage, too, the mechanism of reflexive abstraction is essential. Recall that reflexive abstraction refers to the mental act of reconstructing and reorganizing on a higher level that which was transferred from a lower level. The baby is busy coordinating schemes. These coordinations are transferred from the plane of action to that of representation through the process of reflexive abstraction. For example, the baby learns to coordinate the complex actions of eating—holding the spoon, moving the spoon from plate to mouth, and placing the food in the mouth—totally engrossed in his or her actions. At the representational level, instead, we see toddlers imitating the actions of eating while, at the same time, carrying on "conversations" in the sandbox, often with little actual eating taking place. The toddler conceptualizes the event—that is, represents it mentally—and acts it out through motions and words.

According to Sinclair, the expert psycholinguist of the Genevan School, the processes of repetition, ordering, and associative connecting that assist the child in the coordination of sensorimotor schemes are *themselves* the source of the structures that make language possible (Piaget, 1970d). However, the Genevans don't see language as the source of the shift from practical intelligence (plane of action limited in space and time to the immediately present) to representational thought.

Language Learning. We are now going to consider some experimental evidence for the claim that various aspects of language, such as syntax (sentence structure), have their roots "in the type of knowledge gathered from the subject's own organized activity" (Inhelder, 1976d, p. 164). Sinclair and Bronckart (1972) presented children ranging in age from 2 to 6 years with various constructions of two nouns (N) and one verb (V). For example:

> *NVN*: boy-push-girl; girl-push-boy.
> *NNV*: boy-girl-push; girl-boy-push.
> *VNN*: push-boy-girl; push-girl-boy.

The children were asked to show with dolls what the combinations meant (the combinations were presented verbally to them). The older children were told that the experimenters were not speaking good French (remember that the study was conducted in Geneva) and that they were to guess what the experimenters' words meant. It was thought that the children would use their basic assumptions about language, especially the common structure of subject-verb-object (SVO), to guess the meaning. The question was: would the children use the word order as a guide to the meaning of the sentence, or would they act randomly?

The experimenters expected that the children would use one of two constructions: boy push girl, or girl push boy. That is, it was expected that the children would infer and then use either the agent/patient construction or its patient/agent transformation—a possible grammatical representation of transitive verbs. In fact, this did not happen, for the children's strategies changed with age in a way that more properly reflected the children's developmental views of the meaning of the boy/girl relation.

The younger children in the experiment consistently said that the two dolls were walking. By viewing both dolls as walking, the children acted as the agents of the activity and completely ignored the reciprocal relation between the dolls. In essence, the younger children failed to grasp the implication of agent/patient conveyed in the experimenter's directions. This strategy of avoiding a transitive construction occurred with the older children, too, but not as frequently. The empirical findings of this study suggest that more than linguistic competence is required when children describe action. Whether children will even use a language structure depends on how they interpret object relationships.

The older children, who were starting to decode (interpret) the item as "the boy pushes the girl" or "the girl pushes the boy," showed an interesting order of strategies. First, the children established a link between the verb and the noun nearer to that verb in an agent/action relationship. These children seemed to operate according to the following rule: find the verb; the noun nearer the verb must be the agent; the other noun farther away must be the patient—that is, the one receiving the action. Older children and some of the younger children selected the noun nearer the verb (but not necessarily following the verb) as the patient of the action, with the other noun as agent. With the oldest group, the proximity of verb and noun became less important; the first noun became agent, and the second became patient, regardless of the verb's position.

What do these results mean in the light of genetic epistemology, which bases knowledge on action? If one saw language as the result of an innate factor, one would expect the traditional subject-verb-object order to dominate the results even at the younger age levels. But this was not the case in the experiment above. On the other hand, if one saw language as the result of imitation—that is, as based on environmental input—one would expect such nonsense items as "push-boy-girl" to be interpreted at random with no consistent pattern to be found. Again, this was not the case.

However, if a middle-ground, interactionist position is taken, the emphasis is on the importance of the general cognitive structures composed of the systems of actions established during the first two years of life (as outlined in the discussion of the substages of the sensorimotor stage). There is a correspondence, then, between the language learning of the preoperational stage and the construction of knowledge of the sensorimotor stage. Both are based on children's acting on the environment rather than on their copying what they observe in that environment. If we look at the experiment above from an interactionist perspective, we see that the younger child uses a very free order of the three elements and that the older child constructs "order" out of the elements that do not conform with ordinary sentence structure. Thus, language learning, as an aspect of the symbolic function, is based on how the child acts on the environment and changes that environment through action. Sinclair (1976) has repeatedly demonstrated how the child's cognitive level dominates his or her use of grammar. Recall from Chapter Three Sinclair's experiment, in which she showed that the language of conservers differs from the language of nonconservers.

Symbolic Play and Language

Children between the ages of 2 and 5 must make a multitude of complex social adaptations. A large number of the messages directed to them are meant to tell them "how to behave" or, if you prefer, "how to be civilized." The role that language plays in this process of social adaptation is enormous. The child is spoken to and eventually is expected to respond verbally or behaviorally. Each day the growth of language is obvious. But the importance of language in the child's learning process should not overshadow the essential interplay of language with other areas of the symbolic function, especially symbolic play.

Of all the activities involving the use of the symbolic function, *symbolic play* (which is largely pretend play) is the one in which children most actively *structure* reality (Piaget, 1952b; Piaget & Inhelder, 1969; Inhelder, 1976d). In their dealings with the world, children are required to follow certain linguistic conventions in order to be understood. Consequently, the child must infer, "ferret out," the implicit organization of the structures of adult speech, whereas parents and older peers attend closely to a child's perceptible linguistic competence. Thus, children learn to communicate by trying out their version of the language on more proficient speakers, who, in turn, provide models and give feedback. The joy and freedom of symbolic play resides in the very fact that children can structure what they say as they please; the only conventions they follow are their own. The following examples of symbolic play illustrate the value of these activities for learning.[6]

Jacqueline at the age of 1 year scratched at the bedroom wallpaper, which was decorated with birds. Then she shut her hand as if she were

[6]Examples of symbolic play interpreted in light of the new equilibration model are provided by A. D'Onofrio (Unpublished manuscript, Piaget Seminar, Department of Educational Psychology, Temple University, Philadelphia).

holding something and ran to her mother saying "Look!" She opened her hand and pretended to give her mother something. When her mother asked Jacqueline what she had brought, the child answered "A birdie" (Piaget, 1952b). What is interesting about this example is the reproduction of a sensorimotor scheme outside its usual context and usual objective. The scheme is one of offering an object to another person. But the offering here is really a pretend gesture, for there is no bird to be given. Piaget calls this type of scheme a *symbolic scheme*, a primitive form of symbolic play. In such play the child is using schemes that are very much a part of her behavior but out of the ordinary surroundings for that behavior. Other common examples of symbolic schemes occur when a child pretends to sleep or to eat. Later the child will move to true symbolic play when, for example, she puts a doll to sleep or feeds a stuffed rabbit.

Examples of symbolic schemes that form a bridge to true symbolic play emphasize the spiral-like nature of the stages, ever building on each other with no clear-cut separations. In fact, longitudinal research (Inhelder, 1976d; Nicolich, 1977) reveals the very early appearance of such symbolic schemes in pretend play. Such early forms of symbol use support the idea that attention should be directed toward a general symbolizing capacity (Sinclair, 1976) that provides the foundation for early language. Analysis of early examples of pretend play gives evidence that it is possible to find parallels between children's actions and their first verbal utterances. The roots of language, then, are to be found in the sensorimotor stage.

Another value of symbolic play, also closely linked to language learning, is the gradual separation of what is *symbolized* from the person doing the symbolizing (the *symbolizer*). By making this separation, the child is able to bring relations together in novel ways—an essential aspect of learning. Piaget (1952b) is especially fond of this example of Lucienne's pretend play at age 4:

> Lucienne, standing at my side, quite still, imitated the sound of bells. I asked her to stop, but she went on. I then put my hand over her mouth. She pushed me away angrily but, still keeping straight, said, "Don't. I'm a church [the belfry]" [p. 125].

Lucienne has developed a symbolic "language" and has assimilated reality in a novel manner.

Finally, pretend play is important in that it may function as a means of denying or ignoring a disturbance—the level 1 or alpha behavior of contradiction (see Chapter Three). Piaget (1952b) observed Jacqueline at age 4 in the following sequence:

> Jacqueline was impressed by the sight of a dead duck which had been plucked and put on the kitchen table. The next day I found Jacqueline lying motionless on the sofa in my study, her arms pressed against her body and her legs bent: "What are you doing, Jacqueline? Have you a pain? Are you ill?" [At first she did not answer questions; then in a faraway voice she said:] "No. I'm a dead duck" [p. 133; text in brackets from Piaget & Inhelder, 1969, p. 60].

In this example, Jacqueline seemed to need to reenact her encounter with a dead animal in an immediate sequence of symbolic actions. She neutralized the unpleasantness through play. From the point of view of the cognitive-phenocopy model, Jacqueline brought the external (exogenous) reality into greater proximity to her ability to understand the disturbing situation. By assimilating the exogenous actuality of the animal, Jacqueline internalized her understanding, making it endogenous knowledge, through the mechanisms of play. Play assisted her to accommodate to facts. It is evident, then, that symbolic or pretend play is valuable in its own right, apart from any language experiences that such activities provide.

The Constituent Function

A constituent function is an elementary structure through which a child organizes the covariations of the properties of objects. Constituent functions are actually tools of assimilation that we have chosen to discuss in order to emphasize further the "positive achievements" (Piaget, 1972b) of the preoperational child. For a basis of understanding, consider the following experiment:

> Let us take as an example a string, pulled down by a weight at end b [see Figure 4-4]. The child discovers easily the co-variation involved: if the segment a becomes shorter, then the segment b becomes longer. He discovers just as easily the co-property, which is even an identity: "it's the same string," which gets shorter in the segment a and longer in the segment b. And, significantly, he discovers this well before arriving at the conservation of length $a + b$. This conservation, no matter how long the segment b or a may be, is reached at about 7 or 8 years of age, while the co-variation and identity are affirmed at 4 or 5 years of age. Here, then, is an example of the absence of operational quantification and conservation, since the quantities remain ordinal or in relation to one another: "longer" and "shorter" are still judged in terms of "farther" and "not so far," based simply on the endpoints, but that in no way precludes the use of functions or qualitative identity [Piaget, 1968, pp. 23–24].

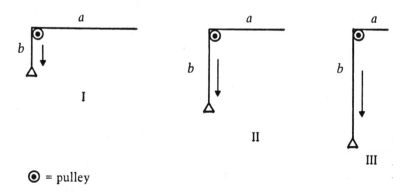

$\odot$ = pulley

$\triangle$ = weight

Figure 4-4. The weight-string problem involving qualitative identity. (Adapted from Piaget, 1968, p. 23.)

A function is found when there is a dependency between the variations of two terms that are relational properties of objects. This functional dependency, or relation, is commonly given in the formula $y = f(x)$, which means that y is the function of x. In the above example, the formula becomes $a = f(b)$ when the child correctly predicts that pulling one of the ends will make segment b longer and segment a shorter. Modifying one of the variables will cause the other variable to be modified, too, because the two variables are *functionally* dependent on each other.

What enables the young child to understand functional dependence? First, in this example the movement is one-directional—that is, based on one-way correspondences.[7] The child doesn't need concrete operations that are truly reversible to understand the functional dependencies inherent in actions such as pulling a string around a corner. Second, such functional dependencies are built on the schemes of action of the sensorimotor period. Action becomes directed toward a goal—that is, the constructing of the means/end relationships that we outlined in our discussion of the final substages of the sensorimotor period. But such means/end relationships imply that the child is operating from an understanding of order: what is further away is "longer" regardless of the starting point. An understanding of order relies on correspondences but not on transformations. Therefore, the solution of the covariation problem above is an example of Type IA interaction (see Chapter Three). The child pulls on the string and observes the correspondence between segment b and segment a. He or she relies heavily on observables (empirical abstraction) when understanding this functional dependence. The logico-mathematical understanding of order (reflexive abstraction) is based on qualitative identity: the properties of an object are understood without conservation of quantity.

To further understand what qualitative identity means, recall that in this experiment the child grasps that an increase in segment b means a decrease in segment a. However, the string itself remains the *same* string; therefore, qualitative identity is preserved. But the child may say that segment b gets longer as segment a gets shorter. Thus, he or she fails to *conserve* the total length $a + b$ because of a lack of **quantitative identity**—that is, an identity based on true **reversibility** (see Chapter Five).

In sum, because the child at the preoperational stage is able to deal with problems involving the constituent function, or functional dependencies, he or she has a powerful tool available to understand relationships. However, the tool is limited because it is based on qualitative identity, a semilogic of one-way relationships that is not the logic of reversible operations.

Some of the most fascinating protocols of the Genevan School are based on problem solutions that reveal the presence of qualitative identity and the absence of quantitative identity. Piaget and Voyat (1968)

[7]A function in this sense entails a one-way mapping. Mapping is a process of finding one-to-one correspondences between the elements of two sets according to common properties. Note that if y is a function of x, it is not implied that x is a function of y.

conducted a series of studies on children's ability to understand the identity of an object during various transformations. In one experiment, children were presented with a wire. As the children were watching, the wire was first bent into an arc and then stretched out in a straight line. After each transformation, the children were asked whether the wire was the same wire they had seen before. Children at the age of 3 and 4 had no doubt that it was the same wire. Some of the 4- and 5-year-olds expressed doubt that it was the same wire. Other children at this level, and even older ones, said that the wire was the same but explained that it was longer or shorter, depending on the transformation. Pau, 5 years old, gave an interesting answer:

> *Adult* (bending the wire): Now is it the same?
> *Pau:* Yes, it is the same wire, but it's not always the same thing. There is one that is longer and one that is shorter. It is always the same, but you relarge [sic] it.

Note that Pau "constructed" the term *relarge* to get himself out of the dilemma.

Dee, 5 years old, was offered a countersuggestion by the experimenter to test the stability of her answer:

> *Adult:* One girl told me that it was something else when it was like this [arc].
> *Dee:* She said a silly thing. She doesn't know that the round [arc] is smaller than the straight. (Dee means that the girl thinks the arc varies only in length). It is always the same wire [protocols adapted from Piaget & Voyat, 1968, pp. 36–38].

These children were convinced of the identity of the object in spite of the changes in its shape. Thus, they demonstrated the presence of the qualitative-identity concept. However, they didn't demonstrate the presence of the quantitative-identity concept, which is based on an understanding of true measurement and compensations (what gets longer at one end must get shorter at the other), which are instruments of quantification (Piaget & Voyat, 1968).

Correspondences and Representational Thought: Summary

In the preceding section on constituent functions it was noted how the children discovered the covariance of dependency between functions. Such a discovery is based on correspondences as the means of comparisons. The children noted a necessary correspondence between "lengthening" and "shortening." One-to-one correspondences (for example, pairing eggs and egg cups) was an older topic of study for Piaget (Piaget & Szeminska, 1952). Recently the Genevan School has emphasized the importance of correspondences because they provide the learning foundation for the understanding of transformations. In

Chapter Five we will note how the emphasis on correspondences has led to new Genevan training studies in conservation of quantity.

In addition to the role that correspondences play in problems based on constituent functions, it is possible to recognize their key role in all aspects of the symbolic function. Inhelder (1976d, p. 161) presents insightful examples of 2-year-olds constructing relationships among objects in pretend play: "Having put the doll in the nursing position, Peter puts the broomhandle in its mouth as if he were giving it the bottle." Here is a symbolic substitution of one object for another based on comparisons.

It is at the stage of representation that the child must rely most heavily on the comparisons that he or she makes when interacting with the environment. As explained in Chapter Two, the Spiral of Knowing may be understood as a progressive replacement of exogenous knowledge by endogenous construction. Correspondences are part of exogenous knowledge, an essential part of the spiral. Transformations are always due to endogenous regulatory mechanisms. However, the structures—the tools of assimilation—are the result of progressive constructions based on the interaction of exogenous mechanisms (correspondences) and endogenous mechanisms (transformations) (Piaget, 1974a, in press).

Recall that in the preoperational child this progressive construction of knowledge is aided especially by the two powerful sets of functions— symbolic and constituent. Preoperational children must be viewed as competent when they interact with objects in new learning activities.

CHAPTER FIVE

Concrete Operations: Learning-Theory Aspects

Chapters Five and Six deal with operational structures—that is, those internalized actions that are reversible. This Piagetian definition, like many of the others we encountered before, means little without explicit examples. One of the main purposes of these two chapters is to present examples of operational structures, so that it will be possible to contrast them with the structures of the preoperational period. Also, to understand further the mechanisms of learning, especially reflexive abstraction, it is necessary to understand how these structures become richer and richer as they are incorporated into previous ones. We hope that these two chapters will promote both understandings.

Remember that it is important to weave together Piaget's logical and biological models (see Chapter Two). Too heavy a concentration on the logical model should be avoided because the model is at present in a state of transition and rethinking at the Center for Genetic Epistemology (Piaget, 1977g; Sinclair, 1977). Since our concern is the study of the learning theory of Piaget and Inhelder, the stress will be on the dynamics of the biological model, especially as reported in the revised model of equilibration (Piaget, 1977b, 1977d).

Introduction

As we noted in our discussion of the Spiral of Knowing in Chapter Two, there is no abrupt transition to concrete operations; the foundations of each stage are found in the previous stages. Each stage may be thought of as a process of reordering and recombination and as richer than the previous stage (Piaget, 1974a). This transition or projection to a higher stage and the accompanying process of reordering—that is, the mechanism of reflexive abstraction—are at this stage both related to concrete objects. But is the presence of objects necessary? Sinclair (1971a) makes a critical point:

> Concrete in the Piagetian sense means that the child can think in a logically coherent manner about objects that do exist and have real properties and about actions that are possible. He can perform the mental operations involved both when asked purely verbal questions and when manipulating objects. The latter situation is far preferable to the former, mainly for reasons of clarity, but the actual presence of objects is no intrinsic condition [pp. 5-6].

Thus, this "manipulation" of concrete objects may be physical or mental. The important point is that initially the operations are concrete, for they are used directly on objects, so that the objects may be manipulated. Manipulation may take various forms: putting objects together into a class (round objects into a pile), separating a collection of objects into subclasses (dividing round objects into small and large), setting up correspondences between objects or relationships (selecting a form of the right size in which to place each of a set of discs), ordering objects (placing sticks of various lengths into a series from short to long), ordering events in time (knowing the sequence of events in a story in logical order), and measuring objects in space (finding the height of a tower of blocks on a table).

The various operations we listed above, such as putting objects into classes or subclasses or ordering from small to large in a seriated fashion, would not be operations, however, unless they were mentally reversible. *Reversibility* is at the very core of the understanding of an operation. This is a Piagetian concept that is often misunderstood. Remember that the "reversing" is not what is accomplished with the objects "out on the table." Reversibility has its roots in a mathematical concept that in everyday thinking becomes observable, for example, in the conservation experiments. Thus, conservation is the empirical manifestation of the mental process of reversibility.

An experiment by Inhelder, Sinclair, and Bovet (1974) based on conservation was described in Chapter Three. Note that, in the experiment, reversibility was not the *physical* reversing of the water (see Figure 3-2) but the *understanding* that it is possible to mentally reverse the original quantities of water to their starting points at A and A'. Those children who could mentally reverse manifested conservation by verbal statements such as "Nothing was added or taken away" and "We started out with the same amount." Such children, even if puzzled by the transformation in E, could still grasp that the quantity of water didn't change in spite of the fact that the glasses were of different shapes or that in E there appeared to be more water. The amount of water was conserved; it remained *invariant*—that is, unchanged.

In this chapter we will probe the meaning of reversibility as related to the broader issue of equilibration, or self-regulation. Our aim is to show that reversibility, manifested in conservation, is linked by definition to operations such as seriating objects or placing them in classes.

Conservation of Quantities and Equilibration

In an earlier essay on logic and equilibrium, Piaget (1957) stressed that conservation is easily explained by probabilities: it is more probable that the child will think that a tall, thin glass contains more water than does a low, wide glass, although the two glasses contain the same amount of water. In his revised model of equilibration, Piaget (1977b) now stresses that conservation is attained by compensatory (counterbalancing) adjustments, or regulations. These regulations balance the affirmations (the observables) and negations (to be constructed) of the transformations (see the discussion of states and transformations in Chapter Three).

The clearest example of the balancing of affirmations and negations appears in the conservation of a continuous quantity such as clay.[1] The entire balancing process may be labeled *construction of conservation* and involves four levels.

The Construction of Conservation

Level 1. The experimenter presents two identical balls of clay to the child. After establishing that the two balls are identical, the experimenter rolls one of the balls into a long sausage. The child at this level (around the age of 5) will no doubt concentrate on the fact that the ball has become longer—the *positive* aspect (affirmation) of the transformation—and will fail to notice that the ball has also become thinner—the *negative* aspect. Thus, when the experimenter changes one of the balls into a sausage, the child will state "You made it bigger," meaning longer (Piaget, 1974c, in collaboration with Othenin-Girard).

Level 2. At this level the child still concentrates on affirmations. However, in the experiment with the two balls of clay, the child begins to notice that materials like clay and water are not so easily separated into discrete components as were, for example, the marbles in Piaget and Inhelder's experiment illustrated in Figure 2-2 (Chapter Two). At level 2 the child begins to develop a sense of the transformations involved in continuous quantity. Noticing that the sausage is thinner than the ball constitutes an unstable equilibrium: first, the child notices length, then he or she notices thinness. But the child fails to coordinate length and thinness; the processes of lengthening and thinning are treated as separate actions. We see, therefore, evidence of the half-logic of constituent functions we discussed in Chapter Four.

See Figure 5-1 for a demonstration of the lack of coordination of level 2. Here Cri, in taking off almost half of the longer clay sausage, sees the increase in length as an increase in quantity. He sees the actions of

---

[1]Continuous quantities—for example, clay and water—are not so easily separated into discrete components as are discontinuous quantities—that is, objects that are separate and countable.

Adult (shows Cri two identical balls of clay and makes sure that the child agrees that they are equal): Now watch. I am going to make two sausages out of these balls. (Rolls one of the balls several times, so that it is longer and thinner than the other.) Now, do we have the same amount to eat?

Cri (5 years old): No.

Adult: What can you do so that we'll have the same amount to eat?

Cri (takes off almost half of the longer sausage): Now we have the same amount to eat (concentrating on the unchanged sausage and on the remaining section of the other sausage).

Adult: Do you think so?

Cri (looks very carefully): No, you have more, because it's fatter (referring to the unchanged sausage).

Adult: What can we do so we have the same amount to eat?

Cri: I don't know.

Adult: If you remake them (suggesting that the sausages be rolled back into their original ball shape), will it make the same amount?

Cri: Yes.

Adult: Look at that on the table (the piece that Cri took off from the longer sausage). Will it be the same amount?

Cri: No, it (the fatter sausage) is still missing some; you'll have to put it back.

Figure 5-1. Example of level 2 in the construction of conservation. (Adapted from Piaget, 1974c.)

adding and subtracting as independent and doesn't realize that by *logical necessity* such actions are, instead, interdependent. What is gained in length (added) must be lost in thickness (subtracted). We will return to this important point of logical necessity in relation to reversibility.

In sum, even though children at level 2 notice both length and thickness, their equilibrium, or level of understanding, is unstable. They fail to grasp the necessity of the coordination (reciprocal relation) between length and thickness (Piaget, 1974c, 1977b).

Level 3. Piaget and Inhelder's (1971) research on mental imagery led to the identification of an important intermediate stage at approximately age 6 (level 3). Children at this level were able to predict that stretching the clay ball would make it thinner. It was as if the interactions with the clay resulted in a feedback from the object and, consequently, in a change in the next observation (see models of equilibration in Chapter Three). However, conservation and, of course, true reversibility were not present. What was observed was a pseudore-versibility (*renversabilité*), or empirical reversibility, which can be defined as a return to the starting point.

The misunderstanding of the concept of reversibility has led to confusion in U.S. research (see the discussion of research studies based on Piagetian theory in "Anglo-American Training Studies in Conservation" in Chapter Seven; see also Peill (1975) for a review of these studies). How does one distinguish between true reversibility and pseudoreversibility? Recall Cri's answer (Figure 5-1) when his attention was directed to the piece of clay sausage left on the table. He suggested that, to arrive again at two equal balls of clay, "you'll have to put it back." Such a "putting back" is an example of pseudoreversibility—that is, an empirical (actual) return to the starting point when there is a failure to conserve (Inhelder, Sinclair, & Bovet, 1974). It was evident from Cri's earlier behavior that he was not able to conserve—namely, that he didn't realize that the change in appearance didn't alter the original amount of clay.

How do levels 2 and 3 differ in the construction of conservation? Remember that at level 2 the lengthening and thinning out of the sausage were thought of as sequential and unrelated acts. At level 3, instead, the child understands that the two events are interdependent. In Chapter Three we emphasized the necessity of focusing on transformations instead of concentrating on static states such as comparing the initial event in a task with the final outcome. At level 3, children "fill-in" the events between the initial and the final states—that is, the transformations involved. The grasp of the transformations, however, is qualitative and not quantitative. By *qualitative* we mean that the child doesn't have the mathematical understanding that the lengthening and thinning out cancel each other, so that quantity is conserved.[2]

In sum, at level 3 there is evidence of pseudoreversibility with prediction of conservation. Transformations are grasped on a qualitative but not on a quantitative level (Piaget, 1977b).

Level 4. At the final level of the construction of conservation, the child makes inferences about the logical necessity of the conservation involved in a task. Often children at this level (around 7 or 8 years of age) act surprised when they are asked a "stupid" question such as "Do we have the same amount?" (after a ball has been rolled into a sausage).

In an experiment on mental imagery (Piaget & Inhelder, 1971) in which children were asked to anticipate the changes in the shape of a ball of clay, those at level 4 made many verbal statements indicating awareness of the need to attend to the *necessary* connection between lengthening and thinning out. Note the response of Gan, age 8, in Figure 5-2.

Gan's statements reveal his understanding of the *necessary* relationship between length and thickness: "It will be longer but not fat" (implying that it will be thin). The two transformations of lengthening and thinning are understood as compensating each other quantitatively (in contrast to the qualitative compensations of level 3). This construction of conservation—a new level of understanding—was not arrived at by simply observing the clay. By making the necessary inference that an increase in length (affirmation) must be counterbal-

[2]In a more technical sense, this may be expressed as the absence of quantitative compensation or the absence of operational reversibility. Piaget (1977b, p. 69) says "Operation T implies the existence of T^{-1} and the product of $T \cdot T^{-1} = 1$." An inverse or negative function, therefore, means a complete compensation of negations and affirmations.

> *Adult* (shows Gan a ball of clay and asks him to anticipate whether there will or will not be the same amount of clay in the ball when it is changed into various shapes): Suppose I change this ball into a sausage?
> *Gan* (8 years old): It will be the same amount, because it is the same clay. It will be longer but not fat (thick).
> *Adult:* Suppose I change the ball into a pancake?
> *Gan:* Flatter and bigger (broader).
> *Adult:* Will there be as much clay?
> *Gan:* Yes, because before they (the ball and the pancake) were the same.
> *Adult* (shows Gan a sausage and three balls of different sizes to choose from. The child is asked to anticipate which one of the three balls one would get if the sausage were transformed into a ball): Which one would you choose?
> *Gan:* The sausage is longer and thinner, and that one (pointing to one of the three balls) is shorter but fatter, and that one (pointing to another ball) is also longer but thinner. That makes the same ball, because there's just as much clay.

Figure 5-2. Example of level 4 in the construction of conservation. (Adapted from Piaget & Inhelder, 1971, p. 276.)

anced by a loss in width (negation), the child achieved conservation of quantity.

These four levels of the construction of conservation may be viewed as the progressive transition from awareness of states to awareness of transformations. At each of these levels a reorganization (reconstruction) was necessary to move to a higher level. This brings us back to the basic mechanism of reflexive abstraction, with its two aspects of projection and reflection (see discussion of reflexive abstraction in Chapters Two and Three and Figure 2-3). At the early level the exogenous factor dominates. As the child moves to a heightened equilibrium of conservation, the endogenous factor dominates. By necessity, the balancing of affirmations and negations wins, and conservation is conquered!

The Construction of Conservation and the Three Results of Regulations

Let's now look more closely at the regulations (adjustments) that are inherent in the transitions from one level of conservation to another (Piaget, 1977b, 1977g; Inhelder, Blanchet, Sinclair, & Piaget, 1975). In Chapter Three we noted that the factor of equilibration in the development of thinking may be compared to a feedback mechanism. The child interacts with an object; often the results of that interaction give information to the child that instigates a modified action on his or her next trial. This feedback process was illustrated in Chapter Three with the example of a slingshot. Similarly, in the construction of conservation, regulations are tied to a feedback process. In order to clarify the nature of the regulations related to conservation, we will outline the three results of such regulations: commutability, vicariance, and compensation.

Commutability. This first result is the understanding that "what is added on one side of the object—for example, at the end of the sausage which has grown by lengthening—necessarily corresponds to what has been taken away from another" (Piaget, 1977b; authors' translation from the 1975 French edition, p. 117).

In Chapter Four we saw the importance of correspondences, or comparisons, in the development of understanding. The emphasis on the correspondence between what is taken away at one end and what is added at the other end has led to a new set of experiments related to commutability. These experiments have been conducted to determine how the understanding of such correspondences may lead to an earlier understanding of the transformations involved (Easley, 1978; Inhelder et al., 1975; Piaget, 1978b).

> In order to examine our hypothesis about the relationship between correspondences and conservation, we've been doing some new experiments lately with Bärbel Inhelder. This time when we have the ball, we don't just push it into the form of a sausage; we take a piece off. Then we ask children if there is the same amount now in the ball, they of course say no. Then we put the piece back on the other side [see Figure 5-3], and we ask now if there is the same amount as there was before. A surprising thing is that from age 5½ about three-quarters of the children conserve.... That is much more precocious than in the classic form of the experiment [Piaget, 1978b, p. 14].

Piaget goes on to emphasize that children's new understanding of conservation generalizes to the sausage shape. Moving the pieces of clay transforms the ball into a sausage, and, when one piece of clay is removed from one end and placed on the other end of the sausage, the children who conserved in the first task (Figure 5-3) conserve also in the second task (Figure 5-4). We can clarify the idea of commutability by using symbols. If A is the part that is moved and B the part that remains, then, according to Figure 5-3, $A + B = B + A$. The identity of the whole is conserved even though there is a different arrangement of the parts.

The protocol contained in Figure 5-5 is an interesting example of a child (Osc, age 5½) who doesn't conserve at first when the pieces of clay are moved around. In spite of his subsequent progress, later in the protocol Osc gives a nonconserving answer when the experimenter shapes the clay into a long sausage: "There is more when it is too long" says Osc.

Ultimately Osc gains the insight that moving bits of clay from one end to the other end of the sausage doesn't affect the total amount of clay, which remains constant. That is, Osc understands that a change in form does not result in a change in mass. The identity of the amount of clay is preserved. It should be noted, however, that Osc's later responses indicate that he is not yet a true conserver; rather, he is in transition

Step 1: Ball of clay.

Step 2: Remove a piece.

Step 3: Ask "Same amount?" (Step 1 versus Step 2)

Step 4: Place removed piece on other side of ball.

Step 5: Ask "Same amount as before?"

Figure 5-3. Training in commutability: Correspondences may lead to an understanding of transformation.

toward that stage. He is overwhelmed by the power of affirmations (seeing the sausage becoming very long) and remains for some time in a stage of equating the positive aspect of length with a judgment of "more clay."

The basic feature of all these experiments is that the child must begin to realize that the sum of the parts of the ball or sausage must be conserved in spite of a change in position of those parts—the commutability result. A common justification that children give in conservation experiments, when asked why they know that they still have the same amount, is "Nothing was taken away, and nothing was added." A related justification may center on the length, as in clay, with a statement that the same amount of clay is present even though the length is in evidence.

Vicariance. The second result of the regulations involved in conservation is closely related to the first. Vicariance involves the ability to understand that, no matter how the parts are arranged, the same whole is involved. This aspect of commutability, however, is concerned with the identity of the parts that are moved and of those that stay in place. Thus, when a child makes a conserving statement such as "You can make the sausage out of the ball, and that's why it's the same amount,"

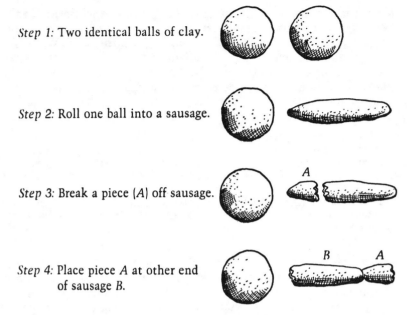

Step 1: Two identical balls of clay.

Step 2: Roll one ball into a sausage.

Step 3: Break a piece (A) off sausage.

Step 4: Place piece A at other end of sausage B.

Figure 5-4. Training in commutability and conservation: Moving A to B results in more precocious conservation.

Osc (after adult breaks off a piece of clay and moves it): There's more; it's bigger . . . You take it off each time here, and you put it back here.
Adult: So that makes more?
Osc: Yes.

After one month Osc shows progress.
Osc (after adult breaks off a piece and moves it): Always the same thing. When you take off a piece, there is less, and, when you put it back, there is the same.

Figure 5-5. Progress in the conquest of conservation when parts are moved. (Adapted from Inhelder, Blanchet, Sinclair, & Piaget, 1975.)

both vicariance and commutability are involved in the statement, which is based on true reversibility.

Compensation. The third result of the regulations in the construction of conservation was expressed by Gan in Figure 5-2: "It will be the same amount, because it is the same clay. It will be longer but not fat." This compensation—that is, the balancing of the relationship between length and thickness—was noted in a qualitative manner at level 3 of the construction of conservation. Thus, compensation in the development of cognition comes before measurement or quantification.

Earlier we stressed that the child must grasp the correspondence between what is added in length (affirmation) and what is lost in diameter and observed as "thinness" (negation). Compensation, as the balancing of affirmations and negations, is highlighted in the answers of 8-year-old Rao (Piaget, 1974c, in collaboration with Othenin-Girard, p. 55; authors' translation):

> Rao watches Silly-Putty (an American plastic substance that rolls into long, thin strings) being changed into a long sausage. When Rao is asked to compare the sausage with a ball, originally of the same size, and tell whether the two have equal amounts of substance, he gives an affirmative answer, because nothing was added or taken away. "It's stretched, that's all. . . . If you press it back together, it will come back to the same thing." This argument of compensation is based on Rao's understanding that the increased length (what is added) is balanced, or compensated, by the greater thinness (what is subtracted).

We notice here the interrelationships of commutability, vicariance, and compensation. Rao understands that, in essence, the particles (molecules) of clay had to move in the stretching action. Neither the identity (commutability) nor the rearrangement (vicariance) of particles change the whole. The lengthening and thinning (the rearrangement) actually balance each other and, therefore, are seen as compensating each other quantitatively (compensation).

The above studies outline the detailed conquest of conservation. The conquest is attributable to the child's gradual awareness of the central relationship between increasing length and increasing thinness. However, at first the child concentrates on the lengthening (affirmation). As the child becomes aware of the thinning (negation) and of the fact that thinning and lengthening are one and the same action, the action is canceled, or compensated: what is added (lengthening) corresponds to what is taken away (thinning).

An effective way of summarizing the child's conquest of conservation is to return to the alpha, beta, and gamma behaviors of contradiction (see Chapter Three). At level 1 the thinning is ignored or repressed (alpha behavior). At level 2 the thinning becomes a disturbance (beta behavior) but is overcome by a tendency to note first the lengthening and then the thinning. At level 3 lengthening and thinning begin to be understood and *anticipated* as one and the same action (gamma behavior). However, only at level 4 is the complete compensation of lengthening and thinning understood quantitatively, so that there is a correspondence between the affirmations and the negations. In other words, reversibility is a result of the regulations; namely, lengthening and thinning are one and the same action (Piaget, 1974c, 1978b).

We can state that, with the conquest of conservation, the child is capable of inverse operations. The newly attained conquest may now act as a regulator for the next level of complexity of conservation tasks. For example, conservation of weight and volume is attained later, as the child moves up the Spiral of Knowing (Piaget, 1972b; Piaget & Inhelder, 1969).

Two Key Structures: Seriation and Classification

As children advance in the Spiral of Knowing, two key structures become central at the level of concrete operations: seriation and classification. There are, of course, other areas of Piagetian research dealing with this stage of development, which basically concerns the child's interactions with objects in a concrete manner (as opposed to interactions based on the probable or possible, as in formal operations). These other areas include time, space, causality, motion, and speed. For the purpose of our learning-theory approach, our discussion will be limited to seriation and classification in relation to the compensatory regulations—that is, to the broad issue of equilibration. It should be pointed out that one of the reasons why it is important to stress that the two operations of seriation and classification are basic to the stage of concrete operations is that both operations are the foundation of the child's understanding of numbers.

In Chapter Three contradiction was defined as incomplete compensation—that is, failure to balance affirmations and negations. In the preceding section we have outlined the step-by-step balancing of the affirmations and negations leading to the conquest of conservation. Such balancing was described as complete compensation. Here, too, in order to understand the child's eventual grasp of true seriation and classification, complete compensation of affirmations and negations will be necessary.

Recall that a compensation is an action in the opposite direction of a given effect. In other words, it is an action that cancels an effect; for example, the *increase in length* of the ball of clay when it is changed into a sausage is compensated, or canceled, by a *decrease in width*. Regulations may lead to compensations by either positive or negative feedbacks. Think of the first day you "conquered" the problems of riding a bicycle. Consciously or unconsciously you began to notice that positive corrections of balancing in the opposite direction from an anticipated fall kept you moving on two wheels.

Compensations by negative feedback fall into two categories (Piaget, 1977b): (1) operations of seriation, made up of relations, and (2) operations of classification, made up of classes. In the following discussion, the negative feedback of *reciprocity* is the regulation for the operation of seriation, and the negative feedback of *inversion*, or *negation*, is the regulation for the operation of classification. In both cases the regulations, as an aspect of the general mechanism of equilibration in development, are the *source* of the operations.

Seriation

The structure of seriation was often used as an example to clarify various concepts in previous chapters. Seriation has been studied extensively because of the simplicity of the tasks and the richness of the strategies it offers. Recently Piaget (1977b) has reexamined the earlier research on seriation (Inhelder & Piaget, 1964; Sinclair, 1967) from the viewpoint of equilibration—especially the necessity for compensation of affirmations and negations following disturbances.

The children in these experiments are instructed to seriate ten sticks in order of increasing length. (The labels A to J for the sticks are used here to facilitate the description of strategies, but they were not used in the experiments themselves.) The subjects range in age approximately from 4 to 8. Remember, however, that age is not of prime importance in discussing the results of these tasks.

Level 1.   Children place a few sticks in parallel and vertical fashion but fail to achieve any definite order. It is as if differences were ignored, even though the instructions point to them.

Level 2.   Children construct pairs made up of one large and one small stick, such as AC or EJ, but with no connections between the pairs. Next, the children begin to form groups of three; again, there is no coordination among the groups. The ten sticks are divided at first into "small" and "large" and later into "small," "medium," and "large." Here we note that the children begin to follow the instruction to "arrange the sticks from smallest to biggest." However, since there is no coordination among the triplets, no sign of operational reversibility is in evidence. Emphasis is on *positive* properties (large versus small) but not on the fact that any one item may be at the same time "larger than" or "smaller than" another. Thus the *negative* property of "less" as opposed to "more" is not brought into consideration.

Transitional Level 2-3.   Interesting strategies emerge at this level. Some children construct stair steps, paying careful attention to the top and neglecting the bottom! Other children construct figures in the form of a roof (upward and downward slopes) and eventually pay attention to the need for a horizontal line at the bottom. Finally, others make a series of four or five sticks and don't know what to do with the others.

From the viewpoint of learning in the broad sense, what is important about these examples is that each compromise is a compensation following a disturbance. Sinclair (1967) highlighted this level by investigating the verbal "labeling" that the children used for the sticks in their completed series. They would start out with great enthusiasm— "quite small," "a bit small," "medium small," "medium," and "large"—then they would tell the experimenter that they didn't know what to call some of the others. The last stick, however, would be identified with a description such as "surely, the very largest." Sinclair described this labeling as a "prerelationship," for the children didn't understand true relationships that encompass bidirectional movement in a series. Thus, when Sinclair asked the children to describe the series in both directions, they couldn't do it. These children lacked the understanding of the "double property of an intermediate item"—for example, that stick C is both larger than stick B and smaller than stick D. Note that the children's one-way movement—that is, the series being constructed and labeled from "small" to "large"—is an example of the semilogic of constituent functions that was described in the previous chapter.

Level 3. Children at this level complete the entire series, but they do so by a trial-and-error method. What is missing is the understanding of transitivity (see Chapter Two). If stick *A* is shorter than stick *B* and stick *B* is shorter than stick *C*, it necessarily follows that stick *A* is shorter than stick *C*. Tests for transitivity as described in Chapter Two are failed at this level. In addition, even when children are able to complete the series, they cannot insert additional sticks into the array without starting over again.

According to Piaget, corrections and regulations are more manifest at this level than at any other. From the viewpoint of the understanding of progressive equilibration, this is the most meaningful stage. One finds a synthesis of similarities and differences: "There is as yet no comprehension of the compensation of positive characteristics and negations, in other words, of the necessary relation of 'more' [the mores] and 'less' [the lesses]" (Piaget, 1977b, p. 133).

Level 4. Children at this level demonstrate that transitivity is acquired by passing the additional tests (as explained in Chapter Two). The strategy used at this level is to search for the smallest stick, then search for the smallest of the sticks that are left, and so forth. This strategy implies both transitivity and the reversibility inherent in an operational structure: any stick is longer than all the preceding ones and also shorter than all those that follow it in the series.

In order to understand the increasing nature of equilibration in the ever-expanding Spiral of Knowing, it is necessary to study carefully the children's step-by-step progress to level 4. Equilibration and the regulatory mechanisms of cognitive development are not grasped by studying the finished product—that is, level 4. In actuality, two progressive compensations are intertwined in the levels that precede it. First, there are initial disequilibriums between the similarities and the differences. Second, the affirmations and negations must be balanced. Piaget (1977b) symbolizes the balancing by labeling the "less-than" relationship between stick *A* and stick *B* as *a* and the "less-than" relationship between stick *B* and stick *C* as *a'*. The following formulas emerge: $a + a' = b; b - a' = a$. What these formulas symbolize is the two-directional awareness necessary for the solution of seriation. Such awareness is not possible unless the child has constructed the relationship of transitivity.

At levels 2 and 3 the child struggles with similarities and differences. Not until level 4 is the child able to grasp the two-directional series of "the mores" and "the lesses," thus "conquering" the disturbance by balancing affirmations with negations.

Here, too, it is possible to consider the levels of seriation in relation to the three types of contradiction behavior. At level 1 the differences are ignored, so there is no disturbance (alpha behavior). At levels 2 and 3 the differences in the seriated objects are integrated into the child's understanding, but "the mores" and "the lesses" (the bidirectional nature of the series) are not related (beta behavior). This is why children at these levels are disturbed by the question "If there are seven sticks longer than this shortest one, how many sticks shorter than this longest one are there?" The reciprocal relation between "shorter than" and "longer than" is not understood. The child can't see that, if there are seven sticks longer than the shortest one, of necessity there must be seven sticks shorter than the longest one.

When children comprehend that "the mores" and "the lesses" compensate each other exactly, they can engage in inverse operations. They are able to *anticipate* the array and insert new elements into the existing array (gamma behavior). The regulation, or gradual equilibration, involved is compensation by reciprocity, or a reciprocal relation best demonstrated in transitivity: $A < B, B < C$; therefore, $A < C$. The attainment of transitivity, however, is a result of the initial disturbances and not the source of it.

Classification

In the preceding section on seriation, attention was focused on the ordering of objects according to their *differences*. In this section on classification, attention will be focused on the grouping of objects according to their *similarities*. In the traditional classification studies of the Genevan School, the children are generally asked to put the things that are alike together (Inhelder & Piaget, 1964; Piaget & Inhelder, 1969; Piaget, 1972b). Three basic levels have emerged from such studies.

Level 1.   The youngest children, before the age of 5 or 6, perform very much as children at level 1 of seriation. For example, if given differently colored shapes such as squares, triangles, and circles, a child may start by lining up all the squares. If the last square, however, is yellow, the child may switch categories (from shape to color) and line up several yellow shapes (see Figure 3-1 and accompanying description). This irregularity indicates that there is no overall plan. Another procedure may be to use the shapes to form a figure—for example, a house. Such a configuration is called a *figural collection*. The figure is an imagined expression of the extension of the class—that is, the set of members of that class.

Level 2.   At level 2 (approximately before age 8), called the level of *nonfigural collections*, children start forming classes and subclasses. For example, they begin to put circles, squares, and triangles in separate groups. However, they are not able to cope with the concepts of "all" and "some." In a traditional study, children may be given pictures of 12 flowers, 6 of which are violets. If children were asked to show the flowers and then the violets, they would have difficulty. If they were asked "Are there more flowers or more violets?" they might answer "Violets." What they don't understand is the relation of the violets (*some* of the flowers) to all of the flowers. Another way of expressing this is to say that the child has difficulty understanding the hierarchical relation between the part, or subclass (violets), and the whole, or entire class (all the flowers). This is why these studies are often referred to as **class-inclusion** studies. If A represents the subclass of violets and B represents the entire class of flowers, the inclusion relation is expressed as $A < B$.

Level 3.   When children reach level 3, around the age of 8, they demonstrate the operation of classification. They are able to understand that A has to be less than B, for there is another subclass (A') of flowers that are not violets. The following section presents a step-by-step analysis of the mechanisms involved in this achievement.

Class Inclusion and Contradiction

The Genevan School has probed several times the mechanisms involved in the attainment of class inclusion. In other words, answers were sought for the question "How does the child come to understand the relationship between a subclass and the entire class?" or "How does the child become capable of a genuine operatory classification?"

In Chapter Seven we will outline research on class inclusion by Inhelder, Sinclair, and Bovet (1974). This research was designed to explain the effect of training in class inclusion on the acquisition of conservation (see Figure 7-1 and accompanying description).

In the following study by Piaget (1974c, in collaboration with Montangero) class inclusion was investigated within the framework of contradiction. The research question, based on the new model of equilibration, was "Is failure in class inclusion due to a disequilibrium between affirmations and negations?" This study is therefore directly related to learning in both the narrow sense of experience and the broader sense of growth in cognitive development.

It was known from previous work by Piaget and Inhelder that young children (age 4 or 5 and sometimes older) often gave answers containing a specific form of erroneous inference: inclusion was thought of as symmetrical. For example, suppose that a child is shown blue squares, red circles, and blue circles (see Figure 5-6). The child is able to make the correct statement that "all squares are blue." However, the child then erroneously concludes that "all the blues are squares." What is involved in this contradiction is incomplete compensation.

According to Piaget (1974c), the child appears to form an important connection between "square" and "blue." This connection may be thought of as an *affirmation*—that is, attention to the positive characteristics of objects. The negation, or the "nonsquareness of the blue objects" (the blue circles) is overlooked. Again, the example stresses how significant the capacity to construct a negation is to a proper construction of the problem. Expressed differently, neither the subclass

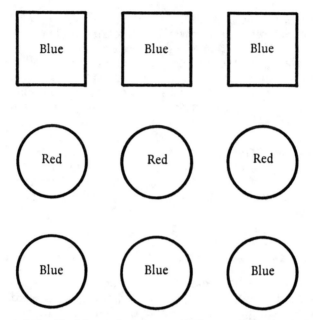

Figure 5-6. Problem of erroneous inference. The symmetrical inclusion is made that, if "all squares are blue," then "all blues are squares." Note that the blues are *both* squares and circles. The "nonsquare" blues are, of course, circles.

of blue squares nor the subclass of blue objects that are not squares will be understood in relation to the entire class of objects unless the negation has been constructed.

To probe the assumption that such failures in class inclusion are due to lack of compensation between affirmations (link between squares and blue objects) and negations (nonsquareness of blue objects), an experiment on contradiction was designed (Piaget, 1974c).

The experimental material consisted of 11 cubes: 5 red (all with bells), 3 yellow (1 with bell), and 3 blue (1 with bell). The children were permitted to handle only the red cubes, and, by handling them, they could hear that each cube contained a bell. The children were also told that the blue and yellow cubes might or might not contain bells. All the cubes were then placed behind a screen so that the children could still handle them but could not see them.

The cubes, still hidden behind the screen, were placed one by one in each child's hand. If the child thought that the cube was red, he was instructed to place it in a container also hidden behind the screen but within the child's reach. This container was a paper tube with room for only 7 cubes. It is obvious that, to perform the task, the children would have to infer the color of the cube from the sound of the bells. Equally obvious is that a blue and a yellow cube would also end up in the container with the 5 red ones. (Remember that the tube had room for 7 cubes; because the children were handling the cubes behind the screen and inferring their color from the sound of bells, the blue and yellow cubes containing bells would also be placed in the container along with the red ones.) .

This feature of the experiment introduced contradiction for the following reason. When the procedure behind the screen was completed, all the cubes were placed in front of the children. Again the children were asked to place the red ones in the container. When they had done so, the experimenter asked the children if they were satisfied with their performance. Next, the experimenter employed countersuggestion, pointing out to the children that, when the tube was behind the screen, it was completely filled but that now, when the tube was in full view, it was only partly filled. In this exchange between experimenter and children, the children were challenged to question the assumption that, *if there was a bell sound, there must also have been a red cube.* The children now had to supply an explanation for the discrepancy.

Piaget's interest in the children's attempts to explain discrepancy in this type of problem is twofold. He is interested in the cognitive level of children who are able to resolve the contradiction correctly. And he is perhaps even more interested in the levels through which children pass in the process of resolving the contradiction. The next few paragraphs describe how children at different levels of awareness interpreted the contradiction and how they resolved it.

At the end of the session the children were asked the standard class-inclusion questions (such as "If I have a bouquet of flowers and half of them are violets, do I have more violets or more flowers?"). Now let's compare the findings at the various levels in order to understand the mechanisms involved in the comprehension of true class inclusion.

Level 1A. Val (age 5) placed 7 cubes with bells (the 5 red ones, the yellow one, and the blue one) in the container behind the screen. She explained that she knew that the reds had bells but the yellows and blues did not. It was evident that she was aware that there was no room in the container for any more cubes. When, after the cubes were brought from behind the screen, Val placed the 5 red ones in the container (with room now for 2 more), an interesting conflict occurred. Each time the cubes with bells were in the container behind the screen, there were 7). Each time the cubes with bells were placed in the container in front of the screen, there were only 5 (all the red ones). The child vascillated back and forth until she remarked "That's odd." But when the experimenter asked "Do you think there could be blues and yellows that have bells?" the child answered no. "How can you be certain?" the experimenter asked next. Val replied "Because they are not red."

Two points about this study in contradiction are important at this level. First, there is the clear liaison (affirmation) between the *reds* and the *bells.* Such a liaison is so strong that the contradictory evidence of 7 cubes in container behind screen and 5 in container in front of screen is ignored. The children cannot fully understand the concepts of "all" and "some" in relation to each other.

Second, the same action of forming a class of cubes with bells leads to different results. The fact that the child ignores the different results is an instance of alpha behavior—coping with contradiction by ignoring it. Therefore, there is absence of logically necessary compensation—a failure to understand that the 2 extra red cubes with bells must be balanced by adding nonred cubes with bells.

Level 1B. Children at this level started with the same explanations as those at the previous level: the reds have bells, the yellows and blues do not. As the experiment proceeded, they saw the contradiction inherent in holding that there could be 7 cubes with bells behind the screen but only 5 in front of the screen.

However, although the children were disturbed by the contradiction—that is, placed in a state of disequilibrium—they didn't completely form the negation. The class of nonreds with bells was still difficult. For example, Lin (age 6) admitted that there *could* be some cubes with bells that were not red, but she didn't state clearly that, of necessity, there would *have* to be. What was most important at this stage, however, was the learning that was modified through action. In other words, the regulations modified the initial affirmations so that a beginning of the construction of the negation (nonreds with bells) was in evidence.

Level 2. Children at this level realized quite early that, since the container behind the screen was filled with 7 cubes with bells when initially only 5 red cubes with bells were observable, some of the nonred cubes must contain bells. When questioned, the children also realized that it was difficult to determine which cubes were in the container behind the screen—the red or the nonred. For example, Flo (age 7) stated that she thought there were 5 red cubes in the container behind the screen, but she could not be certain. The children at this level passed the standard class-inclusion questions (more flowers or more violets), which were not passed by children at the previous levels.

Regulatory Mechanisms and the Concept of Class Inclusion

In Chapter Three and earlier in this chapter we emphasized that the concept of class inclusion is a result of the balancing of affirmations and negations—the overcoming of contradiction so that a compensation may be reached. Let's consider this balancing in terms of the symbols used by Inhelder and Piaget (1964; Piaget, 1977b).

In the upper section of Figure 5-7, class B and subclass A are clearly affirmations—the observables. Class inclusion is impossible, because A is identified with B; that is, *cubes with bells are $A = B$.* Therefore, there is no compensation between the affirmations $(A$ or $B)$ and the *possible* negations—namely, a subclass of nonreds that may contain bells. Children at this level are not disturbed when they equate A with B.

When the new subclass of nonreds (see A' in lower section of Figure

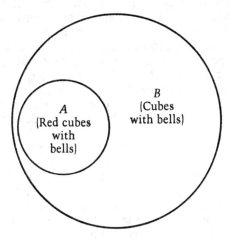

No compensation $(A = B)$

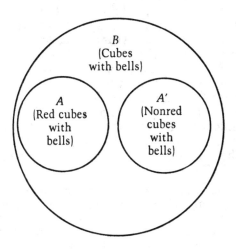

Compensations: $B = A + A'$; $A = B - A'$; $A' = B - A$

Figure 5-7. Negation as regulation for the operation of classification. $(A, B,$ and A' represent sets of possible cubes.)

5-7) is understood as necessary—that is, when the child understands that the whole class of cubes with bells is made up of reds and nonreds (hence the formula $B = A + A'$)—then the negation has been constructed. Subjects at this level understand, but may not be able to express in symbols, the compensations following from $B = A + A', A = B - A',$ and $A' = B - A$. What this means is that the subclass of nonreds is not obvious but must be inferred from the results of the actions during the experiment.

To reach this level and be able to balance the affirmations with the negations, children need to be aware of the contradiction between equating A with B and, at the same time, noticing a nonred subclass of cubes with bells. Such is the role of disturbance in the Spiral of Knowing. Instead of returning to the same level of understanding after becoming aware of the contradiction, the child is in a state of reequilibration. Through the process of reflexive abstraction, with projection to a higher level and reorganization at that higher level, compensation is reached through a negation—that of establishing the nonred subclass with bells (A').

Note, too, the three levels of contradiction. First, the children ignore the disturbance (alpha behavior) by equating A and B. Then comes a gradual realization of the necessity of the nonred subclass (A'), which is manifested through the reaction to a disturbance factor (how can there be 7 cubes with bells behind the screen and 5 cubes with bells in front of the screen?). This reaction to the disturbance is the beta behavior. Finally, by compensating the establishment of the nonred subclass in relation to the red subclass and the whole class (B), gamma behavior is reached.

It is important to stress the great variation in ages within levels 1A, 1B, and 2 of the children who participated in this experiment. Overall, the children ranged from 4 to 9 years of age. There were 6- and 7-year-olds at both levels 1A and 1B and 7-year-olds at level 2. Because of our learning-theory approach to the understanding of the research of the Genevan School, we can't repeat often enough that strategies are more important than age-level distinctions.

Finally, we wish to remind the reader that all the terms we used in analyzing the results of the above experiment (Piaget, 1974c), such as *balancing of affirmations* and *negations, compensations,* and *contradiction,* are aimed at clarifying the broad, middle-ground factor of equilibration. The following is a cogent summary of this factor in relation to the Spiral of Knowing:

> In general these stages enable the equilibration process of cognitive systems to be understood. At every level the systems are based on compensations, but their significance is deeply modified, and consequently they clearly characterize distinct degrees of equilibrium: the first of these three levels shows unstable equilibrium and a highly restricted field; the second reaction shows equilibrium displacement according to many forms, hence, a great number of possibilities are available for a passage from any level to the following one; and the third type of reaction shows a flexible but stable equilibrium [Piaget, 1977b, p. 69].

CHAPTER SIX

Formal Operations: Learning-Theory Aspects

As we survey from a learning-theory perspective some of the theory and research on formal thought at the adolescent level, we need to keep in mind the dynamics of the Spiral of Knowing. The last stage of cognitive development is never finalized as long as new understandings lead to reorganization of past understandings. "Possibilities are constantly coming into being and . . . they have no static characteristics" (Piaget, 1976c, p. 2).

Equilibration doesn't lead to a static equilibrium at any developmental stage. But, if each stage of cognitive development can be defined as the opening up of possibilities, it is the stage of formal operations that offers the greatest number of opportunities.

The first aim in this chapter is to clarify the features that characterize the thinking process of the preadolescent and adolescent. We'll look at these features through strategy analysis—that is, by asking how the adolescent approaches the solution of problems and how this approach differs from that of the previous stage of concrete operations.

The second aim is to place formal thought within the wider context of the form/content distinction. This distinction will then be related to the new level of reflexive abstraction characteristic of this age and which is called *reflected abstraction* (Piaget, 1974a, 1976b, 1978d).

Strategy Analysis

When we compare performance at the concrete-operational level with performance at the formal-operational level, the analysis that is of greatest importance is the analysis of strategies. Piaget (1977b) defines strategies as reasoning methods. Therefore, the analysis of strategies focuses on *how* the problem is attacked. Does the person proceed systematically or unsystematically? How many possible solutions does he or she propose? Can the person give an explanation of how he or she solved the problem and offer a general rule for the solution of similar problems?

Note that the central question is not what logical structures are used at a particular stage. Stages are descriptive. To start with logical structures that should be present at a certain age level and then argue that such structures should *explain* behavior is to make the stages explanatory—that is, predictive (Gallagher, 1979). Recall from the preceding chapter on concrete operations that equilibration is the source of the operations. Also, equilibration is the basis of the regulation of cognitive development. It is necessary to focus on strategies to note examples of regulations that appear in the solution of problems.

We are going to do our analysis of strategies by presenting two tasks that illustrate the different strategies employed at the concrete-operational level and at the formal-operational level. The tasks represent two logical structures that gradually become regulators during the stage of formal thought. The first task is the Combination of Colorless Liquids, which relates to the combinatorial structure. The second task is the Snail and Board, which relates to the so-called **INRC group.**

The Combination of Colorless Liquids

The purpose of this experiment was to study the various strategies children used to solve a problem whose solution involved the correct combination of four liquids.[1] The experimenter gave the subjects four numbered bottles containing (1) diluted sulphuric acid, (2) distilled water, (3) oxygenated water, and (4) thiosulphate, which acts as a bleaching agent. Because the four liquids were both colorless and odorless, the four bottles appeared identical except for the numbers that identified the contents on each bottle. The experimenter also presented a small bottle (labeled g) containing potassium iodide and a dropper. Finally, two unmarked glasses were placed before the subjects, one containing (1 + 3)—that is, sulphuric acid plus oxygenated water—and the other containing (2)—that is, distilled water.

The experimenter told the children to watch while a few drops of (g) were added to each glass. Oxygenated water oxidizes potassium iodide in an acid medium; therefore, the resulting mixture (1 + 3 + g) has a yellow color. It was this yellow mixture that constituted the "correct solution." The experimenter told the children to work alone until they could produce the yellow color. It was possible, of course, that during the experimenter's demonstration some subjects might have grasped the key to the solution of the problem—namely, that there was something about the colorless liquid in (g) that produced the final yellow color. What none of the subjects could have known, however, was the combinatorial

[1]The following description of the experiment (which was originally described in Piaget and Inhelder, 1958) is an adaptation from Gallagher (1973), pp. 167–169.

nature of the problem—that is, *which* and *how many* combinations of liquids from bottles (1), (2), (3), and (4), together with *(g)*, resulted in the yellow color.

Concrete-Operational Strategies. Note the strategy of an 8-year-old child named Curt. He began by trying, in no observable order, all of the following double combinations: (1 + g), (2 + g), (3 + g), and (4 + g). Of course, the resulting mixtures were colorless. "What's wrong?" Curt asked. "I tried everything."

The experimenter suggested that Curt use liquid from the numbered bottles plus *(g)*. The child tried, again in a random way, such combinations as (1 + 2 + g), (2 + 4 + g), and so forth. After several attempts, he tried (1 + 3 + g) and expressed delight when his efforts resulted in a yellow liquid. However, Curt's trial-and-error method proved costly, since afterward he couldn't remember the correct combination. Later, after finding again the "lucky" (1 + 3 + g) combination, he lost it once more by adding (4), the bleaching agent. Puzzled, Curt looked at the experimenter and speculated "Oh, maybe I added too much from the small bottle." But he didn't test his hypothesis.

Several characteristics of the way a 7- to 11-year-old thinks were exemplified in the strategies Curt used when he was confronted with this problem. First, the child's method lacked an overall plan. After the somewhat systematic beginning of double combinations failed, the child proceeded in a random fashion that only accidentally led to a "hit." Second, Curt's spontaneous method was elementary, since he just associated each bottle in turn with the liquid in *(g)*. Only the experimenter's prompting led to a triple combination such as (1 + 2 + g). The child didn't understand the importance of trying all *possible* combinations. Finally, he became so centered on the importance of *(g)* that he couldn't decenter—that is, realize that the addition of (4) bleached away the color he had obtained. The bottles became all important as elements in themselves, and Curt was unable to consider attributing the absence or presence of color to the *combination* of several elements.

To summarize, let's return to the distinction between empirical and reflexive abstraction. The 8-year-old child in this experiment centered on the empirical features of the task. But the solution to the problem required a projection, or reorganization at a higher level. In order to become aware of the possible combination of several elements and their interrelationships, necessary to produce the "correct solution," a systematic strategy was needed.

Formal-Operational Strategies. We focus now on the strategies of Angie, approximately 14 years old. After having been instructed by the experimenter to produce the yellow solution, Angie too began by combining each of the numbered bottles with *(g)*. "Maybe I forgot to use each solution" she commented after no yellow color appeared. "I'll write them down as I go along."

After combining all the bottles successively with *(g)* and listing the results, Angie moved on to triple combinations—that is, liquid from two bottles in combination with *(g)*. When she mixed (1 + 3 + g), "Oh, it's turning yellow! You need (1), (3), and the drops" she exclaimed.

"Where is the yellow?" the experimenter asked and then, pointing to *(g)*, "Is it in there?"

"No, they go together" Angie answered.

Next, she was quizzed on the effect of liquids (2) and (4). She responded "I don't think that (2) has any effect, but I'll make sure. If it has no effect, the yellow color will remain after I add liquid (2) to this (1 + 3 + g)."

After proving her point, Angie said "I think that liquid (2) is water. I'll take some water from the faucet and make sure." Having added the water, she concluded "See? The new combination (1 + 3 + g + water) is yellow as before. So liquid (2) must be water."

She made further observations: "Perhaps liquid (4) is water, too. If it's water, no change will occur." After adding (4) to (1 + 3 + g), she commented "No, now the color is gone. I think something in (4) keeps it from coloring. Let me try (2) and (4) again." She combined (1 + 2 + 3 + g) and (1 + 3 + 4 + g). "Look! Liquid (2) causes no change in color, so it must be water. But (4) keeps it from coloring. Now I can complete my list."

Note the strategies that distinguished the thinking of the adolescent from that of the child during the solution of the problem. First, the adolescent systematically proceeded to explore the results of all possible combinations. It is important to emphasize the *systematic* nature of the strategy even more than the finding of all possible combinations. An overall plan of approach—that is, a systematic plan—gives evidence of what Piaget (1974a, 1976b, 1978d) labeled *reflected abstraction*, which is the special abstraction beyond reflexive abstraction at the formal-thought level. The focus here is on the need for the statement of a principle. Second, the adolescent attempted to determine the effect of one or more liquids on another—that is, their interrelationships. Relationships can be understood only when variables can be separated.

As an example, review the younger child's performance in trying to solve the problem. When the yellow color disappeared after the addition of liquid (4), the child failed to devise a method of experimentation to determine why. The adolescent, however, established a testable hypothesis based on an implication, or logical conclusion: "If (4) is water, no change will occur." The adolescent was able to suggest the possible effect of one liquid on another—a relationship. At the same time, she demonstrated the ability to separate mentally the effect of one variable on another. The "if . . . then" statement is important because it manifests a deduction from the hypothetical, or possible. The adolescent is capable, then, of hypothetical-deductive thinking: suggesting possible relations even before the practical test confirms the proposed possibilities. After the practical test, the adolescent is able to return to the starting point to propose another hypothesis, thus manifesting reversibility.

In summary, three interrelated characteristics of adolescent thinking have emerged from the above analysis of strategies: (1) the ability to determine possible combinations of variables that solve the problem, (2) the ability to suggest mentally the possible effect of one or more variables on another when a certain relationship is suspected among the variables, and (3) the capacity to combine and separate variables in a hypothetical-deductive framework ("if this is so, this will happen"), so that a reasonable possibility is recognized before the test is made in reality. This reversible maneuvering between reality and possibility is the fundamental property of adolescent thought (Piaget, 1957, 1972b, 1976c; Inhelder & Piaget, 1958).[2]

Snail and Board

As we saw in Chapter Five, at the concrete-operational level the negative feedback for the regulation of seriation is reciprocity, whereas for classification it is inversion, or negation. Each of these forms of regulation rules separately; that is, reciprocity is related to seriation, while inversion, or negation, is related to classification. What is lacking is an integrated system, a set of operations that permits more freedom of movement from one area of operations to another.

This improved system at the next level of the Spiral of Knowing needs to be more complete and synthesized. Like the combinatorial structure—the structure we analyzed in the previous task and which permits the realization of the possible—the structure we analyze now includes all the combinations of inversions and reciprocities. This second new structure that characterizes the formal-operational level is the four-group transformation. It is called the *INRC group* because it deals with four regulations: identity (I), negation (N), reciprocity (R), and correlativity (C). In mathematical theory the four-group is called the *Klein group*. For our purposes, it is not necessary to give the mathematical derivation. We will, instead, link the structure to the regulations of the formal-operational stage.

Consider the example of the Snail[3] and Board, which involves the INRC structure. In this experiment (Piaget, 1970e; Piaget & Inhelder, 1969) children are asked to compare the paths traveled by two moving bodies—a snail and a board. In order to compare the paths correctly, the children must intuitively grasp that the paths traveled by each body will be composed of distances that are mutually related (correlative). The distances covered by the snail and by the board can be considered as the space displaced by each object, and these displacements must be constructed mentally. The children must also compose the spatial relations *between* both paths, since the snail and the board are moving simultaneously, thus affecting the comparative distances between them.

---

[2]Note that the testing of hypotheses is not listed as a specific characteristic of adolescent thinking. Small children test hypotheses in very concrete situations (see Chapter One of this book and Karmiloff-Smith & Inhelder, 1975). The key factor is the strategy used.

[3]This snail is not to be confused with *Limnaea stagnalis* of Chapter Two, which is only a phenocopy cousin!

In the experiment a snail is placed on a plank made of cardboard. The child is told that the snail will move slowly enough to allow the child to keep an eye on it. However, the experimenter will also try to trick the snail by moving the plank as the snail walks. Thus, in order to make fruitful comparisons of the two paths, in actuality the child must predict the relative positions of the snail and the board as sets of simultaneous displacements. At about 9 or 10 years of age, children begin to see immediately that they must coordinate the space displaced by the snail with that displaced by the board.

Figure 6-1 shows the respective displacements in the experiment. The snail is placed on the guideline, and the child must predict the

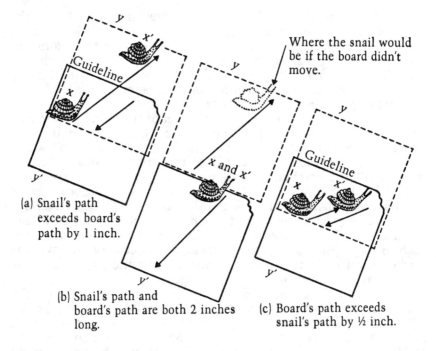

(a) Snail's path exceeds board's path by 1 inch.

(b) Snail's path and board's path are both 2 inches long.

(c) Board's path exceeds snail's path by ½ inch.

Where the snail would be if the board didn't move.

x = starting point of the snail
x′ = finish line of the snail
y = original position of the board
y′ = final position of the board

Figure 6-1.   Diagram of the paths of the snail and the board.

snail's finishing point. He or she is asked whether the snail will arrive to the right or to the left of the guideline. The child's prediction depends on whether the snail travels a longer or shorter distance than the board while the board is moving in a direction opposite the path of the snail.

Young children (approximately age 7 to 11) often experience difficulty with this problem. In tasks where board and snail move equal distances (as in section (b) of Figure 6-1) or move unequal distances in the same direction, the children are more often successful because they can compose and relate each path in successive stages. Section (b) of Figure 6-1 demonstrates the simplest example of the snail-and-board experiment. The snail and the board move in opposite directions, but at distances of 2 inches each, respectively. The snail makes no progress with regard to the guideline, because the movement of the board compensates exactly for the movement of the snail. Thus, the starting point and the finish line (x and x') remain the same for the snail, which stays in the same position.

However, the same children may fail to make correct predictions in the tasks involving unequal distances and opposite paths, because they must coordinate two systems of comparison simultaneously—that of length and that of direction. In section (a) of Figure 6-1, the snail and the board move *unequal* distances. If we start with the path of the snail from starting point x to the finish line x', its trajectory represents a *direct transformation* of its position by 2 inches. This displacement must be visualized as an identity, or totality, against which the unequal movement of the board (1 inch from y to y') can be compared as a reciprocal and unequal distance. The child is required to construct the snail's movement to a finish line at the right of the guideline as a positive gain over the path of the board.

Conversely, in section (c) of Figure 6-1, the snail and the board again move unequal distances: however, the path of the board exceeds that of the snail by ½ inch. In this form of the task the child is required to construct a net loss (*negation* of distance) for the snail. Since the child was told to focus on the snail, the movement of the board has to be interpreted as correlative motion. The failure of younger children to make simultaneous comparisons of relative gains and losses based on inversions, reciprocity, correlativity, and negation may occur because concrete-operational children use the board as a single point of reference. They may forget that the motion of the snail is also a correlative point of reference for the path of the board. Children who make incorrect predictions because they are misled by the guideline and don't grasp the importance of relating, or coordinating, two points of reference are limited in their understanding of the simultaneous aspects of the task. They depend on a style of processing characterized by comparisons of successive states rather than simultaneous transformations (previously discussed in Chapter Three).

Ger (10½ years old) got the problem of unequal distances correctly: "Here . . . because you drew the card back farther than the snail went forward: he ended behind the guideline" (Piaget, 1970e, p. 113). Ger understood that simultaneous comparisons of distance and directionality are essential to making a correct prediction. The distance of the snail and the board and their opposite directions are two sets of reciprocal relations that are correlated in space and thus must be coordinated simultaneously. At the level of concrete operations, children typically compose the displacements successively—first those of the snail, then those of the board. Finally, they work out the coordinations or inverse relationships of distance (longer/shorter) and direction (forward/backward) in isolation. In formal operations, adolescents are more likely to grasp immediately that the relative direction and relative distance of the snail's path are correlated with the distance and direction covered by the board. That is, they can integrate the precise reciprocal relationships between the pairs of inverses (Piaget, 1977e). Therefore, the stage of formal operations demonstrates a distinct qualitative improvement, because a child at this stage can coordinate two systems of reference in an integrated solution.

In formal operations, adolescents grasp the complex interrelationships of the problem of the Snail and Board. To make a correct prediction, they establish a set of distance compensations (longer with shorter) and another set of directionality compensations (forward with backward). Then they establish a reciprocal relation between the sets of compensations (see Klein in Piaget, 1977e). Although their operations are identical to those of concrete-operational children, their ability to find the higher, integrating structure between operations is the distinguishing hallmark of their formal thought. At the formal-operational level, adolescents will also gradually understand the importance of the reciprocal relation involved in two movements that cancel each other out.

It is possible now to be more specific about the meaning of the acronym INRC:

I = Identity, or direct transformation (movement of snail to right)
N = Negation, or inverse transformation (movement of snail to the left)
R = Reciprocity, or reciprocal transformation (movement of board to the left)
C = Correlativity or inverse of the reciprocal transformation (movement of board to the right)

Every operation is at once the inverse of another and the reciprocal of a third, so that the four transformations are integrated: direct, inverse, reciprocal, and inverse of the reciprocal (correlative). Such integration truly frees the person from any step-by-step combinations of inversions and reciprocities. In other words, form is freed from content (see next section), so that operations may now work on operations. All combinations of these operations on operations are possible; thus, the two structures—the combinatorial system and the INRC group—work together.

We have described a task in which subjects must imagine the displacements in space of a snail and a board moving simultaneously. The subjects were expected to see how the paths of the snail and the board referred to each other. The observable information in the problem suggested correlative spatial relationships that had to be construed. Moreover, the problem required the integration of two systems of motion—that is, of the snail and of the board—through the manipulation of a double-reference system (Piaget, 1977e).

Formal Thought and the Form/Content Distinction

How can we look at formal thought, as manifested by the combinatorial system and the INRC group, from the viewpoint of a learning-theory approach based on reflexive abstraction? In the pages that follow, this question will be answered by referring to three research areas of the Genevan school: constructive generalization (Piaget, 1978c), reflexive abstraction (Piaget, 1977e), and awareness, or consciousness (Piaget, 1976b). The same general theme permeates each of the three research areas. This theme, which is the essential aspect of formal thought, is best summarized by Wason's (1977) statement: "Content gradually becomes subordinated to form with the growth of knowledge" (p. 119).

For the purpose of a learning-theory approach, this form/content distinction has two broad meanings with regard to formal thought. The first is that the form, or structure, of an argument may be followed apart from its content. To illustrate this point, Piaget (1978c) used the following example of a paradoxical statement of implication: "If vinegar is consumed, beards will grow longer." Young children perceive this statement as a joke and will not search for any possible meaning. Adolescents, however, understand that such a statement can become meaningful if more information is found that links the ingestion of vinegar to the growth of hair.

Because of the structural foundation consisting of the combinatorial system and the INRC group, adolescents are able to deal with the possible. Recall that each set of structures, when achieved, acts as a regulator for the next level of the Spiral of Knowing. Younger children will deal with the above statement by focusing on its absurdity; that is, they will approach it in a very concrete manner. According to the form/content distinction, the form of the argument—the "if...then" (if vinegar, then beards) statement of implication—is seen by the adolescent as *possibly* valid. The content of the statement can be easily changed while the form remains the same: vinegar could possibly promote freckles!

The second broad meaning of the form/content distinction is directly connected to the mechanism of reflexive abstraction. The essential function of cognitive mechanisms is to construct forms and then forms of forms. This means that the upward movement of the Spiral of Knowing is increasingly abstract and free of content (Piaget, 1974a). Recall that in Chapter Two we probed the meaning of biological phenocopy in relation to cognitive phenocopy. At the biological level it wouldn't be possible to separate form from content. However, as human thought develops, the movement toward complexity is really a movement that frees form from content. The three research areas of the Genevan School discussed in the following sections clearly show that this "freeing" is a central feature of formal thought.

Experiment on Constructive Generalization

Bourquin (Piaget, 1978c) conducted an experiment on the discovery of the center of gravity with subjects from 12 to 15 years of age. The subjects were asked to find the point of equilibrium of variously shaped objects, such as circles, rectangles, and discs of irregular shapes. At the beginning the subjects were permitted to use the edge of a table to discover the lines of equilibrium and thus the center of gravity, which is at the intersection of these lines. Then the subjects were asked to place the shapes on a cylindrical support of 5mm in diameter so that they balanced.

Note the answers of Cla, age 12 (incomplete protocol adapted from Bourquin, in Piaget, 1978c):

> *Adult* (gives Cla a rectangular board): You have to find the middle—the point of equilibrium.
> *Cla* (divides the long side in two and points out the two medians): There, where these two lines join in the center.
> *Adult:* How many of these lines are possible within the rectangle?
> *Cla* (places the rectangle along a diagonal on the edge of the table): That makes four lines (possible).
> *Adult:* Is that all?
> *Cla:* Yes, I think so. You can't make any more lines.

Cla tries several discs of irregular shapes and various rectangles and comes to the conclusion that, if a shape has equal sides and equal angles, one can "do more things with it."

However, after manipulating the irregular discs, she decides that only one line of equilibrium can be drawn. Further manipulations lead her to change her mind and make a summary statement about the discs and the rectangles: "Everywhere there is an infinite number of lines that cross the same point. To find the equilibrium, one must find [and that's enough] two lines, not necessarily in the [spatial] middle of the figure."

Contrast the conflicts and hesitancies of Cla with the quick, self-assured answers of Mil, age 15½:

> *Adult* (starts with the diagonals): How many possible straight lines are there?
> *Mil:* An infinity.
> *Adult* (shows rectangles that are thicker on one side and therefore off-centered): Where will the point of equilibrium be?
> *Mil:* If there is more weight on one side, the center will not be at the intersection of the diagonals.

For adolescents who are at Mil's level of thinking, it is normal to state that the figures may be turned in all directions and that all the imaginable lines may be understood as passing through the center. Cla, however, by reflecting on her activity of turning the irregular disc on the side of the table, is able to generalize from regular shapes to irregular shapes and thus move gradually to almost the same level of understanding as Mil's. Just as the little boy on the beach advanced in knowledge by projecting to a new level and reorganizing, so Cla constructs an understanding based on her activities: "There is an infinite number of lines everywhere, because you can always turn it."

In order to find the center of gravity, the subjects in Bourquin's experiment had to generalize from the concept of the infinite balancing lines of a circle to that of the infinite balancing lines of rectangles and irregular discs. The tricky aspect was the necessity to generalize from the operation of turning and not from specific empirical properties (uneven sides or irregular shapes) of any content with which the subjects worked. Another way of stating what the subjects had to accomplish is to say that they had to concentrate on constructing a general rule, or *form*, that would go beyond the initially perceived *contents* of circles, rectangles, and irregular shapes. Constructive generalization in this experiment is centered on an infinity of possible diameters.

Finally, the experiment is a clear example of the meaning of cognitive phenocopy: exogenous knowledge (the finding of a few lines of intersection) is replaced by endogenous knowledge (the finding of the intrinsic property of an infinity of lines of intersection).

The most significant aspect of Bourquin's experiment is that it is an example of constructive generalization (Inhelder, 1977; Piaget, 1978c). In our earlier discussions we emphasized the meaning of reflexive abstraction as a new organization of thinking in the face of a new problem. Reflexive abstraction is always accompanied by constructive generalization—introduction of new combinations, such as operations on operations at the formal-operational level. This means that, by "reflecting" on the projected and reorganized thoughts of a previous level, the adolescent moves to higher and higher levels of understanding.

Constructive generalization is quite different from inductive generalization, which extends an already existing concept by arguing "from some to all": "This happens in some cases; therefore, it will happen in all cases." Just as reflexive abstraction is based on learning from actions and not from objects directly, so constructive generalization is based on extending the new organization: "The relationship between reflexive abstraction and constructive generalization is necessarily a very close one; each abstraction leads sooner or later to constructive generalizations, and each generalization is based on reflexive abstractions" (Inhelder, 1977, p. 337). (See "Genetic Epistemology and Developmental Psychology," by Inhelder, in Appendix B.)

Recall that the older subjects in Bourquin's experiment enriched their comprehension by means of operative actions. Such enrichment of comprehension was accompanied by an increase in content: the more intersection lines the subjects found, the more objects they found that had these infinite intersections. Therefore, enrichment in comprehension leads to an increase in content through the application of meaning to other contents. This is the movement from exogenous knowledge (empirical abstraction) to endogenous knowledge (reflexive abstraction) that was emphasized in connection with cognitive phenocopy (Chapter Two).

It should be noted that constructive generalization is not unique to adolescence and that it is found at all levels of development. Inhelder (1977, pp. 336–337) gives the following example of constructive generalization on the part of younger children:

> The child is given ten sticks of different lengths correctly seriated and is asked, "How many sticks are there that are bigger than this tiny one?" The child easily shows the smallest stick and correctly counts the others. Then the experimenter shows the biggest stick and asks, "And how many are smaller than this one?" The 5- to 6-year-old will then count the sticks again, whereas one or two years later he will laugh and immediately answer, "Nine also, of course!" Such constructive generalization is the main mechanism of progress in mathematics, and it is striking that it should already be present in the child.

What makes constructive generalization so essential a factor at the formal-operational level is the new structural organization that was demonstrated in the Bourquin experiment. What is of key interest here is not the common assimilation of new contents to forms already constructed, which was demonstrated in the seriation and classification experiments described in Chapter Five. Of interest here is the construction of *new* forms and *new* contents—the structural reorganization of reflexive abstraction at the formal-thought level. This reorganization is illustrated in the following experiment on analogies.

Experiment on Reflexive Abstraction (Analogies)

Piaget (1977e, in collaboration with Montangero and Billeter) investigated children's understanding of analogies. The focus was on the distinction between empirical and reflexive abstraction that becomes more and more evident at the preadolescent level.

In this experiment 29 children between the ages of 5 and 13 were presented with a number of pictures that were to be paired. After the subjects had taken the important step of identifying the pictures, they were asked to put together those that went well together. Next, the children were asked to arrange the pictures into 2 × 2 matrices (see Figure 6-2). If a child had difficulty in finding relationships such as "Dog is to hair as bird is to feathers," he or she was asked questions such as "What allows the bird to stay warm in winter?" If the child still had difficulty, three of the cells (see Figure 6-2) were filled, and the child was asked to fill the fourth cell with one of the three pictures. If the child succeeded in finding the right picture, he or she was given a counterexample. Thus, in Figure 6-2a the subject was asked "Does a bike pump go as well here as the handlebars?" Such counterexamples, as diagrammed in Figure 6-2, were introduced to determine how strong the relationships could be held by the child in spite of the adult's suggestions for another possible answer.

The important procedural point to be stressed here is that at all steps of the experimental session the method of critical exploration was used;

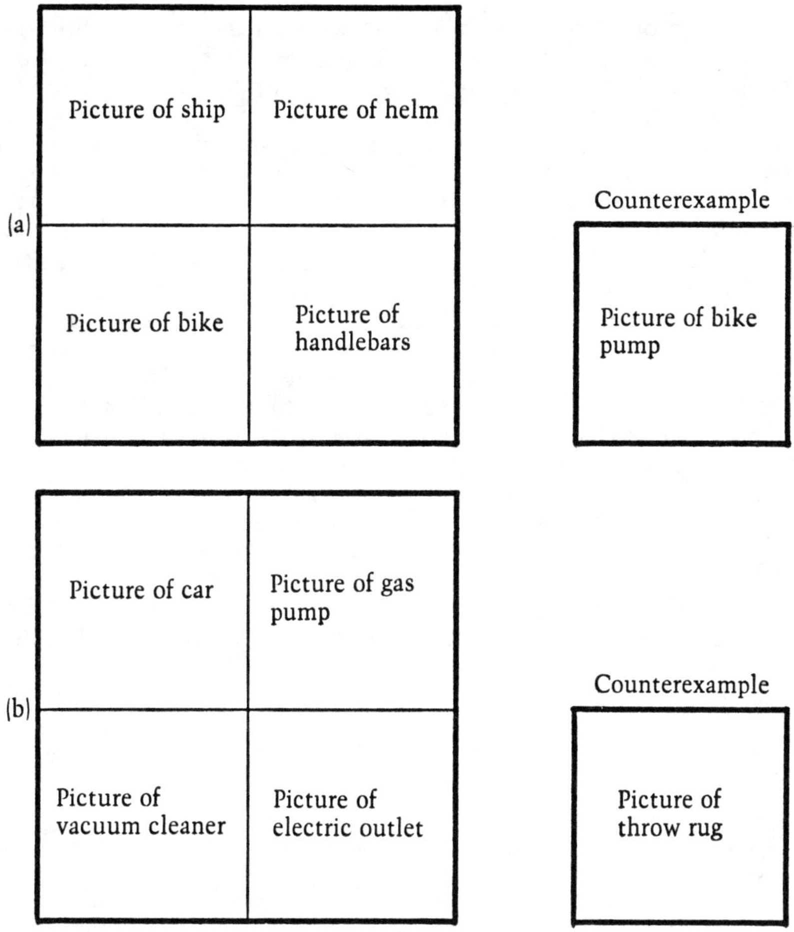

Figure 6-2. Examples of correlates. (Adapted from original research report submitted by Montangero and Billeter for inclusion in Piaget, 1977e.)

that is, the subjects were asked why they thought the pictures went together. According to Piaget, the results led to the identification of three distinct levels. The younger children at stage 1 (ages 5 and 6) were more likely to arrange pairs but ignore the complete analogical form. For example, they stated that the dog needs hair to keep warm and the bird needs feathers to fly. The relationship between dog and hair (*A* is to *B*) was not compared to the relationship between bird and feathers (*C* is to *D*). For Piaget this is an example of empirical abstraction—attending to the observable characteristics—which prevents true solution according to the analogical form of *A:B* as *C:D*.

Piaget (1977e) argues that the awareness of form is hindered by the young child's emphasis on observable features and consequent neglect of the intrinsic properties of the objects to be compared. Growth in solution of analogies, then, is due not to summation of facts gained from observation of such separate contents as *A, B, C,* and *D* but to a building up of form, which goes beyond contents. What is necessary for progress, then, is reorganization at each new level. In a constructivist model such a reorganization is due to reflexive abstraction. For example, Piaget reported that, in the analogy *auto : gas pump* as *vacuum cleaner : electric outlet,* many young children tended to look for obvious, observable pairings, often based on function. Other young children connected the four terms in a series, such as "Auto fits with gas pump, and vacuum cleaner fits with electric outlet." Upon further questioning, it became obvious that the "fits with" was not so much the awareness of form as a pairing of terms two by two, with failure to educe the relationship. Such pairings, which Piaget labeled *successive relationships,* are analogous to the seriating of sticks one to another, without the form of transitivity to raise the action to a new level of understanding.

Children at stage 2 (approximately ages 8 to 11) were able to complete the matrices. But when the countersuggestions were made, the analogical form proved to be weak and the answers were changed. However, according to Piaget, the ability to complete the matrices demonstrated reflexive abstraction—a projection to a higher level of that which is drawn from a lower level. Such a process entails a coordination. In the case of analogy problems the solution is based, as previously emphasized, on the coordination of two separate relationships (Piaget, 1977e).

At stage 3 (approximately age 11 and older) the children were able to resist the countersuggestions. The form *A:B* as *C:D* is stabilized, and it is possible for the subjects to *reflect* on their answers by consciously explaining the hierarchical relation obtained from consideration of both parts of the analogy. In addition, it is possible for children at this stage to understand that the qualitative form used in the problems is based on the mathematical (quantitative) form that is the origin of the notion of an analogy as a double ratio (for example, 3 is to 6 as 4 is to 8: $3/6 = 4/8$).

In addition, further research on reasons for selection of answers (Gallagher, 1978a, b; Gallagher & Mansfield, 1980; Gallagher & Wright, 1977, 1979) has confirmed that children at level 3 are more likely to state a rule that links *A* to *C* and *C* to *D* (the inverted form of an analogy). For example, the relation that must exist between auto and vacuum cleaner and gas pump and electric outlet (see Figure 6-2) is that the first set needs the energy source of the second set. Children at this level may state a rule such as "The machines get energy from them" or "The last two are energy givers." Younger children are more likely to spell out a reason that follows the linear form of the analogy: "The auto runs on gas, and the vacuum cleaner runs on electricity."

The older children seem to grasp the structural symmetry of the analogy that permits both a regular form (*A* is to *B* as *C* is to *D*) and an inverted form (*A* is to *C* as *B* is to *D*). The ability beginning at preadolescence to give reasons in an inverted form (*A:C* as *B:D*) is another example of constructive generalization. There is evidence of flexibility in construction of contents (the individual terms *A, B, C,* and *D*) due to a stability of form that permits both a regular and an inverted reason when children are asked to explain why they selected a certain answer.

Experiment on Awareness: The Hanoi Tower

In Chapter Three we mentioned a problem-solving game called the Hanoi Tower (Piaget, 1976b). We said there that, in order to play the game successfully, children need to develop a strategy. Here we concentrate on the dramatic difference between the strategies used by younger children and those used by older children. An analysis of such strategies clarifies concepts central to the form/content distinction, the movement from exogenous to endogenous knowledge, and the special aspect of reflexive abstraction ("reflected" abstraction at the formal-operational level).

Three posts—*A, B,* and *C*—are vertically attached to a baseboard (see Figure 6-3). A graduated set of discs with a hole in the center (largest at

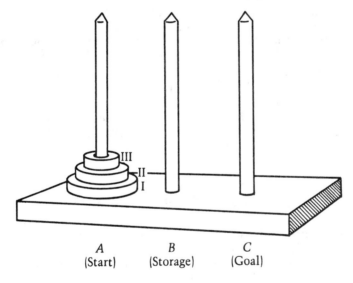

$$
\begin{array}{ccc}
A & B & C \\
\text{(Start)} & \text{(Storage)} & \text{(Goal)}
\end{array}
$$

Figure 6-3. The Hanoi Tower. Move discs from *A* to *C* according to rules.

bottom to smallest at top) are placed on *A,* the starting post. The player is told to move the discs from post *A* to post *C* observing the following rules: (1) only one disc at a time can be moved; (2) no disc may be placed on a smaller one; (3) discs may not be rested on the table; and (4) discs may not be held in hand while another disc is being moved. (The reader is encouraged to figure out the winning strategy before reading the next section.)

Success depends on the player's awareness of post *B* as an intermediary ("storage") post as the various moves are made. For our purposes here, emphasis is on the striking difference in difficulty between the task involving only two discs and the task involving three discs. It is as if the problem actually changed in form with the addition of an extra disc.

A study of the protocols reveals three main stages. The children at level 1 (ages 5 and 6) managed to solve the problem involving two discs by trial and error. These children were unable to solve the three-disc problem even after many trials. Their failure was due to lack of transitivity—the use of *B* as an intermediary post between *A* and *C*, so that II (see Figure 6-3) could be placed *on top* of, not *underneath*, I on *C*.

At level 2 (ages 7 to 9) the two-disc problem was easily solved. However, the three-disc one posed special difficulties. Children at this level didn't demonstrate an overall plan; that is, they failed to grasp the form of the problem.

Children between 11 and 12 clearly demonstrated level-3 strategies and easily solved the three-disc problem. What was new at this level was the ability to express verbally the procedural rule behind the solution. This is how Rob (age 11½) stated the rule for a four-disc problem:

> You always take away the smallest one (IV), then the middle one (III), then you put the small one on the middle one and you can get at the big one (II); that makes a small pyramid there, and then the way is clear and I can start all over again; it's the same story afterward (with disc I) [Piaget, 1976b, p. 298].

Rob was able to describe a general model, or *form*, that he could apply as the content of the problem changed (from three to four discs, from four to five discs, and so on). This ability to state the form of a problem is due, according to Piaget (1974c, 1976b) to reflected abstraction. The reorganized level (reflexive abstraction) is brought to awareness, so that a principle may be expressed verbally.

Some Concluding Comments

The emphasis in this chapter was on strategies—the reasoning methods by which the adolescent approaches problems. We stressed, for example, that the adolescent isolates variables and systematically tests hypotheses rather than list all possible combinations.

Such an emphasis reflects the current shift in the Genevan School's approach to the formal-operational level—a shift from stress on structures related to stages (Piaget, 1953) to stress on mechanisms (Piaget, 1977b; Sinclair, 1977). This stress on mechanisms is expressed by a series of questions in the psychological or behavioral realm: Given that adolescents are capable of reflected thought—that is, thought not bound by observable characteristics—how will their performances change (Piaget, 1974a, 1976b)? Also, how will adolescents approach problems of causality, which, of necessity, include abstracting from the interaction between subject and objects (Piaget & Garcia, 1974)? How will these newly found abilities be affected by careers that lead to specialization of certain thought patterns (Piaget, 1972a)?

Therefore, the research and speculation about the formal-thought level is in a state of change. Piaget has been attentive to criticism of his overemphasis on structure—an overemphasis that perhaps was a weakness of the first expanded volume on the formal-operational stage (Inhelder & Piaget, 1958). Some European critics (Henriques-Christofides & Moreaum 1974; Wermus, 1972) were effective in pointing out both the strengths and the weaknesses of that stage. Others, instead, who may be classified as belonging in the "logic-testing camp," were too intent on pointing out weaknesses and thus failed to see the dynamics of an interaction approach to the study of cognition. (For a discussion of this point see Falmagne, 1975; Overton, 1975.)

New trends point to vitalization of the model and of the research in formal-operational thought. An analysis of the "possible" (the ever-expanding Spiral of Knowing), which includes the possibility of error, was formulated by Piaget (1976c, in collaboration with Voyat). Research on the form/content distinction places research on formal thought within an expanding spiral in which each operation becomes a regulation for the next. Recall the meaning of the two characteristics of reflexive abstraction as related to the expanding spiral (Chapter Two). Every "reflecting" of content presupposes the intervention of a form or reflection in the sense of reorganization. The contents transferred to a higher level require the construction of new forms. The construction of new forms is due to the reflection or reorganization at a higher level. What may be seen, then, is a continual succession of contents, forms, reelaborated contents, and new forms along the Spiral of Knowing (Piaget, 1977e). The formal-thought stage, then, is an opening up of possibilities rather than a static state of completed structures.

CHAPTER SEVEN

Genevan Learning Theory: The Research Foundation

Now that we have examined the stages of development and the challenges children encounter in the course of their intellectual growth, we shall consider the role that learning plays in the developmental process. You will remember that the Genevans distinguish between two types of learning: learning in the strict sense and learning in the broad sense (Piaget, 1959). In the strict sense, learning is defined as the acquisition of knowledge from experience, or, we may also say, from empirical abstraction. The child extracts from objects properties relevant to a given situation—for example, the weight of the pebbles on the beach.

Learning in the broad sense includes both learning in the strict sense and equilibration; thus it embraces all of cognitive development (Inhelder, Sinclair, & Bovet, 1974). Knowledge is gained not only by abstracting the properties of objects. What a child notices about the objects is in itself determined by the child's ability to relate the factors to his or her own *activities*.[1] In learning in the broad sense, therefore, objects act only as supports; information is derived from the coordination of mental actions one carries out on the objects—that is, from reflexive abstraction.

As noted earlier, Piaget is not an "armchair philosopher." His theory is based on his own and his colleagues' experimentation in which children are observed and interviewed while they solve problems. The Genevan research in learning is designed to examine what children learn through reflexive abstraction—the logico-mathematical framework or *form* of knowledge—rather than the content of concepts.

[1]Remember that *activity* in the Piagetian sense does not necessarily mean the manipulation of objects. *Activity* also refers to a mental process in which people think about (assimilate and internalize) objects and experiences (Piaget, 1977e).

Spontaneous Learning within the Context of Development

Because the studies of Inhelder et al. (1974) were so successful in clarifying the mechanisms by which children move through and within the stages of development, we have already examined two of them in Chapter Three (one on the conservation of liquids and one on the conservation of length). Another important achievement of these Genevan researchers was to shed some light on the connections among different types of cognitive constructions. We shall discuss two experiments that elucidate these links by examining the influence that training in class inclusion has on conservation and vice versa. (The development of both class inclusion and conservation has been described in Chapter Five.)

The Influence of Class Inclusion on Conservation

In conservation problems, children must understand that quantity remains constant despite changes in the physical properties of an object. This understanding requires the linking of the initial and final states by a reversible mental transformation. In class-inclusion problems, on the other hand, all information is available at the outset. The problem "lies in the need to apprehend the logical simultaneity of two different-level classes" (Inhelder et al., 1974, p. 171). This means that, given a class B (for example, flowers) composed of two unequal subclasses A (daisies) and A' (tulips), a class-inclusion task is for the child to tell whether there are more flowers or more daisies (see Figure 7-1). Children who rely on figurative aspects answer that there are more daisies. Because they do, in fact, see more daisies, these children lose track of the superordinate class of flowers. It is as if they forgot that tulips are also flowers. Recall the explanation in Chapter Five of the necessity of balancing affirmations and negations in class-inclusion tasks. Only by constructing the negation $B - A' = A$ can the child understand that the objects in A are simultaneously daisies and flowers.

Inhelder et al. (1974) selected children between the ages of 5½ years and 6 years, 8 months from a larger group on the basis of pretests in conservation of number and quantity as well as the class-inclusion problem we just described. Incidentally, selected children had failed the class-inclusion task but had at least reached the level of quotity[2] in conservation of number.

The experiment, which included six training sessions (each a half-hour long), worked like this. The experimenter gave a basket with some pieces of fruit to a doll; the fruit was of two different kinds (subclasses)—

[2]*Quotity* is a term coined by Greco (cited in Inhelder et al., 1974) to describe the level at which children know how many objects are in one collection after they have counted the number in a second, equal collection but when they still believe that there are more objects in one of the two collections. Quotity precedes the acquisition of conservation of number.

B = flowers

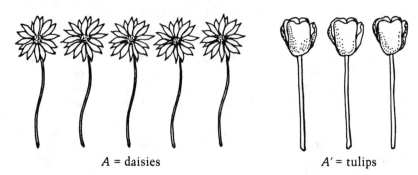

A = daisies   A' = tulips

Figure 7-1.   Class-inclusion task: Are there more flowers or more daisies?

for example, peaches and apples. He then asked the children to put "more (or fewer) peaches but just as many pieces of fruit" into the basket of a second doll. The second part of the training consisted of a number of questions aimed at helping the children compare the number of items in the superordinate class of fruits with the number of items in one of its subclasses. (Recall that children usually lose track of the superordinate class and compare the subclasses with each other.) Questions such as "Does one doll have more apples?" were alternated with "Does one doll have more pieces of fruit?" to encourage rapid decentration from subclass to superordinate class. In the third part of the training only one collection of fruit (apples) was used, and the children were asked to determine whether more apples or more pieces of fruit were in the doll's basket. All of the children received the first part of the training. Only those who had difficulty with the first part received the second and third parts. As in most Genevan research, the method of critical exploration was used; therefore, the questions and the order of presentation varied considerably from child to child.

Before the results of this experiment are described, it is important to note the system of presentation used by Inhelder and her colleagues in this study, because it characterizes much of their work. The basic sequence of items goes from the most difficult to a less difficult one, and, if no success is attained, to an even less difficult item. The last item is frequently so easy that the child solves it spontaneously. Pascual-Leone (1976) describes this "problem-solving learning method" as *graded learning loops.* If the child fails the early, more difficult items but succeeds on the final item, the graded series is implemented in the reverse direction. The strategies used to solve the easy items plus the experimenter's encouragement to compare the items in the loop (usually by asking for justifications) frequently help the child discover solutions to the more complex items.[3]

[3]Pascual-Leone (1976; Pascual-Leone, Goodman, Ammon, and Subelman, 1978) is careful to note that children's ability to gain insight in the more difficult problem solutions

Encouraging the child's active coordination through the use of conflict situations in which contradictions arise between predictions and reality and between subschemes (such as number and length or class and subclasses) in the learning-loops paradigm is a learning procedure unique to the Genevan school.[4] The Genevans are not interested in finding methods of maximally accelerating learning but in investigating the role of learning as part of the developmental mechanisms (Inhelder et al., 1974; Pascual-Leone, 1976; Kuhn, 1974).

What did Inhelder and her associates find? Posttesting (done immediately and again after three to five weeks) consisted of the tasks used in the pretest plus (1) a conservation-of-weight task, (2) several additional questions on class inclusion extending to three-level problems (such as dachshunds plus collies to form the class of dogs and dogs plus a cow, a pig, and a goat to form the superordinate class of animals), and (3) an intersection problem in which counters were placed into circles and the children were asked why they thought that the experimenter put the round red counters in the intersection (see Figure 7-2). This task was included to make sure that, when a child said

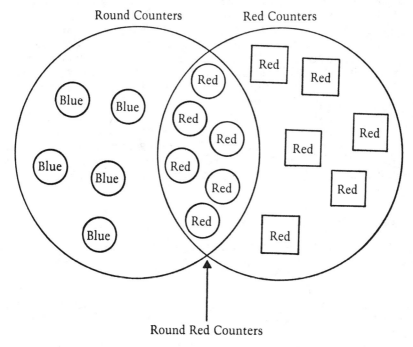

Figure 7-2. Schematization of the intersection of sets.

---

may depend on their information-processing capacity. This growth may be more closely related to what Pascual-Leone calls the "power of mental centration" (similar to the concept of short-term memory or, perhaps, to the ability to keep a number of items in mind simultaneously) than to schemes as described by Piaget.

[4]See the experiment on conservation of liquids in Chapter Three.

"Dachshunds are dogs," he or she understood the relation as an inclusion and not simply as an intersection (see Inhelder, Bovet, & Sinclair, 1967). *Intersection* refers to the members held in common by two equivalent sets (for example, the counters in Figure 7-2). An inclusion requires a hierarchical relation in which one set in its entirety constitutes a portion of the larger, superordinate set (for example, tables and furniture, skirts and clothing).

The results of the experiment indicated that many of the children made progress in the class-inclusion task and some performed better on the second posttest than on the first. Those who were more advanced on the pretest progressed further than those less advanced, so that the final order of the children's performance on the posttest was approximately the same as the order on the pretest.

This finding is common to many of the Genevan experiments and indicates that progress in learning is dependent on the child's initial level of competence. Throughout their research the Genevans found instances of children who successfully completed the training sessions but were unable to perform the very similar problems given on the posttests. These findings did not point to true regressions, because the children had not, in fact, lost ground. They had simply responded only to the specific situation presented during training and were unable to understand the correspondences between the tasks they had performed during training and the tasks on the posttests. On the other hand, some children performed better on the second posttest than on the first. The Genevans argued that the progress begun during training had a delayed effect; that is, the progress was continued spontaneously by these children. What is important is that the vast majority of children performed better *after* training. This finding provides a convincing indication that learning constitutes an important and integral aspect of the mechanisms of development (Inhelder et al., 1974, p. 245).

The Influence of Conservation on Class Inclusion

In the second experiment, children were trained on conservation of quantity. The first tasks of this experiment used discontinuous materials—that is, countable collections of objects—in this case, toy houses and trees. The children were asked to put a tree on the table each time the experimenter placed a house there. The experimenter was careful, however, to put the houses into different spatial configurations than those the children made with the trees. The children were then asked whether they could put a tree next to every house and, if not, whether there were more houses or more trees. If the children answered incorrectly, they were asked to recall the procedures used in putting the items on the table. These procedures involved situations in which one-to-one correspondence was maintained and situations in which the correspondence was interrupted by the experimenter's putting down a house out of sequence. More difficult situations, in which the items were countable only theoretically (such as beads in covered glasses) or were continuous (water), were also used.

For this experiment, 20 children between the ages of 5 and 7 were selected on the same basis as in the first experiment. The posttests given to these children were also the same as in the previous study. Of the 20 children, 9 made very clear progress on the posttests in conservation and 3 made no gain. The remaining 7 made partial gains. Again, progress was dependent on the initial level, and some children showed more progress on the second posttest than on the first, indicating that it took somewhat longer for them to internalize what they had learned. Although children made progress also on the class-inclusion task (for which they had not been trained), gains were twice as frequent for the conservation problems. Moreover, it seemed that children either made no progress on the class-inclusion task or achieved complete competence.

In these two experiments, the children made about equal progress when the problems for which they had received direct training were considered. But when the "no-help" task was considered, the children trained on the inclusion problem made more progress on conservation than those trained on conservation did on class inclusion.[5] Inhelder et al. (1974) concluded that exercises in class inclusion can have a more marked effect on conservation performance than vice versa.

The Two Aspects of Concrete-Operational Activity

Piaget and Garcia (1974) have noted that activity at the level of concrete operations has two aspects. First, there is the actual result of the activity (referred to as the *causal aspect*). In the preceding two studies, the actual results, or causal aspects, are the collections of pieces of fruit and the groupings of the houses and trees. The second aspect of concrete-operational activity is the logical aspect. In these studies, the logical aspects are the hierarchical ordering of classes and the maintenance of equivalence in the face of perceptual distortion. When children are able to separate the causal and temporal aspects from the logical ones, they become aware of what is common to many different actions. They realize, to use an analogy, that 3 has the same meaning whether one is counting elephants, years, or miles, whether one counts rapidly or slowly, or whether one does the counting today or tomorrow. Similarly, classes are hierarchically ordered whether one is discussing tools, animals, or furniture. Children who are able to separate the causal and logical aspects of a problem are in fact substituting endogenous for exogenous knowledge (see Chapter Two). Their logical structures are becoming content free. A more advanced level of content-free thinking was described in Chapter Six in the course of the discussion of the Combination of Colorless Liquids and the Snail and Board.

It may be that in the experiments we just described the training procedures facilitated the children's ability to differentiate between the particular causal action and the logical operation. In both cases the

---

[5]The nature of the posttests is important. The class-inclusion posttest included only one task with either different material or a three-level inclusion. The conservation tasks included conservation of liquids and weight, which usually develop over a period of several years.

logical operation involved the conservation of *quantity*. As we said earlier, Inhelder et al. (1974, p. 258) also suggested that the class-inclusion training had a more direct effect on the acquisition of conservation than vice versa; the reason, they thought, was that the training in class inclusion emphasized both the logical and the causal/temporal (simultaneous) aspects of the problems. The conservation problem, on the other hand, takes place over time (since the transformation is carried out) and has a much more compelling perceptual element.

The Transitional Levels of Learning. Although these results are obviously important to an understanding of the role and process of learning, the Genevans were as interested, or perhaps even more interested, in the behavior of the children *during* the training sessions themselves. The class-inclusion tasks in the first experiment enabled Inhelder and her associates to study the transitional process in the achievement of class inclusion. The children fell into five groups, and the performances of the groups were hierarchically ordered as follows: (1) children who made the same collection as the experimenter and gave the doll only apples or who said that the problem was impossible; (2) children who took account of only one aspect of the problem and gave more apples, without regard for the total number in the collection; (3) children who understood that, if they increased the number of items in one subclass, they must decrease the number in the other but for whom the compensation remained qualitative (these children didn't manage to make the total number of pieces of fruit in their collections equal that of the experimenter); (4) children who avoided the necessity for compensation by making a collection equal to that of the experimenter but containing only one type of fruit (these children seldom had difficulty finding an alternative solution); (5) finally, children who achieved a correct solution either by understanding the problem immediately or by reversing the number of peaches and apples. If, for example, the experimenter had two apples and three peaches, the child would construct a collection of two peaches and three apples.

This type of careful analysis carried out by Inhelder et al. contributes to a clearer understanding of the dynamics of the learning process rather than simply focus on the more static final results. One can see from the sequence of transitional levels that children use alternative schemes to attempt to solve a problem and that it is only when the schemes are coordinated that progress is achieved. Similar levels have been delineated in the gradual acquisition of conservation (see Chapter Five).

The Influence of the Environment

Although the primary emphasis in the Genevan studies has been on the actions of the child, the contributions of the environment have not been ignored. Language, although not a sufficient condition for learning, plays a major role as a vehicle for thought, memory, and the direction of attention (Inhelder, Bovet, & Sinclair, 1967; Inhelder et al., 1974). Children's interactions with reality awaken their curiosity and provoke feelings of conflict when the outcome of an event doesn't correspond to their predictions. This element of surprise induces children to attend to previously undiscovered aspects of a situation and to question their own early impressions.

Summary

In sum, the Genevan studies reviewed in this chapter and in Chapter Three indicate that children attempt to assimilate new situations to an existing scheme. Progress is made when children attempt to apply simultaneously a second, conflicting scheme and realize that they have two contradictory answers to one problem. We have also seen that learning in one domain, such as class inclusion, facilitates learning in a second, related area of knowledge, such as conservation. The fact that the child's own activity is the primary impetus for growth can be noticed in the dependence of progress on the child's initial level of functioning and on delayed gains (observed on the second posttests).

The environment, too, plays an important role in growth by promoting interest and conflict. The situations most likely to elicit progress are those in which children compare modes of reasoning that vary both in their nature and in their complexity. Finally, these studies call into question any learning paradigm that purports to isolate knowledge into its component parts for training purposes. It is through the integration of related aspects of learning that growth occurs.

Anglo-American Training Studies in Conservation

In contrast to the Genevan studies, which look at learning in the context of development, are a series of Anglo-American[6] studies that examine learning for its own sake. As Voyat (1977) pointed out, the Genevans and the Anglo-Americans are working at cross-purposes: "Piaget sets out to discover, analyze, and explain the way in which the child *constructs reality*, whereas the American 'common sense' approach persists in thinking that this development can be precipitated and directed by the appropriate external manipulation, by the correct 'programming'" (p. 343).

As a result of the pragmatism of Anglo-American thinking, a rather substantial body of literature has been published that addresses the question of inducing and accelerating various aspects of cognitive

---

[6]The term *Anglo-American* is used as a convenience to refer to researchers throughout the English-speaking world, particularly the United States, Canada, Great Britain, and Australia.

development, in particular the conservations. Although most of this research purports to adhere to statistical rigor, few studies resist criticism on methodological grounds.[7] It is their theoretical weaknesses, however, that are of interest to our discussion of learning and development. The problems that exist in these studies are illustrative of the misconceptions that occur when Anglo-American researchers, often unknowingly, assimilate Piagetian constructs into an empiricist paradigm.

Reversibility

The most vulnerable of these constructs seems to be reversibility. As early as 1941, Piaget and Inhelder distinguished between logical reversibility and empirical return. Empirical return differs from true reversibility in that, "although the return action is the inverse of the transforming action, it neither cancels out this transformation nor compensates for it; it is merely a second action which, for the child, is completely independent of the first" (Inhelder et al., 1974, p. 33 and Chapter Five in this book).

A number of Anglo-American training studies have confused reversibility and empirical return (for detailed discussions see Peill, 1975; Zilkha, 1976). The following is an example of the kind of procedures employed in such studies. Liquids are placed in equal containers, and the amounts are determined to be equal. Liquid is then poured from one glass into a taller, thinner (or shorter, fatter) glass. The children are asked whether the amounts would be equal if the liquid were poured back into its original glass. Many children who are unable to conserve on pretests are able to answer such questions about empirical return. If they are not, they are given practice observing the results of the repouring, and then they are asked the question again. Correct responses have been taken as evidence that the children are conserving.

Logical reversibility, however, requires that the inverse action be carried out *mentally* and that both the pretransformation and posttransformation states be accessible simultaneously. In fact, the conserver reasons in terms of the pretransformation state. Ironically, such research simply demonstrates that it is not knowledge about empirical return that enables children to conserve.

---

[7]Many North American experimentalists find the research methodology used in Genevan experiments a source of amazement and frustration. As Kuhn (1974) pointed out, in the Genevan research, problems are not presented in a consistent manner, training procedures are long and complex, the number of subjects in a given experiment is generally small, and data are frequently incomplete. Seldom are any statistical analyses carried out. Kuhn also pointed out, however, that the Genevan learning studies have aims different from those of the Anglo-American studies, in that they are generally the *source* rather than the test of hypotheses. Peill (1975, p. 183) goes so far as to say that "if each child is questioned adequately, there is little need for statistical analysis of grouped data." The Genevans, who are structuralists, share this view. They are interested in finding the similarities across many children and many instances; they are not concerned with the study of individual differences, which makes the use of statistical techniques a necessity.

Reinforcements

Another problem exists in Anglo-American studies that attempt to teach conservation by giving rewards to children or by using empirical feedback. A typical study of this kind might allow children to test their answers in a conservation-of-weight task using clay balls by weighing the deformed balls on a balance scale. This method assumes that what the child needs in order to conserve is correct information (Zilkha, 1976). Piaget, however, argues that actions must be internalized and assimilated into previous structures and that old assimilation schemes must be reorganized if the experience is to be meaningful in terms of development. These training techniques don't take integration into account. What probably happens is that these children acquire only an isolated response.

Misleading Cues

Avoidance of misleading cues has been another approach to training. One popular technique for conducting such studies has been to perform conservation experiments behind a screen, so that the child cannot see the transformation. Certainly children are more apt to give conserving responses under such circumstances. All these experiments require is an understanding of qualitative identity—namely, that it is the same water or the same clay (for an extended discussion, see Chapter Four). Elimination of the perceptual cues, however, constitutes insufficient proof of conservation. Children with well-developed cognitive structures integrate information into more highly differentiated structures; they don't ignore it.

Prerequisite Skills

The most popular method of inducing conservation has been the training of prerequisite skills. Proponents of this method assume that one can teach conservation by teaching the less complex skills that underlie the concept. For example, these Anglo-American researchers teach children addition and subtraction, identity, and/or reversibility and expect that the child will be able to coordinate these components into a concept of conservation. This kind of instruction ignores the limiting effects of the child's developmental level.

Inducing Conflict

Finally, the method of inducing conservation that appears to be most closely related to Piagetian theory is that of introducing conflict into the experimental situation. Two major lines of research have been used in Anglo-American research. A typical strategy in the first line is to provoke conflict by bringing two judgments into juxtaposition. For example, if a child says that the clay sausage is heavier than the ball because it is longer, the experimenter may take a piece off the sausage. The sausage is still longer than the nondeformed clay ball, but in the child's judgment it is also lighter because a piece has been removed.

The second line of research has been to use groups of peers to solve conservation problems simultaneously. (Some of these studies are described in detail in the section on peer interaction later in this chapter.) The thinking behind such a strategy is that the child will be forced to notice elements of the situation that he or she has previously ignored.

These studies suffer from two problems. First, there is no way to be certain that the child is actually experiencing conflict, since conflict in the Piagetian sense is a subjective phenomenon. Second, even if conflict (or contradiction) were to make the child aware of the hitherto unnoticed dimensions, awareness doesn't seem to be sufficient to induce conservation reasoning (Peill, 1975).

Conservation Criterion

Another problem in Anglo-American training studies is the criterion used to classify a child as a conserver (Peill, 1975; Zilkha, 1976). Piaget describes conservation as a *symptom* of the acquisition of concrete-operational structures. Many training researchers are satisfied that the child is conserving if he or she simply acquires an isolated response. They are, therefore, concerned only with performance, or learning in the strict sense. Such training may teach children verbal rules. Bruner (1964), for example, suggested that, if the child is to succeed in conservation tasks, he or she must have a verbal rule to protect against the compelling perceptual cues. Some researchers, therefore, have taught children rules such as "They are the same because nothing has been added and nothing has been taken away." Within the context of the training, children are often able to apply such a rule and to appear to be giving conservation responses. What this type of research ignores is that conservation is the *outcome* of development and not an end in itself. Children may be able to give appropriate responses in any given situation, but they may not have constructed the logic to understand their own responses. It is this kind of learning that easily leads to forgetting.

Although new and more sophisticated training studies are still being designed (see, for example, the work of Murray, Ames, & Botvin, 1977, on the acquisition of conservation through cognitive dissonance), attention has shifted from attempting to induce conservation to determining the criteria for just what constitutes a conservation response. In a series of papers Brainerd (1973, 1974, 1977, 1978) has argued that judgments alone are preferable to judgments plus explanations because they lead to (1) fewer false negatives (conservers being judged nonconservers in an experiment) and (2) lower rates of error. Brainerd further argued that explanations require a level of verbal sophistication in addition to the ability to perform the conservation task; therefore, they complicate the task in an unreasonable manner.

Some have disagreed with Brainerd's position. Reese and Schack (1974), for example, critiqued Brainerd's position on theoretical grounds by asserting that the use of explanations does, at least, eliminate false positives (the attribution of conservation ability when it is not warranted) and questioned Brainerd's insistence that the elimination of false negatives is more important. Gallagher and Reid (1978) have demonstrated empirically that judgments plus explanations constitute the more accurate criterion. They showed that the use of explanations contributed significantly to the variance in performance on a conservation-like task designed to make the use of reversibility manifest even after the variance attributable to judgments had been taken into account.

Summary

Both the training studies and the recent preoccupation among Anglo-American researchers with defining the nature of an acceptable conservation response suffer from two deficiencies. First, they are based on the implicit assumption that the major source of learning rests in the environment and not in the child's actions. Second, they force Piagetian concepts into standardized tasks that make it difficult to determine *how* the child reasons. Instead, they focus on whether the child *has* conservation or not. These strategies embody "a subtle but real reversal of Piaget's intentions, which were never to treat intelligence as a progressive accretion of specific reactions, but rather to analyze it as an overall structure" (Voyat, 1977, p. 345).

The Invention of Conservation of Substance: Peill's Studies

E. J. Peill (1975), an Australian, has carried out a number of studies designed to elucidate the process children go through to *invent* conservation of substance. Unlike most Anglo-American researchers, she has not misinterpreted principles of genetic epistemology. To test hypotheses related to the possible steps in acquisition, Peill developed four models. According to the first model, consistent with Bruner's theory, the child begins by using a one-dimensional perceptual criterion (for example, the height of the clay ball) and moves directly to what Peill calls the *NAS criterion*—namely, that nothing was added or subtracted during the transformation. This model also predicts that perceptual judgments are irrelevant to conservation acquisition even though they may occur as a consequence of having attained conservation.

The second model proposes that the child must become aware of contradictory judgments of pre- and postdeformation amounts based on alternating perceptual criteria (for example, the width versus the length of the clay sausage). The child will then find perceptual criteria unsatisfactory and will begin to use the NAS criterion. The third model, consistent with Piaget's theory, suggests that the child learns to resolve the contradiction between alternating perceptual judgments by interpreting changes in dimensions as exactly compensating each other, while simultaneously constructing the NAS criterion.

The fourth and final model predicts that the child overcomes the contradiction in perceptual judgments by using a more complex, coordinated perceptual criterion. As a result of making perceptual compensation judgments, the child can finally develop the NAS criterion. Piaget's model is considered a special case of the fourth model, because it is quite possible that the child might learn about the uniqueness of reversibility by the time he or she is ready to make judgments of perceptual compensation. It is only this temporal sequence that distinguishes the third and fourth models.

Peill's research program was designed to test each of the models vis-a-vis five questions for which a different pattern of responses was predicted (pp. 175–177): (1) At what stage in conservation acquisition does the child become unsure of *A* versus *B'* perceptual judgments?[8] (2) Which situations make it easier for the child to use the NAS criterion? (3) At what stage in conservation acquisition are deformational and perceptual information each sufficient for the child to make an equality-amount judgment? (4) Does the child make perceptual compensation judgments that are always consistent with his or her judgments about the effects of deformation on appearance? (5) Does the child make perceptual compensation judgments only if he or she knows about the uniqueness of reversibility?[9] Peill's conclusion was that the fourth model (with modifications) and the third model (seen as a special case of the fourth one) were consistent with her findings.

The process children appear to follow in the acquisition of conservation of substance is as follows. Children initially make a decision based on a single, one-dimensional perceptual criterion, such as height. They then use alternative perceptual criteria but find a contradiction in that solution and begin to make perceptual compensation judgments. An intermediate conserver, for example, cannot make a conservation judgment on the basis of the NAS criterion alone. He or she requires information about the deformation and understands in a *qualitative* way that an increase in width can balance, or compensate for, a decrease in length. An intermediate conserver, therefore, would need to learn about the uniqueness of reversibility in order to acquire the NAS criterion. (It is interesting to compare this description with that offered by Piaget, which is reported in Chapter Five.)

Peill's work has made an important contribution to the study of Genevan theory. Her research is clearly defined and carefully executed. She seeks not to train skills in isolation but to understand the process of the child's "invention" of conservation in its natural context. Her work,

[8]*A* and *B* represent the two balls of clay prior to deformation. *B'* represents the *B* ball after deformation.

[9]Uniqueness of reversibility refers to the child's knowledge that a short, fat clay sausage, for example, can be rolled to look like only *one* of a set of thin sausages of equal diameters.

in a sense, attempts to go one step beyond the Genevan learning studies in that it hopes to clarify how children's discoveries lead them to invent the NAS criterion and, therefore, conservation. Peill's work represents one of the few in-depth Anglo-American studies carefully detailing the development of a cognitive operation.

Studies on Memory

Piaget and Inhelder's work on memory is one area of research that clearly supports the Genevan emphasis on reflexive, rather than empirical, abstraction in learning. Piaget and Inhelder (Piaget, 1968, 1973b; Inhelder, 1969, 1976c) hypothesized a relation between memory and operativity. They suggested that the memory code changes in the course of the development of cognitive operations. They tested this premise by showing a stimulus to children at different developmental levels and asking them to recall the stimulus after several weeks and again after several months without having seen the stimulus again. Both cross-sectional and longitudinal data were collected. Although Piaget and Inhelder conducted many individual studies that varied in both the form of the presentation (pictures and events) and the content (including additive, multiplicative, causal, and spatial structures), only one—the best known of them—will be reviewed here.

Children between the ages of 3 and 8 were shown a set of ten seriated sticks (Piaget & Inhelder, 1973). One week later and again six to eight months later, the children were asked to describe the series of sticks by outlining it with their fingers and by drawing it. One group was asked to describe the series verbally. After the children had completed their descriptions, they were asked to reconstruct their "memory" with actual sticks.

After one week the youngest children drew sticks of more or less equal length. Children 4 to 5 years old drew sets of sticks that were all divided into two groups, large and small, or they arranged the sticks by pairs—one large and one small—or they arranged them in threes, with a small, a medium, and a large stick in each set. Five-year-olds succeeded in drawing correct series, but with only a few elements in each. Children 6 to 7 years old most often drew correct configurations. These results are consistent with what children of similar age do when asked to make or draw a series of sticks when they have *not* seen one. The drawings also corresponded to children's verbal descriptions (Sinclair, 1967a). The conclusions drawn from this aspect of the study were that memory images are linked to operatory schemes that control the images and dominate the perceived model (Inhelder, 1976c).

The longitudinal data indicated that, contrary to commonly held expectations that the memory trace would weaken over time, a large majority of the children drew better drawings after eight months than after one week. This finding suggests that the action schemes constituted the memory code and that the code was modified as cognitive structures were modified (Inhelder, 1976c).

The interpretation which seems to be called for is the following. First of all, a memory-image is not simply the prolongation of the perception of the model. On the contrary, it seems to act in a symbolic manner so as to reflect the subject's assimilation "schemes," that is, the way in which he *understood* the model (I say "understood," and not "copied," which is an entirely different thing). Now in six months, in the case of seriation or ordering, such as we have in this experiment, this operational or preoperational scheme of assimilation evolves, as the child has continued to compare objects of different sizes, etc., outside and well beyond the experiment which we presented to him. Then the new scheme of the next level serves as the code which has changed, which is better structured than it was before and which gives rise to a new image which symbolizes the current state of the operational schema and not what it was at the time when the encoding was done [Piaget, 1968, p. 5].*

This quotation points out two essential aspects of Piaget and Inhelder's explanation of the relationship between development and memory. First, it indicates that memory of an activity is modified by the child's developmental view of a problem. A child who performed a task when she was operating at a less sophisticated cognitive level at a later time remembers the structure of the problem as if she had solved it at the more sophisticated level she has now achieved. The passage of time, rather than eroding memory, actually enhances it. The child's memory of the problem undergoes developmental modifications. Second, the quotation above points out that the child's initial schemes for assimilating the problem have themselves been transformed and projected to the next level of development. Thus, the child's assimilatory structures, having evolved, now permit her to represent the task more accurately from memory.

In a review of research examining memory from a Piagetian perspective, Liben (1977b) questioned the findings of Piaget and Inhelder on grounds that later studies have failed to support a strong relationship between memory and level of operativity. She suggested that the Genevan research may be confounded by the effects of repeated testing. Since most long-term memory studies have found a high incidence of regression, Liben concluded that some images may be more faithful to perceptions than to cognitive understanding. Perhaps, as Liben suggests, both operative level and authentic memory must be invoked to explain children's performances on memory tasks.

In a later article, however, Liben (1977a) reported that operative training during the retention interval enhances memory and that participation in a memory task affects later operative performance (p. 507). Both these findings support the position of Piaget and Inhelder regarding the fundamental relationship between memory and cognitive development. Liben noted that some of the reasons for the disparity of findings between the studies of Piaget and Inhelder and those of later researchers may be due to such methodological contrasts as the duration of the retention interval, the age range studied, and the testing schedule.

*From *On the Development of Memory and Identity* (Vol. 2), by J. Piaget. Copyright 1968 by Barre Publishing Company. Reprinted by permission.

Summary

What is important to our discussion of the relationship between learning and development is that no additional learning in the strict sense took place during the retention interval. Instead, any gains must be attributed to the child's coordination of mental actions—that is, to reflexive abstraction.

Studies on Consciousness

Recent research in Geneva has examined the point at which a child becomes consciously aware of a situation and has attempted to answer the question of how consciousness occurs (see also Chapter Six). In our discussion of Genevan research on learning, we have seen consistently that, for growth to occur, the child has to become aware of contradiction. For example, children who remain unaware of a conflict between the one-to-one correspondence process and the various spatial configurations in the conservation-training experiment described earlier in this chapter simply dismiss one part of the problem instead of integrating it into a solution (Inhelder et al., 1974). The research on consciousness indicates that *becoming cognizant* of an action scheme transforms that scheme into a concept (Piaget, 1976b).

In one study, children were given a large plastic disc (a tiddlywinks) and were asked to use it to snap a smaller disc into a box on a carpeted floor. As soon as the children had achieved their goal, they were asked to describe the event in detail. Later, discs and box were put on a table, and the entire experiment was repeated without the benefit of a resilient carpet. When the children found that the small disc didn't jump, they were asked to explain why. Finally, the children were given boxes of matches, a chess pawn, and a role of adhesive tape and were asked to predict what would happen if they pressed on the edges of these objects. After the children had carried out the experiment, they were asked why these objects fell over backward, whereas the disc on the carpeted surface jumped into the box.

Young children about 5 to 7 succeeded in snapping the disc into the box; they also realized that the disc jumped because they had pressed it. They were unable, however, to differentiate this pressure from a simple push forward. They conceived of the trajectory as a horizontal movement that rose suddenly as it approached the box (see Figure 7-3). A successful action leads to an adequate concept of that action only to the extent that it conforms to the children's understanding of causal ideas (which are in fact different from the actions themselves).

By the time they are 7 to 8 years old, children become able to conceive of the trajectory as a curve. They understand that the pressure on one side of the disc results in compression on the carpet, so that the other side of the disc is set off at an angle. Since the surface of the table allows no compression, the disc simply slides horizontally. Children at

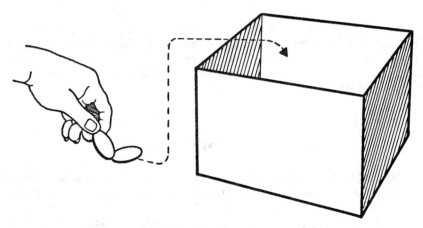

Figure 7-3. Imagined trajectory of disc.

an intermediate stage grasp that the disc sinks into the carpet, but they cannot understand why the resulting depression helps the disc to jump.

Finally, at approximately 10 to 12 years of age, children understand the rotation of objects. In this case, they understand that, when the object is thin (a disc, for example), the slope of the compressed carpet projects the object forward but, when the object is thick (a box of matches or a chess pawn, for example), pressure on one side of the object simply raises the other side but doesn't cause the object to jump.

Since children as young as 5 or 7 were able to perform the task, we cannot suggest that it is the observable elements of the event that lead to the greater understanding demonstrated by 12-year-old children. We see instead the beginning of a coordination: the carpet is depressed by the child's pressing on the disc; the "dent" in the carpet in turn acts on the disc and makes it jump. There appears to be, therefore, an ordered sequence of regulations, or progressive corrections, described by Piaget as a "constant search for equilibrium" (1976b, p. 146).[10]

Summary

The study described above and the one on the Hanoi Tower described in Chapter Six highlight the interaction between the child and his or her environment. "The subject only learns to know himself when acting on the object, and the latter can become known only as a result of ... the actions carried out on it" (Piaget, 1976b, p. 353). It is this *interrelation* that explains the harmony between thought and reality.

[10]This equilibrium should be interpreted not as a static state but as the very temporary state described within the Spiral of Knowing. Any state of equilibrium is transitory, because it provides the basis for asking new questions, which in turn lead to disequilibrium and consequent reordering.

Success and Understanding

Two important results of the studies on consciousness were (1) the indication that there is an interval between the successful active performance of a task and the conceptualization of that same task and (2) the indication that knowledge is acquired, so to speak, from the periphery to the center—that is, from the accommodation to objects made on the basis of the results of an action to internal regulations. In his later research on success and understanding, Piaget (1978d) attempted to confirm his earlier findings and to extend his inquiry to more complex problems, which are of necessity solved more gradually.

To succeed is to *understand in action* sufficiently well to be able to accomplish an activity. Even young children, when asked to propel a ball from a sling into a target, were able to do so. Hence, they succeeded. To understand, on the other hand, is to succeed in a situation *at the level of thought,* not action. To understand is to know the *why* and the *how* of the interrelations observed. In the example of the projected ball, understanding means comprehending the relations among the trajectory of the ball, the point of its release, and the position of the target (Piaget, 1976b). Few young children are able to understand such interrelations, even though they are successful in coordinating these three variables at the level of action.

One example of the problems examined in the research on success and understanding was the use of playing cards to build a house and a figure T (formed by one vertical card and one oblique card). After the activity the children were asked why the cards stood and what would happen if one or another of the cards were removed.

The younger children (approximately ages 5 to 6) were about to build the figures but couldn't explain how the cards retained their balance. At first the children didn't mention that some cards were placed obliquely. Although they used oblique supports, they were unaware that such positioning had a causal relation to the card's standing. In addition, the vertical card seemed to be regarded as in some way superior: the oblique card supported it!

At a higher level, spatial progress is made. Children mentioned the oblique position of some of the cards and established a causal relation. They didn't, however, comprehend the reciprocity (mutual support) of the oblique and vertical cards. These children, too, seemed to consider the vertical card as privileged.

Older children recognized that, in situations in which the two cards were symmetrical, the cards' actions were reciprocal. These children understood quite clearly that the two cards held each other up. The vertical, however, still maintained its "privilege"—in this instance, the privilege of restraining the oblique card rather than being supported by it. In addition, since the relations between "being supported" and "supporting" were still unclear, the children at this level didn't understand that the removal of a third card would not cause the first two to fall.

More advanced children (about 9 to 10 years of age) were able to construct a correct response to the problem. They denied the privileged position of the vertical card and argued instead that the vertical and the oblique cards leaned on and supported each other (although the children recognized that the leaning was not the same in the two cases).

Summary

Several important conclusions can be drawn from this experiment. First, even children who can succeed in an activity do not necessarily understand it. The delay observed in the studies on consciousness has been confirmed. Second, the evolution of understanding follows the expected course from the periphery to the center. Progress is made from initial gropings, without any plan, to a growing ability to anticipate—that is, to make inferences on the basis of past experience. Third, knowledge is gained through successive approximations. The opposition between closer and closer practical physical coordinations and mental coordinations is reduced by successive wholes (for example, no child could understand the forces exerted on or by a single card, unless he or she understood the relation between the cards at the outset). Finally, the ability to anticipate and to make choices constitutes the link between practical activity and conceptualization. The important aspect of learning in this situation is not observable but depends on reflexive abstraction.

Studies on Social Interaction

U.S. Studies

Piaget (1951, p. 205) has argued that "affective life, like intellectual life, is a continual adaptation, and the two are not only parallel but interdependent, since feelings express the interest and value given to actions of which intelligence provides the structure." Whereas Piaget has directed his efforts primarily at understanding the development of cognitive structures, some U.S. researchers have examined the effects of affective, particularly social, factors on the child's intellectual development. These researchers reasoned that, since intellectual life and affective life are interdependent, children with a high frequency of positive social encounters will have an intellectual advantage over less popular children and over those who are emotionally disturbed. Their research revealed that popular children are to some extent more likely to attain conservation than their less popular agemates (Goldschmid, 1968a; Rardin & Moan, 1971). Neale (1966) found emotionally disturbed children to be slower in overcoming egocentrism. The problem with this early research is "the American problem" that Piaget so often laments—a concern with *amount* rather than with the nature and quality of the interactions.

In 1972, Murray published an interesting study that examined the use of social interaction in the absence of any systematic instruction as a possible training procedure for conservation. He asked three children—two conservers and one nonconserver—to solve jointly a series of standardized conservation problems (Goldschmid & Bentler, 1968). In both immediate and delayed (one week) posttests, many shifts from nonconservation to conservation responses were observed.

A related line of research used social-interaction studies to test Piaget's theory of equilibration. Since Piaget (1971a) holds that the organism has an inherent tendency to move toward more stable and better integrated levels of equilibrium, attempts to change the child's thought (if the new notion is not too far above the child's current level of development) "should be more successful when he is exposed to concepts that reflect a higher rather than a lower stage of development" (Silverman & Geiringer, 1973, p. 815). Turiel (1966) and Kuhn (1972), for example, found results that supported the equilibration model, as they had operationally defined it, in studies using adults as models. The children in these studies were more influenced by performances slightly above, rather than below, their own level. Silverman and Stone (1972) and Silverman and Geiringer (1973) performed similar studies with similar results but investigated the influence of peer interactions rather than that of adult models.

Miller and Brownell (1974) extended the work with peer interactions. Second-graders were paired on the basis of pretests of conservation of length and weight—one conserver and one nonconserver per pair. The children were asked to resolve their differences on the conservation tasks and on two control questions. As would be expected from Piaget's theory of logical necessity, it was found that conservers prevailed more often on conservation tasks but not on the control questions. Few of these children, however, stated feelings of necessity. Those children who won the arguments most often explained or simply asserted their own answers. Conservers were likely to give logically adequate justifications, whereas nonconservers often gave variants of a perceptual theme, such as "It's thinner."

From the perspective of social-learning theory, Rosenthal and Zimmerman (1972) argued that conservation responses could be extinguished through the influence of a model giving nonconservation responses. As Turiel (1966) and Murray (1972) point out, however, it is one thing to change surface responses but quite another to alter cognitive structures.

Genevan Studies

A rather new line of social-interaction research by Doise and his colleagues Mugny and Perret-Clermont has been conducted in Geneva. In his discussion of social psychology, Piaget (1965, cited in Doise, Mugny, & Perret-Clermont, 1975) constructed a model to demonstrate that the structures underlying social interactions (for example, those involving values or idea exchanges) are identical to those of cognitive operations. Piaget (1965) insisted that the development of social logic and the development of individual logic are two inseparable aspects of a single reality, and, therefore, no causal relation can be established between them. Doise and his colleagues (Doise et al., 1975) disagreed and tested the hypothesis that social interaction does indeed exert a causal influence on cognitive development.

In a review of the work of this group, Doise and Perret-Clermont (1975) summarize their work as demonstrating the following three points:

1. Groups tend to develop a more coherent organization of criteria than individuals do when asked to formulate preferences or judgments.

2. Children working in groups reach levels of structuration that individuals working alone cannot attain, and the cognitive structures formed are internalized and reactivated in other situations. For example Mugny (reported in Doise et al., 1975) performed an experiment in which two groups of children between 6 and 7 years of age were presented with a model village and told to reconstruct the village on a table set at an angle of 90° so that a man coming out of the lake (a mark) could find his house. Four different items were devised; two were classified as simple and two as complex, depending on the transformational structures they required. The children performed the task both singly and in pairs (same sex and same school class). Results indicated that pairs of children made more progress than individuals and that the success of a single child could not account for the success of the pair. The authors offered two reasons to explain the superior progress of groups. First, the interference that each child's actions created for the others helped them integrate aspects of the problem that might easily have gone undiscovered when children acted alone. Second, integration of different points of view was more likely to be required in the group situation. Individuals, on the other hand, could concentrate successively on one aspect of the task and then on another without coordinating them.

In a closely related experiment, Perret-Clermont (Doise et al., 1975) asked a nonconserver to pour juice for two conservers who were to make sure that the sharing was fair. Two equal glasses plus one that was wider and shorter than the others were used for the sharing. The conservation-of-liquid posttest also included a taller and thinner glass. A high percentage of the 37 children progressed from nonconserving to transitional to conserving performances on the posttest. A second posttest one month later indicated that most children either maintained the progress they had demonstrated on the first posttest or had advanced beyond it. Interestingly, arguments given by children who had advanced in the posttests were often not those offered in the social situation, implying that cognitive reorganization had occurred.

3. The third finding of the studies by Doise and his associates has been that the construction of new coordinations depends on the individual's resolution of conflicts between his or her own centrations and those of others. These researchers took issue with the interpretations of much of the research cited earlier, which suggested that an adult

model or interaction with a child at a higher level of development was needed to effect cognitive growth. They argued instead that the existence of the "conflict of communication" itself was sufficient for progress to occur in the interaction. Contrary to the thesis advanced by social-learning theorists, they also argued that the effects of modeling could not be explained as the result of passive imitation but rather as a cognitive elaboration, or reconstruction.

To test these propositions, Mugny, Doise, and Perret-Clermont (1975) selected 6-year-old children who hadn't demonstrated conservation performances on tests of both equal and unequal lengths. These children were randomly assigned to one of three groups. In the first group (*C*), a collaborator of the experimenter offered a conservation response after the child had given his or her nonconservation response. In the second group (*NC*), the collaborator gave a response different from the child's but equally incorrect and based on similar reasoning. For example, when the child argued that stick *A* was longer because it extended beyond the end point of *B* (see Figure 7-4), the collaborator responded that *B* was longer because it extended beyond *A* in the opposite direction. The third group were controls.

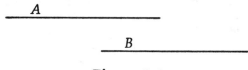

Figure 7-4.

The findings supported the hypothesis that children in the *C* group would make the most progress on a posttest but that children in the *NC* group would make significant progress as well, indicating that a superior model is facilitative but not *necessary* to achievement of progress. Because it was found once again on both immediate and delayed posttests that children gave explanations for their responses that had not been advanced during the period of social interaction, it was argued that it was not the imitation of a model per se but the consequences of the social interaction itself that led to cognitive restructuration. These studies will be reexamined in Chapter Eight, when their relevance to education will be discussed.

Cross-Cultural Research

Cross-cultural research has contributed to our understanding of the rates and sequences of cognitive development in societies throughout the world. In addition to providing information about stage theory, it has helped us understand the impact of such variables as schooling, urbanization, and social class on cognitive development. Since Piaget's

(1966) original discussion of the importance of cross-cultural studies, much work has been done, but the results have not always been so clear-cut as one would have hoped.

The First Three Stages

Cross-cultural studies have been conducted to verify the sequence of developmental stages and to explore horizontal time lags within a stage (Dasen, 1972). The few studies dealing with sensorimotor development suggest that there is little variation among children of different cultures (Glick, 1975), although some minor advances and delays can be observed (Bovet, 1976).

The transition from preoperational to concrete-operational thinking has been studied extensively, usually using conservation as an index of the achievement of concrete operations. The results of these studies have been quite varied. Dasen (1972) reports that authors working with such diverse populations as the Tiv in Central Nigeria (Price-Williams, 1961), Europeans in Hong Kong, average Americans, Chinese with no schooling (Goodnow, 1962; Goodnow & Bethon, 1966), and Iranian schoolchildren (Mohseni, 1966) found that all of these groups achieved the level of concrete operations at approximately the same age as Europeans—between the ages of 7 and 8. On the other hand, Tuddenham (1968, 1969) found that Oriental children living in California were superior to European children on at least half of 15 tests of concrete operations. Both Bovet (1968, 1971) and Kohlberg (1968) have found evidence of concrete operations at approximately 7 and 8 years of age in Algerian and Alayal (Formosa) children, respectively. In each case, however, there appeared to be a regression followed by a reappearance of operational abilities several years later. Bovet (1976) explained that the initial conservation was not fully operational and that distinct processes of development may exist. She attributed this deviant type of conservation to an inadequate analysis of the figural aspects of the problem (for example, ignoring the appearance of the liquid after it has been poured into a differently shaped container). Kohlberg suggested that the Alayal, because of magical beliefs, simply became less trusting of their own judgments. Retarded development has also been reported (Dasen, 1972). It appears that non-Western and nonurban children, as well as children of low socioeconomic status, lag two to seven years behind their middle-class Western peers in the development of conservation skills (Kamara & Easley, 1977).

Although divergent findings exist (see Goodnow & Bethon, 1966; Mermelstein & Shulman, 1967; Heron, 1971), many studies support schooling as one of the principal cultural influences on operational development. Bovet (1976) and Bruner and Greenfield (cited in Bruner, Olver, & Greenfield, 1966) reported that better-developed perceptual strategies result from schooling. Bovet suggested that improved perception may possibly derive from activities in which children are taught to attend to the figural aspects of objects, such as building with blocks or stacking bowls. Learning to read and write also necessitates careful perceptual comparisons.

Actually, the effects of schooling on cognitive development are still unclear. It may be that the confusion results from considering schooling per se and not, as would seem to be more appropriate, the *nature* of the schooling (Carlson, 1973). Waddell (1968) and deLemos (1969) have suggested that schooling becomes an important factor when it brings with it cultural stimulation that would otherwise not be available (Dasen, 1972). The more important element, therefore, seems to be contact with Western cognitive values, including urbanization and social class. Mohseni (1966), for example, found children in the city of Teheran to perform on concrete-operational tasks in accordance with expectations for European children but to be approximately two years ahead of illiterate children in the more rural Iranian towns. Other factors that may affect cognitive development but that have not been investigated in relation to Genevan theory are malnutrition, early physical and social stimulation, and linguistic structures (Dasen, 1972).

In most cases of retarded development the causal factors are unclear. Although many children don't achieve conservation within the expected age range, most eventually do (in some studies the age range is so restricted that it is impossible to determine whether children later attained concrete operations). There is evidence, however, that children in some cultures don't attain concrete operations even as late as 18. There is no research to indicate whether these children may at some time during their adult lives succeed in conserving. Studies with adults have demonstrated that conservation may be achieved by many, but not all, persons in a given culture; that some conservations may be achieved but not others (for example, quantity but not weight), or that concrete operations may be demonstrated in one area (such as time and speed) and not in another (conservation). These findings indicate that the research examining concrete operations generally supports the Genevan model, with the rate of acquisition being dependent on cultural factors.

Formal Operations

Results of research investigating formal operations is less clear (see Chapter Six for a description of formal thought). Neimark (1975) summarizes her review of the literature by offering the following points among her "tentative generalizations" (p. 585):

1. There is a stage of thinking beyond the concrete-operational level that is qualitatively distinct from it. Inhelder and Piaget's (1958) description of formal operations appears to be a good first approximation for studying this stage, but refinement and elaboration of the theoretical framework are needed.

2. This advanced stage is not attained by all individuals (either across or within cultures) and may not be stable for one individual over time. Research findings summarized by Papalia (1972), for example, indicate that operational thought declines with advancing age. The

pattern seems to be in reverse of the order of acquisition. Studies showed a sharp decline in conservation of volume, less decline in conservation of weight and substance, and no decline (within the age range tested) in conservation of number.

3. Cultural differences undoubtedly affect the proportion of members of different societies likely to attain formal operations. A consistent finding has been that non-Western groups frequently evidence delay or even nonacquisition.

In a speech given in Italy in 1972, Piaget revised—or, perhaps, it is more accurate to say clarified—his position on formal operations. He noted that all normal people have the potential to develop formal structures but, without adequate intellectual stimulation, they may not realize that potential. He also pointed out that, as people age, their aptitudes diversify and they become interested in a variety of things. These interests may be a powerful factor in determining how the level of formal operations is demonstrated. Poets, for example, may not be adept at solving problems in physics but may demonstrate high levels of reasoning with regard to the infinite possibilities extent in their creation of images, use of rhyme and meter, and so on.

Much of the cross-cultural research has not taken aptitude into account. As Cole, Gay, Glick, and Sharp (1971) point out, when the results of a study indicate a lack of competence, researchers must examine the intelligent adaptive behaviors people engage in every day, in order to determine whether it is the subjects or the *analysis* that is at fault.

Within-Stage Development

Even with all its diverse findings, cross-cultural research supports the reality of the stage theory and of the sequence of stages postulated by the Genevans. When the order of development within a given stage is considered, however, research results don't conform so well to expectations. Piaget (1970b) explains that all children (regardless of the culture in which they live) evidence horizontal *décalage* (Pinard & Laurendeau, 1969)—a time lag in which they are unable to apply the same structures of thought to different contents. The best-known example of horizontal time lags is the acquisition of conservation: conservation of quantity precedes conservation of weight and length, which in turn precede conservation of volume.

Research has not shown this order of acquisition to be stable across cultures. Deviations (for example, conservation of weight preceding conservation of quantity) have been attributed to the influence of day-to-day activities, to familiarity of testing materials, and to the demands of the natural environment and/or cultural characteristics (Dasen, 1972). Evidence of time lags during the period of concrete operations also raises questions about the current predilection to demonstrate consistency among operations or generalization from one task to another at the level of formal operations. As Piaget (1972a) suggests, until a certain level of development, behavior patterns at various stages are characterized by very general properties. But, as individual aptitudes become more pronounced, greater differences can be noticed among subjects. For example, drawings can help to determine the level of intellectual functioning of young children. With adults, however, drawings "gradually become diversified according to criteria of individual aptitudes rather than the general development common to all individuals" (Piaget, 1972a, p. 8).

Summary

In all cultures the children who were studied show, "at one period or another in their development, the same patterns of cognitive assimilation and the same structural coordinations" (Inhelder, 1976b, p. 5). Cultural influences appear to be limited in their effect to the rate of development achieved, the particular route taken, and the ultimate level of development attained.

Piaget and Education: An Overview

Introduction

In this and the next chapter our concern will shift to the implications that the learning theory of Piaget and Inhelder has for education. Chapter Eight emphasizes the principles of the theory that have special relevance for education in general but especially for the normal child. Chapter Nine focuses on special populations of children, such as the mentally retarded, the learning disabled, and the gifted.

The 1960s saw many attempts to apply the developmental theory of the Genevan School directly to both curriculum and instruction. Two factors were no doubt responsible for these attempts to make a direct transition from theory to practice in the classroom. At that time the colorful bandwagon of direct applications of B.F. Skinner's learning principles to instruction moved in to lead the parade to Utopia. Some educators joined the parade, but, instead of Skinnerian principles, they tried to apply Piagetian theory to educational practice.

The other factor was the booming market in educational materials resulting from an empiricist philosophy that advocated the manipulation of those materials in very direct attempts to teach concepts of learning or change existing learning patterns. Piaget's research tasks became marketable kit materials to "sell" cognitive development. And materials to teach conservation found their place on the shelf next to the teaching machine and to the programmed-instruction books of the stimulus-response school of learning.

We agree with Kamii, DeVries, and others (DeVries, 1974, 1978; Kamii, 1975; Kamii & DeVries, 1977; Denis-Prinzhorn, Kamii, & Mounoud, 1975) who said that teaching the tasks reduces the theory to the content of the tasks themselves and results in an obvious distortion.

Also, concentration on tasks that were originally designed to determine qualitative differences in answers at various developmental stages leads to an overemphasis on Piagetian stages and regards them as *the* essence of the theory's relevance for education. The following quotations elucidate these criticisms.

> The tasks Piaget and his collaborators have designed during the past 30 years or so have been intended as means of determining the type of structure which characterizes each level of development. For Piaget, the important thing is the process of thinking and the structure that the process has attained. The answer the child gives is of interest to Piaget only insofar as it tells us something about the underlying process. . . .
>
> The fact that something is teachable does not necessarily imply the desirability of teaching it. For example, it may be possible to teach all the Binet items to children up to a certain level. The teachability of the items, however, does not imply the desirability of teaching them or the conclusion that it is possible to make children more intelligent. The teachability of Piagetian tasks likewise does not necessarily reflect a change in the structure of thought process. Only through longitudinal studies can we find out whether or not the teaching of a Piagetian task at age 6 or 7 produces lasting effects on the further development of all the cognitive structures in adolescence and beyond [Denis-Prinzhorn et al., 1975, p. 12].*

It must be remembered, however, that this emphasis on "teaching the tasks" in an attempt to apply Piagetian theory to education paralleled the emphasis on stages in the Genevan School itself. The educator who studied Piagetian theory was naturally drawn to what was most obvious in the then translated works—tasks and stages. As we mentioned in previous chapters, the early Piagetian writings dealt only sketchily with the details of the mechanisms of equilibration and reflexive abstraction and the concept of conflict as a spark of reorganization of thinking—all now so obviously rich in implications for education. Note, too, that Inhelder, Sinclair, and Bovet's (1974) experiments on learning and training studies were at first scattered in a few journals. Thus, educators were working with what was available—an incomplete theory. It was Furth (1977) who teasingly told Piaget how nice it was that he was getting around to fleshing out such concepts as equilibration! (One guide to Piaget actually stated that equilibration was an important concept but "it will not be treated here.")

In sum, a new era is here. We have clearer writings and more accurate translations of concepts based on mechanisms relating directly to a wider and wider spiral of knowledge, which is fundamentally what education is all about. In the last few years, both in Europe and in North America, some innovative approaches to the implications of Piagetian theory for education have been published. Our aim in the two following sections is to summarize these approaches and encourage further research and writings on the topic.

---

*From *Inside Piaget: Practical Considerations for the Classroom,* by M. Denis-Prinzhorn, C. Kamii, and P. Mounoud. Copyright 1975 by Pragmatix. Reprinted by permission.

Relating Piagetian Theory to Education: Two Directions

The Method of Critical Exploration and Classroom Teaching

An important and exciting movement in instruction has grown out of the Genevan research method, or "method of critical exploration" (for a discussion of this method, see Chapter Two). Such a method is adapted to educational purposes by questioning children about how they would approach a problem and how they arrived at their answers. The teacher presents children with further problems, based on those the children have already solved (or not solved), to see what rules or generalizations the children have formed. Often the children are given a second problem, especially in mathematics, that, if solved by the procedure used to solve the first problem, would lead to an incorrect answer. Thus, by setting up a conflict situation, the teacher notes whether the disturbance causes an adjustment and consequent avoidance of future errors.

The method was first proposed as applicable to education by two Genevans, M. Denis-Prinzhorn and J. B. Grize (1966). These researchers listed three advantages of the method. First, it would provide a means by which individual teachers, by interacting with individual students, could determine the level of cognitive functioning of the student. Second, it would enable the teacher to fit more adequately the program of instruction to the individual child. (Such a method of instruction would, of course, have wide application in special education. See Chapter Nine.)

> The task of the teacher is not to pass on to the students the knowledge that he possesses but to put them in a situation where they can construct the knowledge themselves. It requires, first of all, that [the teacher] make for himself a picture of his 'subjects' that is as exact as possible. . . . The teacher will use the general development as a frame of reference in which he could place each of his students by making precise use of the clinical method [Denis-Prinzhorn & Grize, 1966, pp. 322–323].[1]

The third advantage of the use of this method is that it encourages social interaction between child and teacher and, if used in a group situation, between the child and his or her peers who may be at different levels of understanding. We shall see in the following section the further advantages of the method for group interaction in a conflict-instigating situation.

The method of critical exploration of the Genevan School has most frequently been used in research and writing at the School of Education of the University of Illinois (Easley, 1974). Doctoral candidates, under the direction of such professors as J. A. Easley and K. G. Witz, investigated children's understanding of certain topics in mathematics—for example, fractions and decimals—in order to determine what rules the children used to solve problems. The following is an account of the research Erlwanger (1975) conducted with a sixth-grader named Benny. (For a review and evaluation of clinical studies in mathematics education, see Easley, 1977.)

---

[1]Translation by M. W. Louisell and R. F. Easley.

Benny was of average intelligence but, according to test-score results and his teacher's judgment, in mathematics he performed on an above-average level. Benny progressed through an individualized instructional mathematics program based on programmed learning. As we shall see in the example that follows, Benny saw mathematics as a search for patterns from which he could deduce rules. His "rules," although often based on incorrect concepts, led to "right" answers often enough to keep his teacher unconcerned. When Benny failed to get at least 80% correct answers, he would try to find a pattern in the correct answers and then change the wrong ones to better fit the key. Read carefully the following excerpts from the critical exploration of Benny's understanding of addition of fractions.

Excerpt 7

1. *E:* Let's come back to this one. 4/4 + 5/5.
2. *B:* Is 2 wholes because 4/4 *is one whole*; 5/5 *is another whole.* So 1 whole and 1 whole is 2 wholes.   It's just like saying 1 + 1, which is 2.
3. *E:* But look at it like this one [i.e., 3/4 + 4/5 = 7/9]. The numbers at the bottom are not the same. That's 4 and that's 5. Why did you not use this rule?
4. *B:* Because it is different, see? Like this one—4/4, 5/5 . . . well, they're both wholes, so we know that they have to be 1 + 1, which is 2.
5. *E:* Well, what about 4/4 + 2/3?
6. *B:* 4/4 + 2/3; 1 2/3.
7. *E:* I notice you are not using this rule.
8. *B:* Ya. . . . Ya, because we get a whole one here [4/4]; 2/3 left; 1 2/3.*

Excerpt 8

1. *E:* Do you think it makes sense to have one rule here and another there?
2. *B:* Ya, *because they are different;* fractions are little things.
3. *E:* Suppose I had 2/1 + 1/2. How would you do that?
4. *B:* *That would be 1 whole . . . because 3/3 . . . 1; . . . it's just like saying 1/2 + 1/2 because 2/1, reverse that . . . 1/2; so it will come out 1 whole no matter which way. 1 is 1.*
5. *E:* I see. What does 3/4 + 4/3 give you?
6. *B:* 1 whole.
7. *E:* Now you used your rule here.
8. *B:* Ya, ya.
9. *E:* Is there another way of doing it?
10. *B:* Ya. Say . . . oh! 3/4 + 4/3 is a whole because, see, 7/7 is a whole.

*This and all other quotations from this source are from "Case Studies of Children's Conceptions of Mathematics—Part I," by S. H. Erlwanger, *Journal of Children's Mathematical Behavior*, 1975, 1(3), 157–283. Copyright 1975 by Curriculum Laboratory, Urbana, Illinois. Reprinted by permission.

Note that Benny's "rule" of adding both numerators and denominators works for whole numbers. If confronted with $1/2 + 1/2$, he would find it difficult to answer $2/4$ and then return to $1/2$. "This *has* to produce dissonance, a realization that some accommodation is called for. And this is precisely what Benny does: He draws a boundary around all of this particular kind of troublesome case and makes up a new rule that applies to this case only!" (Editor's note in Erlwanger, 1975, p. 208).

Erlwanger (1974, 1975) concluded that the crucial element is not to be found in the results of tests but in the right or wrong mathematical concepts that children construct for themselves. (Of course, this is true of all school subjects.) It was difficult for Benny to change and learn from remedial tutoring, for he was constantly searching for his own rule system. Thus, an individualized instructional program, without teacher intervention to determine real understandings, was a handicap to Benny.

Piaget (1970c, 1973b) noted that programmed instruction may indeed be conducive to learning. However, it is not conducive to constructing, unless children are permitted to do the programming themselves (see, for example the experiments of Papert, 1973). Even manipulative materials such as the famous Cuisenaire rods used in mathematics instruction may impede learning because of the stress on the figurative, as opposed to the operative, activity (see "The Figurative/Operative Distinction" in Chapter Three).[2] The use of such materials may lead to the erroneous conclusion that "doing" is understanding (Brun, 1975).

In sum, instructional materials may at the outset appear to be the long-awaited answer to children's difficulties in learning certain subjects. However, unless the teacher spends time in the careful questioning of individual children, incorrect concepts on the part of the children may impede their learning. The method of critical exploration as used in a classroom setting reaffirms the continuing importance of teachers. No machines, programmed materials, or educational gadgetry will, in all probability, ever replace them.

It may seem to be a contradiction that, in an age when independent study, programmed materials, and learning centers are in vogue, an argument is made that periods of intensive interchange between teachers and students are necessary. Why not plan lessons in logical sequence, distribute them in prepackaged units, and wait for the "soaking-in" process to take its course?

Brun (1975) warns against the conflict between natural thought patterns constructed by the child and prepackaged educational materials, which may have little to do with such patterns. For example, suppose a teacher plans, as part of a science unit, to "teach" the concept that some heavy objects float while others sink. No doubt the teacher would plan for children to work with many different types of materials in no set order and will discuss with the students their findings. The

---

[2]Piaget reports that the rods are no longer used in some Swiss cantons.

teacher is providing the background for the concept of density. However, the term doesn't need to be used for the children to begin to grasp the basic concept.

Children will bring to this science lesson a wide variety of experience with floating and sinking objects. There is no way for a teacher to control this experiential background, nor is it necessary. And yet, as Brun (1975) notes, some curriculum areas such as mathematics have seen an artificial breaking down of concepts into prepackaged small parts. As we have stressed, if children learn from reflecting on meaningful actions and reorganizing past understandings through a self-regulative process, then the constructing process is their own. Teachers may provide materials and guides, but such artifacts in themselves are no assurance of the rightness of the acquired concept. Through carefully planned questions, the teacher probes to determine levels of understanding. No kits, packages, or detailed lesson plans are insurance against the possibility of misconceptions. How many Bennys are in our classrooms?

Teachers need to learn and come to believe in the ability to progressively understand the thought structures of their students. A common theme in Piagetian writings on education (Piaget, 1970c, 1972d, 1973b) is that the training of teachers is successful only if it includes the careful study of the development of children's thinking. This is how Sigel (1969, p. 468), in an early and important essay on Piaget and education, highlighted this need for teachers to be aware of the dynamics of the child's intellectual growth:

> Although cognitive growth appears to be a continuous process, it proceeds in discontinuous ways with spurts and plateaus of achievement. Thus, for the educator, it is important to be aware of the fact that cognitive structures are not fixed or given but develop and, in the process of adaptation, become modified and reconstituted as new structures at subsequent points in time. The process of structures being built, decomposed, and recombined highlights the dynamics of mental growth. Piaget's system is one of changing gestalts or wholes that are reorganized and redefined in the course of growth.

The subject of the dynamics of mental growth brings us back to the continuing theme of this book—the projecting and reorganizing aspects of reflexive abstraction. It is to that mechanism that we now turn our attention by considering conflict in social-interaction studies.

Social Interaction: Conflict as a Means to Increase Understanding

Some research on social interaction was discussed in Chapter Seven in relation to research on learning. We return to this area here because of its importance for educational applications. Various views have been offered to explain why children seem to improve in the understanding of concepts if they are tutors or participants in group discussions, especially of a problem-solving nature. The common denominator in studies of tutoring and group problem solving is the requirement that children give explanations or state their points of view to their peers. In the majority of these studies, there is little or no teacher intervention.

Interaction with Peers. You will recall that a common reason given in research studies to explain why social interaction facilitates cognitive development relates to the process of model imitation (for a complete review of social-interaction studies from the perspective of the Genevan School, see Perret-Clermont, 1976).

However, it is difficult to interpret some of the findings of both social-interaction and tutoring studies from the viewpoint of a learning theory that gives a central role to the mechanism of imitation. Let's consider the findings of four studies, some of which we discussed in detail in Chapter Seven. In one of Murray's (1972) social-interaction studies, groups of three children, usually one nonconserver and two conservers, were told that they had to agree to the answer for each problem on a standardized test of conservation. When there was disagreement, the children were directed to discuss the problem and explain their points of view. The important finding, relevant to the present discussion, was that social interaction facilitates performance not only for nonconservers but also for conservers. Although Murray does not base his findings specifically on a modeling explanation, he does not emphasize the paradoxical conclusion that some conservers advance when interacting with nonconservers.

In a second study (Allen & Feldman, 1973), low-achieving fifth-graders acted as tutors for third-graders of similar ability. The children who acted as tutors improved in their understanding of the material more when they acted as tutors than when they studied the material by themselves. The results are interpreted as indicating that the tutors saw themselves as teachers and this self-perception enhanced their learning. The authors discredit the idea that the tutees may have taught some material to the tutors.

In a third study, Perret-Clermont (1976) pretested children on a task requiring selection and drawing of figures in various spatial rotation. After pretesting, the children were paired—one "inferior" and one "superior"—to work on a similar task. The surprising result was that the children designated as superior in the pretesting were able to demonstrate more advanced performance after working with their slower partners. Perret-Clermont interprets the findings of her study as an indicator of internal reorganization due to the mechanism of reflexive abstraction.

Such a conclusion is supported by a fourth study summarized by Perret-Clermont. In unpublished research reported by Mugny and Doise of the Genevan School, children in groups of two, after completing tasks involving relations of spatial perspectives, were assigned by a pretest to one of four levels, according to their level of success on the task. The most important finding for our evaluation is that children judged to be most advanced on the pretest profited in interaction with children of the *same* level of ability as well as with children of inferior level of ability.

Application of Research Findings to Classroom Practice. Such findings are very significant for the understanding of the educational process. These experiments may seem unrelated to classroom practice, since the researchers used, as one critic (Allport, 1975) calls them, "informationally impoverished laboratory tasks." On careful reflexion, however, it is possible to view all these studies as providing valuable data on the Piagetian mechanism of reflexive abstraction.

Recall the twin and inseparable facets of reflexive abstraction: projection to a higher level of what was known on a lower level and reorganization of what was known in order to program to a richer level of knowing. As we noted in Chapter Seven, what these studies indicate is that it is neither necessary nor sufficient to "follow" a correct model in order to advance in knowledge. What is important is that through social interactions one is forced to listen to and interact with *different points of view*. Such differences of opinion, wrong or right, force the participants to reorganize what they already know and think of new methods of explanation, with the result that novel constructions emerge, which are richer than the past understandings.

This is how Perret-Clermont (1976, p. 247) summarizes the above points:

> The interactionist and constructivist conception of development ... considers the origin of cognitive structures as resulting not from a passive appropriation by the subject of outside behaviors but [from] a structuring activity on reality which is brought about in a privileged way through the coordinations between individuals. ... Social interaction does not offer solely a kind of "intellectual nourishment" for assimilating but arouses especially an activity of accommodation which is, itself, the creator of novelty.

As already stated in several places in this book, mechanisms such as reflexive abstraction may function in a regulatory manner: that is, they react to disturbance. The conflict situation due to the expression of differing points of view during social interaction, even though on the surface a minor one, may be viewed as a disturbance. The child or adult on all levels of education is placed in a situation of *confrontation* between his or her own reactions and those of others.

Thus, Brun (1975) defines the goal of teaching as the fostering of reflexive abstraction. It is the teacher's role to set up situations in which the projecting and organizing of concepts takes place. When teachers perceive themselves as dispensers of knowledge, as archivists, or as gods of wisdom passing out gems to be preserved for the next generation, they are headed for the museum they have made for themselves. What is needed are teachers who are trained in asking stimulating questions that spark conflict and stir up opposing points of view. Therefore, teachers need to evaluate themselves on the questions their students ask rather than on the sum of right answers they score on their students' tests.[3]

---

[3]For a discussion of conflict in Piagetian theory and education, see Gallagher (1978b).

Such sparking of conflicts and setting up of situations in which opposing points of view are elicited are not part of the kind of teacher education that stresses the danger of confusing children. Children don't live in a completely ordered world. To fear potentially confusing input is to fear that the child is alive. As we mentioned so often in the preceding chapters, when ideas are in conflict, the self-regulatory mechanisms are at optimal level. To send children home with puzzled expressions and unanswered questions to mull over should be high on any teaching objectives list. Perhaps more flexibility is needed in training teachers to write lesson plans. Why do classes end with neat little summaries instead of stimulating questions? A related problem was noted in the protocol of Benny. Here was evidence that a neat, programmed approach to a concept didn't confuse enough. In fact, the child learned incorrect rules, which were not challenged.

Teachers, too, need to grow in the art of teaching by being confronted with conflict. In an insightful essay on the developing teacher, Schwebel and Raph (1973, p. 288) say:

> Developing teachers, sensing that all is not well with the functioning of their class, will begin to question their orientation and procedures. It is a well-known fact, documented recently in dozens of books, that many new teachers respond to their tension-provoking recognition by changing only one variable—the degree of strictness. The teacher becomes "tougher" but otherwise remains unchanged and closes off the opportunity, for the time being at least, of developing by means of a new adaptation under circumstances of disequilibrium.

Another important implication of these studies is that various media—for example, television—may instigate opposing points of view. Such is the conclusion of Fowles and Voyat (1974, p. 78):

> Piaget cites an ambiguous intrusion upon the existing system as an important initiator of cognitive activity.... As Sigel (1969) puts it, an important teaching strategy deducible from Piaget's theory is to "confront the child with the illogic of his own point of view"! ... Taken together these comments suggest [that] stimulus presentations, with certain structures built in, can "trigger" constructive mental activity. It also seems that there is nothing to preclude television from providing those stimuli.

What modern education needs, then, is that we explore all possibilities for the triggering of cognitive conflict. We shouldn't forget, however, that the simple classroom setting of teachers interacting with students and students interacting with other students at all levels of ability is a rich arena for the stimulation of cognitive growth.

Summary

It may not be wise to attempt *direct* applications of the changing and still incomplete learning theory of the Genevan School to education. It is possible, however, to search for broad implications that provide insights into how the theory may be used to evaluate trends in education. This chapter explored two such areas: (1) the value of the method of critical exploration, as adapted for classroom investigations, and (2) the power of social interaction as a means to elevate understandings to higher and richer levels. Both of these areas are fruitful for all ages and curricula. Our discussion has made clear that we are not advocating a "Piagetian method" for teaching reading, social studies, or science. However, if learning *is* reflexive abstraction—that is, a projecting and reorganizing process—then knowledge of the research of Piaget and Inhelder may help teachers at all levels to better understand not only specific learning experiences in interaction with their students but the learning experiences of their entire lifetime as well.

If a learning theory is to have an impact, it needs to stimulate the thinking of teachers. Claparède (1975/1911, p. 160), one of Piaget's "stimulators," incorporated a 1910 quotation from the mathematician Camescasse into his text: "Our schools might be a place of pleasure. Let people say this to themselves: When the school ceases to be attractive to the child, *it is always the school that is in the wrong.*"

CHAPTER NINE

Exceptional Children and Special Education

Traditionally, special educators have shown less interest in Genevan theory than have their counterparts in regular education. Although there appears to be increasing interest in the use of a "Piagetian framework" for understanding disabilities, little effort has been expended in the special class for adapting teaching techniques derived from Genevan theory. It has been assumed, for example, that open education is generally inappropriate for exceptional children, but research aimed at investigating this issue is practically nonexistent.[1]

The paucity of research examining the potential problems and/or benefits of a Genevan-derived educational paradigm reflects seemingly contradictory areas of concern. First, as we have seen throughout this text, the Genevans, and especially Piaget, have directed their efforts primarily toward defining those aspects of knowledge acquisition and of change mechanisms that are common to nearly all children. Emphasis among Genevans has been on homogeneity; emphasis among special educators, on individual differences. Second, special educators have generally been committed to the notion that "special" children (and adults) require a step-by-step, behaviorally defined approach to learning. Genevans have opposed such pupil-passive methods, suggesting that it is dangerous to prevent children from constructing ideas for themselves (Piaget, 1970c, 1973b). Finally, Genevan theory has focused on development rather than on the learning of academic skills and the acquisition of information. Educators (both regular and special), therefore, have been unsure about the actual implications of Genevan theory for educational practice. In this chapter each of these issues will be examined in turn.

---

[1]Knoblock's (1973) work with the emotionally disturbed, however, constitutes one important exception.

Individual Differences

Does Genevan theory provide an appropriate basis for the development of teaching strategies for children (and adults) who deviate from developmental norms? Although the Genevans have not attempted to provide a systematic approach to individual differences (Webb, 1974; Piaget, 1971c), their theory has helped those concerned with exceptionalities to understand them. Many kinds of individual differences are possible, such as differences among children in their rates of development, variations within a given child's development (one child may move through one or more stages at a normal pace, but be delayed in attaining others), or differences in the routes various children take to attain the same stages.

When these differences in rate or manner of development are sufficiently noticeable that they result in a child's being labeled exceptional, one can usually relate the advance or limitation to one or more of the four factors of development. For example, Piaget has repeatedly stated that physiological maturation provides a *condition of possibilities* that places limits on what a child learns from interaction with the environment.[2] When there are disturbances in the functioning of the central nervous system—which is often the case with retarded and learning-disabled children—learning is necessarily impaired. Children with sensory deficits (such as blindness or severely restricted vision), as well as children with physical impairments (such as cerebral palsy or paralysis), may suffer from a disruption of physical experience. Although in these cases reflexive abstraction appears to be *relatively* unaffected in the long run, initial levels of development may be delayed because of the difficulties experienced with the comprehension of affirmations. Disadvantaged and deaf and hard-of-hearing children appear to experience rather severe problems with regard to social experience. Emotionally disturbed and mentally retarded children often exhibit difficulties with the process of equilibration. It should be clear that all these relations are meant only to be illustrative. Certainly one child in any disability category may experience limitations in some or all of these four areas. Gifted children generally appear to benefit from particular facility in all four of them.

Genevan theory provides us with a developmental sequence (not necessarily age-related) that emphasizes *how* children function rather than *what* they know at each stage. It is this attention to modes of functioning, as well as to variations in motivation, interest, and experience, that promises to enrich educational methods. Genevan theory, with its emphasis on equilibration, or self-regulation, can help special educators understand the role children play in their own development. It might also serve to make educators more sensitive to the astonishing variety of avenues children may find useful in learning. Finally, the developmental sequence itself calls attention to levels of functioning and to the necessity for developmentally appropriate goals and interventions.

[2]See Chapter Three.

Characteristics of Special Populations

A great deal of research using a Genevan framework to study exceptional children has been carried out in both Europe and North America. Some of the work has lead to clarifications of Genevan theory as well as to a better understanding of exceptional persons. In the case of special populations, this work has been carried out by "Piagetians" such as Inhelder, de Ajuriaguerra, Schmid-Kitsikis, and Voyat but not by Piaget himself. What have we learned from these studies?

Mental Retardation

The mentally retarded progress through the same stages and in the same order as normal persons, but the rate at which they progress is relatively slow. The ultimate level of development attained appears to be related to the severity of the retardation. The mildly retarded generally reach concrete operations, and the moderately retarded generally reach preoperations, but the severely retarded are unable to advance (even in adulthood) beyond the sensorimotor stage (Inhelder, 1968; Woodward, 1959, 1961, 1962). Cognitive development among the mildly retarded seems to continue between the ages of 16 and 20 but at a decelerating pace (Stephens, 1974). Similar improvements are exhibited throughout late adolescence in moral judgment (Mahaney & Stephens, 1974) and in moral conduct (Moore & Stephens, 1974). Although retardates are less capable of behaving in a moral fashion than normal children of similar chronological age, their moral conduct is equivalent to that of their *mental-age* peers. In general, mental age is a better predictor of cognitive development among retardates than chronological age (Adler, 1964; Carpenter, 1955; Hood, 1962), and level of cognitive development does appear to be correlated, at least, with school performance (Ranson, 1950; Garonne et al., 1969; Swize, 1972).

Development in the retarded appears to be less homogeneous than in normals; that is, the retarded function consistently within a given domain of knowledge but demonstrate considerable variation among and between domains—for example, number and space. Overall, their thought appears analogous to that of younger children. The mildly to moderately retarded, for example, vacillate between higher and lower levels of functioning, tend to solve problems on the basis of their concrete attributes, and are highly susceptible to irrelevant influences such as the tester's approval (Zigler, 1969), the way a question is phrased (Carlson & Michelson, 1973), or whether a verbal or nonverbal response is required (Vitello, 1973). Inhelder (1966) suggests that these children reach only levels of "pseudoequilibrium." Retardates' activity, however, does lead eventually to stable constructions despite vacillations and limited deductive processes (Schmid-Kitsikis, 1976).

When compared to normals, the mildly retarded appear to have particular problems in conservation and classification, which are related to difficulties in categorization, flexibility, and reversibility (Stephens &

McLaughlin, 1974; Brogle, 1971; Marchi, 1971; McManis, 1969; Wilton & Boersma, 1974). Several studies (see, for example, Kahn, 1974; Lister, 1970) have been successful in teaching the task of conservation to retardates, but none has shown that their accurate performance reflects the acquisition of those structures of which conservation is the result in normal children.[3]

What often appear to be random behaviors in the severely retarded actually follow the sequence of substages of the sensorimotor period (Woodward, 1959). The severely retarded don't seem to be able to acquire language until they are able to perform at the level described as substage 6 of the sensorimotor period (see Chapter Four), which confirms Piaget's contention that the development of certain cognitive structures is prerequisite to language development (Kahn, 1975). Severely retarded children who do use language tend to speak in a manner expected of much younger normal children (Sinclair, 1967b).

Emotional Disturbances

Unlike the reasoning of retardates, that of severely emotionally disturbed, or prepsychotic, children is characterized by incoherence and a distorted assimilation of reality (Inhelder, 1966). Because these children often suffer from a conflict between affect and cognition, they don't try to overcome deficient thought mechanisms. Instead, they transform reality to suit their own needs and fears in an attempt to avoid conflict (Schmid-Kitsikis, 1969, 1973). Prepsychotic children don't appear to follow normal developmental patterns. Because of the extreme fluctuations in their behavior, they have difficulty acquiring stable operations at even very low levels of functioning (Schmid-Kitsikis, 1976). The severely emotionally disturbed appear to treat each action separately; this prevents them from coordinating activity and structuring thought in a logical way (Schmid-Kitsikis, 1976; Voyat, 1978b).[4]

Severely emotionally disturbed children who suffer from problems related to organic impairment (such as minimal brain dysfunction), however, display a somewhat different pattern. Brill, Weiserbs, and Reid (1978) found that these children try very hard to solve problems but use ineffective and inappropriate means, such as counting the number of sticks in a seriation task. Furthermore, the performance of severely emotionally disturbed children (with or without organic problems) on tasks of conservation, seriation, and class inclusion appears to be correlated with school achievement, especially in mathematics.

Neurotic children, on the other hand, exhibit normal reasoning processes, but those processes are characterized by extreme oscillations between two successive levels of thought. It seems that the level of their motivation to adapt to reality is an important variable in their

[3]It is important to note that these problems cannot be explained in terms of differences in chronological or mental age between mental retardates and normals.

[4]In gifted prepsychotic children, coherent structures do exist.

performances (Inhelder, 1966). Conservation, however, appears to be a particular problem for the emotionally disturbed (Goldschmid, 1967, 1968a; Inhelder, 1966; Miller, Zumoff, & Stephens, 1974).

Expectations for emotionally disturbed youngsters in other areas of cognitive development are not so clear. Howell (1972), for example, found that the emotionally disturbed had greater problems than nondisturbed youngsters on classification tasks, but Filer (1972) suggests that the performance of emotionally disturbed children equals that of normals on cognitive but not on social-cognitive tasks.

Learning Disabilities

Those persons who are of near-average, average, or above-average intelligence but who have problems in the basic processes related to the use of oral or written language are often described as *learning disabled* (National Advisory Committee on Handicapped Children, 1968).[5] Little research using a Piagetian framework has been carried out with such children. It is clear, however, from the work that has been done that learning-disabled children often exhibit difficulties in figurative abilities. If such disturbances in figurative functioning are severe, a delay in operativity may also be apparent (Klees & Lebrun, 1972). Surprising as it may seem, however, these same children have a tendency to persist in the use of figurative (perceptual) strategies even when such strategies are inappropriate. Kershner (1975), for example, found that poor readers could not coordinate multiple cues or reverse perceptual imagery. In addition, poor readers demonstrated both an inability to decentrate and an overconcern with perceptual features.

Learning-disabled children appear to cope with their language-related problems by accompanying language with action and gesture (de Ajuriaguerra, Jaeggi, Guignard, Kocher, Maquard, Paunier, Quinodoz, & Siotis, 1963; Reid & Knight-Arest, 1979) and by subordinating their deficient figurative representations to cognitive operations. Figurative representation, therefore, tends both to slow down the formulation of operations and to become enriched and dominated by them once they are constituted. Some learning-disabled children who have rather subtle difficulties with motor performance (they are referred to as *dyspraxic*) are often quite difficult to test when the test involves the manipulation of objects. When Schmid-Kitsikis (1969, 1972) asked several of these children to seriate a collection of sticks, they were incapable of doing so. Surprisingly, however, they understood both the problem and its solution. They could explain that first one had to find the smallest stick, then the next-smallest stick, and so on. Their problems were not related to their thinking itself but to the actualization of their thinking.

Knight-Arest and Reid (1978) observed similar behaviors when

---

[5]These problems generally manifest themselves in academic areas related to reading, writing, spelling, arithmetic, and mathematics. They don't include handicaps related primarily to sensory deprivation, emotional disturbance, mental retardation, or cultural deprivation.

learning-disabled nonconservers were each asked to pour juice for two classmates (also learning disabled) who conserved liquids. One of the conservers had a glass that was identical to that of the nonconserver, while the other had a taller and thinner glass (see Chapter Seven for a description of similar research carried out with normal children). The learning-disabled nonconservers put too much emphasis on the figurative aspects of the problem. Unlike the normally achieving children, the learning disabled tended to put the glasses next to each other so they could compare juice levels, to use their fingers to mark juice lines, and to move their bodies into a variety of positions (for example, kneeling or squatting) to observe the juice levels from different perspectives (for example, looking through one glass at the levels of the next two, aligned glasses). It was as if they expected the objects themselves to provide the solution to the problem (Reid, 1978).

Also unlike normally achieving children, the learning disabled (who after a discussion with their classmates were able to give conservation responses on a similar task) parroted explanations heard from their peers but were unable to offer new ones. They appeared to have understood the correspondences between the transformations they had observed during the peer discussions and the later task, but they seemed not to have constructed new levels of understanding.

Cerebral Palsy

Cerebral-palsied children progress through the same stages of cognitive development and in the same order as do normal children. Although nonretarded cerebral-palsied children and normal children progress at approximately the same rate, cerebral-palsied children seem to respond more slowly when performing tasks that require manipulation, need more trials, and have a more limited range of interaction with objects and toys, a lower tolerance for frustration, and a need for more encouragement (Tessier, 1970). That children with a motor disability proceed through the stages just as normals do emphasizes the importance of reflexive abstraction as opposed to activity per se (Piaget, 1977f).

Deafness

For a long time it was thought that deaf children suffer significant delays in the acquisition of cognitive structures because of their difficulties in developing language skills (Oléron, 1956; Oléron & Herren, 1961). Furth (1966, 1971, 1973), however, has demonstrated that deaf children and adolescents can perform tasks requiring concrete operations and even formal operations. He argues that, when deaf people understand what they are expected to do (which often requires nonverbal directions as well as training over a rather extended period of time), they exhibit a development lag of only one to two years. Furth attributes this lag to a lack of adequate cultural stimulation, because the deaf perform similarly to impoverished children who have language. Although conventional language, as Piaget has stated, appears to be an important and effective medium for the transmission of information, it is not *necessary* for the development of operations.

Blindness

Findings that blind children exhibit significant delays in cognitive development (see, for example, Hatwell, 1966; Miller, 1969; Freidman & Pasnak, 1973; Stephens, 1977) may result from problems related to the way the research studies were conducted. Generally blind and sighted children were compared on tasks of haptic (tactile plus kinesthetic) perception involving objects and forms. The sighted children, however, were permitted to see the forms. The sighted children often came from urban environments, and the blind children from rural areas. The blind children frequently began school at a later age. When these problems were eliminated (Cromer, 1973), blind children at least conserved at approximately the same age as sighted children, used similar language, and gave similar explanations for their choices. Unfortunately, studies with blind children seem not to have examined areas of cognitive development other than conservation. Equally unfortunate is that the problems with the research designs reflect conditions in the real world that do indeed put blind children at a disadvantage.

Giftedness

Gifted children appear to be superior in the performance of cognitive tasks that are within the capability of their average-IQ peers but don't move at an exceedingly rapid pace through the stages of cognitive development. Elementary-aged gifted children, for example, usually don't attain the level of formal operations, but they far exceed their peers in their ability to perform concrete operational tasks (Lovell, 1968; Webb, 1974). Similarly, gifted 4-year-olds with a mental age of 6 would be less capable on concrete-operational tasks than average 6-year-olds (Brown, 1973). Even older mentally retarded children with a mental age of 7 would be expected to perform better than 5-year-old gifted children of the same mental age (DeVries, 1973). Quite clearly, therefore, the quality of thought is affected by maturation and experience even in gifted children.

Summary

In summary, Genevan-based research has contributed to the understanding of how children in various special populations progress within and between stages. The mentally retarded progress slowly but normally. Their behavior, however, is characterized by rigidity, oscillations, and difficulty in making inferences. Severely emotionally disturbed children, on the other hand, do not follow normal developmental patterns but, in an effort to avoid conflict, transform reality to fit their own subjective views. Neurotic children progress normally, but their reasoning is characterized by fluctuations between higher and lower levels.

Learning-disabled children appear to have problems with figurative understanding. They do, however, compensate for these problems, and, once operational competence is attained, figurative understanding is subordinated to it. The cerebral palsied, the deaf, and the blind appear to proceed through the stages of cognitive development normally and with only minimal delay. The gifted, who might be expected to race through developmental stages, are not actually capable of doing so. They do, however, perform stage-appropriate tasks in a manner that is far superior to that of their average-IQ peers. What is clear from this review is that, with the exception of prepsychotic children, special populations learn in the same way as normals do.

The Contribution of Special-Population Studies to Genetic Epistemology

It is equally important to point out that this research with special populations has provided tests of some key aspects of Piaget's theory and has, therefore, enriched our understanding of normal development. Among other things, it has generally supported the existence of cognitive stages and the importance of both maturational and experiential parameters. A mentally retarded child, for example, with a mental age of 7 may perform better on a cognitive task than a younger, gifted child of the same mental age (DeVries, 1973). Research with both retarded and deaf populations has confirmed that (1) cognitive structures exist that are prerequisite to language development (see Kahn, 1975), (2) although language is important to the transmission of information, it does not play a predominant role in the acquisition of cognitive structures (Furth, 1966, 1971, 1973), and (3) language, like other manifestations of the symbolic function, is subject to the laws of operational development (Sinclair, 1967a).

As previously noted, research with cerebral-palsied children lends support to Piaget's emphasis on the importance of reflexive abstraction in the development of operations rather than on motor activity per se (Tessier, 1970). Schmid-Kitsikis (1969, 1972) has also confirmed the importance of this distinction between reflexive abstraction and physical activity by demonstrating that dysphasic children (those with normal intelligence but with problems related to motor and spatial factors) could solve complex logical problems so long as the problems didn't involve manipulation of materials.

Finally, research with emotionally disturbed children lends credence to Piaget's belief that emotional and intellectual aspects of development cannot be dissociated. This same research, however (Schmid-Kitsikis, 1976; Voyat, 1978; Brill, Weiserbs, & Reid, 1978) questions the *nature* of the relation between these two aspects. Piaget (1965) postulates that affect can modify the conditions under which a child functions but cannot change the nature or level of his or her performance. He therefore suggests a functional rather than structural relation between affect and cognition. Since, however, psychotic children do not progress through the stages of development, it appears that affect may indeed modify cognitive structures.[6]

The Education of Exceptional Children

Typical Strategies

With the exception of the gifted, the predominant orientation toward the education of special populations has been a behavioral one.[7] This theoretical framework suggests that learning is a result of conditioned links, or associations, between events and a person's response to those events. Associations are formed primarily as a function of stimulus conditions that are external to a basically passive student. Translated into a teaching procedure, this approach suggests that three variables—stimulation, response, and reward—must be manipulated by the teacher. The teacher is the responsible agent who must decide what is to be learned by the student and who must provide and manipulate the external stimuli that will lead to the desired learning. The teacher also must determine in advance what student response is required or appropriate. Finally, the teacher seeks methods for rewarding, or reinforcing, correct and desirable responses.

Well-known teaching strategies based on behavioral principles that have found favor among special educators are behavior modification (Wallace & Kauffman, 1978), precision teaching (Bradfield, 1971), and programmed learning (see Engelmann & Bruner, 1969). In these systems, it is necessary to *task analyze* the skill to be learned—that is, to break the task or skill down into an ordered series of component steps and to teach them sequentially. Each step must be a small one, so that students make few errors and can practice correct responses. Students must respond in a prespecified way and must be reinforced as soon as possible by knowledge of the correctness of their responses, by praise and/or attention, and/or by more tangible rewards and privileges. These types of teaching strategies are so widespread in the field of special education that Public Law 94-142 (The Education for All Handicapped Children's Act of 1975) has actually legislated a behavioral approach to the teaching of exceptional children. The law, for example, requires that specific instructional objectives be specified for each child and that statements

---

[6]Further support for a structural relation is offered by Saarni (in press) in her work with affect, cognition, and social expression in infants.

[7]Guilford's (1967) model of the intellect has provided the primary theoretical basis for developing educational strategies for the gifted.

of annual goals be based on the child's current level of functioning (Deshler, 1976).

Proponents of behavioral approaches to teaching have focused on the apparent problems of special children in perception, learning, memory, and language and have put forth considerable effort in devising remedial education programs in these areas. For a number of years, perceptual-training programs (see Frostig & Maslow, 1969; Kephart, 1971; Getman, 1965) were used extensively with special children in hopes that perceptual problems might be ameliorated and that improvement in academic skills might result. After many years of research, these hopes remain unfulfilled (Hammill, 1972). Four misconceptions seem to underlie this emphasis on perception (Reid, 1978). First, as we have pointed out in earlier chapters of this book, although one must be able to "read" the figural aspects of reality (the affirmations), only the student's activity may ensure comprehension of the dynamic quality of transformations. In learning, therefore, the emphasis must be on the operative rather than on the figurative aspects of thought. Second, few educators recognize that children's levels of functioning affect their perceptions and that, since knowledge is gained through successive approximations, errors provide an important foundation for future advances (Ditisheim, 1975; Inhelder, Sinclair, & Bovet, 1974). Closely related to the second point is that the understanding of topological space precedes mastery of Euclidean forms (Piaget & Inhelder, 1967), which suggests that tests asking children to identify or reproduce geometric forms may be inappropriate for young children (Friedland & Meisels, 1975). Finally, perceptual facility is dependent on the child's ability to form mental images from abstractions of space (Piaget, 1969). Making certain attributes more salient, therefore, is of limited value.

Learning has been another area of concern to special educators, particularly in regard to mental retardation, where the problem appears to be most obvious. Iano (1971) points out, however, that even research conducted from a behavioral (or learning) perspective has failed to support a learning-deficiency hypothesis. When comparisons of the performances of normal and retarded children on simple learning tasks were based on mental age (and not on chronological age) retardates often performed as well as normals. Retardates may take longer to begin learning, but they ultimately learn as well as their mental-age peers (Garrison, 1966; Zigler, 1969). Lovell (cited in Garrison, 1966) suggests that, in retarded children, learning occurs *without* concomitant understanding. Lack of understanding contributes to the slower acquisition of general structures, which poses a problem of development and not learning per se (Iano, 1971).

Recent emphasis in special education on memory and language is also based on a behavioral framework that assumes that knowledge is acquired from the environment, that children store copies of reality in memory, and that language is the essential ingredient in both learning and thinking. Language is, however, only one, albeit a very important one, aspect of the symbolic function (see Chapter Four). Memory represents another aspect. Since children do not simply copy reality, what they store in memory is what they have assimilated, which may be more or less accurate or more or less objective. What appears to be faulty memory, therefore, may result from stimulus deformation rather than from inattention or inability to store and retrieve information. The trouble with emphasizing these representational aspects of functioning—memory, language, and perception—has been that the more fundamental, operative aspects of knowing have been all but neglected in special-class curricula.

Hypothesis Testing

An important teaching framework that is familiar to special educators and appears to be compatible with many educational implications of genetic epistemology is the hypothesis-testing approach to learning. A teaching strategy derived from such a theory regards learning as a very highly active process. The student seeks, invents, and discovers rather than respond. Students must make observations, pose problems, construct hypotheses and test them, reformulate hypotheses that have been disconfirmed, and finally construct generalizations.

Imagine a group of young children who have decided to find out which of a group of various items will float. They first put some of the objects in water and observe them. After they have seen several items sink and others float, they may begin to make predictions about the remaining items. Then, one by one, they check their predictions. Finally, they conclude by deriving broad principles—for example, that metal items sink whereas things made of wood float (Kamii, 1971).

What is the teacher's role in such a teaching framework? The teacher must provide a rich and stimulating environment that will lead the children to ask interesting and exciting questions. The teacher must also encourage children and ensure that individual rights are respected. A teacher should also stimulate students into deeper levels of thought. As noted in Chapter Eight, the method of critical exploration may be effective in doing so.

Henderson (1969, pp. 89–90) pointed out the contrasts between teaching strategies derived from behavioral theories and those derived from hypothesis-testing theories (see Figure 9-1). In a hypothesis-testing

Teaching Strategies	
Behavioral	*Hypothesis testing*
The teacher acts on the student.	The student acts on materials.
Activity is defined and directed by the teacher.	Activity is initiated by the student.
Emphasis is on overt behavior.	Emphasis is on thinking.

Figure 9-1. Differences between teaching strategies derived from behavioral theories and teaching strategies derived from hypothesis-testing theories.

system one is not concerned that the children arrive at correct answers. This lack of concern is a very important difference between that system and one that has a behavioral orientation.[8] If you recall, the behaviorists use a step-by-step procedure, so that children can avoid making errors and can practice correct responses. This procedure is supposed to decrease or eliminate altogether a special child's sense of failure. Perhaps it does, but it probably also decreases or even eliminates the child's sense of excitement about learning. Furthermore, since children learn by resolving discrepancies between the givens in a situation and their own mental coordinations, errors are quite important to growth.

Some contents might be appropriately learned in a step-by-step manner, but operational structures are not developed in that way. Recall from Chapter Four that, when a series of dominoes are stood on end and closely aligned, children must understand from the outset the relations among all the dominoes in order to comprehend that a push on the first will tumble the last. A segment-by-segment teaching strategy would fail in this case, because emphasis would necessarily be on the individual parts rather than on the dynamic aspects of the transformation.

Some final benefits of a hypothesis-testing approach to teaching are that children quite naturally work at levels appropriate for them and that they have every opportunity to use their strengths rather than practice in their areas of deficit. Also, teachers who focus on children's self-regulation of their own learning are likely to view the child as a whole rather than in terms of his or her disability.

The Hypothesis-Testing Approach to Spelling and Reading. Perhaps it is clear how a hypothesis-testing approach to learning may apply to the teaching of social studies, science, and arithmetic. But does it have any import for teaching spelling or reading? Morf (cited in Duckworth, 1973) devised a technique for teaching writing and spelling simultaneously by having a child offer a word to be written and then having the children as a group offer all possible spellings for that word. The word *cousin*, for example, might be spelled *kuzin, coosin,* and so forth. Instead of feeling ashamed for making an error, those who suggest unconventional spellings feel clever! The teacher, of course, must point out the conventional spelling, but children then begin to understand how very arbitrary some aspects of language actually are. The children are also acquiring dictionary skills; in order to look up a word, one must be able to generate possible spellings.

Reading might be approached in a similar way. Reading is both a "top-down" and a "bottom-up" process (Adams & Collins, 1977; Rumelhart, 1976). It is "top down" in the sense that the meaning of the print rests with the reader. One can read only if one can bring meaning to the words and sentences that the author has written. Reading, therefore, is an *interaction* between what the reader brings with him or her and the message the author has attempted to encode in the print. Reading is a construction. The "bottom-up" part of reading is comprehending the

[8]One would not, for example, expect 6-year-olds to be able to determine *why* objects float, even if they were to ask that question themselves.

graphic presentation. No past experience can be brought to bear if the reader is unable to crack the code of the marks on the page that lies before him or her.[9]

Unfortunately, especially among special and remedial educators, the assumption has been made that reading consists primarily of decoding written language into oral language. Considerable emphasis has been placed on analytic and synthetic strategies for sounding words or recognizing their parts—strategies usually carried out as drills and using words in isolation. Rubin (in press) has shown quite clearly, however, that reading is much more than the translation of visual stimuli into oral language. Many conventions and syntactic structures are used almost exclusively in written language. "Top-down" processes—for example, those that utilize semantic and syntactic cues—can greatly aid in the interpretation of print.

Also, emphasis on the part of special educators has been on the perceptual aspects of reading. This approach is most likely a dangerous one, because deficient readers, as noted earlier, tend to persist in the use of highly perceptual strategies even after such strategies are no longer appropriate. As Goodman (1976) and Smith (1975) suggest, children may profitably be directed to make predictions regularly throughout the reading of a passage and to check those predictions by reading the text for meaning. This procedure is clearly a function of reflexive abstraction.

In sum, a hypothesis-testing approach to teaching appears to be consonant with the implications that Genevan theory has for education. There are, however, two major differences in emphasis. First, the Genevans attribute a more crucial role to contradiction and conflict than do the hypothesis-testing theorists. Second, for Genevans the resolution of conflict provides its own motivation. Piaget (1976b) has shown, for example, that only the initial goal is given when children are asked to perform a task. Intermediate goals are derived by the children themselves as they tackle problems and struggle with contradictions.

Conclusions

Although Piaget has sought to describe structures common to all children, other Genevans have used his theoretical framework to great advantage in examining individual differences. Deviations from normal development may be viewed as limitations resulting from one or more of the four factors of development—maturation, physical experience, social experience, and equilibration—and affecting their interaction. Genevan theory supplies a developmental sequence not tied to age and focusing on mechanisms of change. Its emphasis on equilibration helps educators focus on the children's *capabilities.*

[9]For an elaboration of reading as an interaction process see J. M. Gallagher, "Problems in Applying Piaget to Reading, or Letting the Bird Out of the Cage," *Journal of Education,* 1979, *161,* 72–87.

Research comparing groups of special children (specifically the mentally retarded, the prepsychotic, the neurotic, the learning disabled, the cerebral palsied, the deaf, the blind, and the gifted) to normals of the same chronological and mental ages, as well as research examining the variations in the process of equilibration within each group, has provided a basis for understanding the compensations that special children tend to make between their accommodations to environmental stimuli and their internal assimilatory schemes. All children except the seriously emotionally disturbed follow normal developmental patterns. Generally exceptional children progress through the same stages of development and in the same order as normal children. Although variations in rate, final stage attained, and quality of within-stage performance may exist, the process of equilibration is similarly effective in special children in producing higher levels of functioning (Reid, in press-b).

For some time special educators, like their peers in regular education (see Chapter Eight), appeared to believe that the value of genetic epistemology for education was twofold. First, special educators looked for ways to teach special children the Piagetian research tasks on which they performed so poorly. Second, they attempted to determine the stage levels of the exceptional children with whom they worked in an effort to devise developmentally appropriate curricula. Neither strategy proved effective. Teaching exceptional children to conserve or to seriate did not, of course, increase their aptitudes for academic learning. Furthermore, children exhibit time lags at all levels of development; thus, limiting all tasks and interventions to a particular "stage" was too strict an interpretation. Genetic epistemology does, however, offer special educators interesting and profitable methods of examining educationally relevant behaviors as they occur spontaneously in exceptional children (Reid, Knight-Arest, & Hresko, in press).

Finally, although Genevans have concentrated on understanding and explaining spontaneous learning within the context of development, much of their work has clear implications for academic learning. Rather than emphasizing representational skills as behavioral models do, Genevan theory suggests that operational aspects of thought be encouraged. A hypothesis-testing approach to teaching that includes the inducement of conflict/contradiction appears compatible with Genevan theory. Current procedures that lead children step-by-step through learning activities are probably less effective than those that foster choice, anticipation, and the testing of predictions. Active problem solving leads quite naturally to conflict and contradiction, which encourage the child to set additional goals and ask new questions spontaneously. Exceptional children, with the exception of the gifted, may require considerable guidance in their efforts toward compensation. Since Genevan theory encourages teachers to attend to that system of compensation, it promises to provide a new and vital key to educational programming for special populations.

Epilogue

The goal of the preceding chapters was not to give a comprehensive account or an overview of Piaget's theory. The goal was to highlight those aspects of his theory that might prove most relevant to professionals concerned with applying Piaget's ideas in order to better understand and guide children's learning. Because Bärbel Inhelder, through her own research and her collaborative efforts with Piaget, has had a strong influence on the elements of the theory most directly applicable to learning and education, we have drawn heavily on her findings. We have not attempted to draw bold lines between segments of children's developmental achievements; rather, we have emphasized that development is a process closely resembling an ever-widening spiral. That is not to say that stage-related characteristics are nonexistent; but the fact is that they contribute minimally to our understanding of learning. The important question in learning is *how* something occurs. Thus, our major concern has been with the mechanisms of transition—the means by which children progress within and between stages.

We have described two types of learning. One is learning in the strict sense, in which knowledge is gained through direct environmental experience, especially experience with objects, persons, and the culture at large. But Piaget has cautioned that even learning in the strict sense must necessarily occur within a developmental framework. In order to be able to learn, children must have the capacity to assimilate new experience or information; their level of development colors their interpretations of environmental events as our examples in Chapter One clearly show. Learning, therefore, also occurs in a broader sense and results from the interplay among maturation, experience, and the process of self-regulation Piaget has called equilibration. In the course of this broader process of learning, the child first attempts to apply an assimilative scheme to a situation in which such a scheme is either inappropriate or inadequate. As a result, several possible alternatives occur.

The child may be unable to see the existence of a conflict. Piaget (1974b) has given the example of a child who observes the reflected images of two letters (*R* and *A*, presented simultaneously on the same card) in a mirror. The child explains the fact that *R* appears reversed but *A* does not as a selective process on the part of the mirror. For this child the phenomenon doesn't deserve a second thought: the mirror has simply chosen to do it that way! In other words, there is no conflict.

Later, however, conflict does occur as the child recognizes that there is something striking about the reversal of only one letter. The conflict is likely to make the child seek an explanation that solves the problem. Piaget has described the means the child uses to find a solution as a process of achieving exact compensation between affirmations and negations. The affirmations (the empirical facts) tell the child that one letter appears to have been reversed and the other does not. There is nothing in the empirical data, however, that enables the child to understand why. The child, therefore, must *construct* negations (what is not empirically present) through the process of reflexive abstraction. Reflexive abstraction entails the projection of what is taken from a lower level (for example, motor) onto a higher level (for example, thought) and the drawing of inferences that allow the child to reorganize his or her knowledge. Thus, the child will begin to realize that the mirror has no magical powers and that the reason for the apparent contradiction lies within the nature of the letters themselves. There is then a gradual construction of the understanding that the mirror images of symmetrical letters appear unchanged whereas those of asymmetrical letters are reversed.

It is during the construction of the rule that learning takes place. But it is not just learning in the strict sense. Experience is central to learning, because it enables the child to modify the original theory with which he or she has begun the task. But experience is not enough to induce learning. The child's current level of functioning plays the predominant role in determining how he or she interprets environmental events. Only after the rule is constructed does the child achieve a new level of thinking in which he or she is able to *anticipate* the result of holding the "*R* and *A* card" up to the mirror, so that no disturbance is experienced at all.

Our discussion of the stages of development has offered new interpretations of many well-known examples of stage-appropriate behavior in accordance with Piaget's recent explanation of equilibration (in terms of the compensation between affirmations and negations in response to disturbances). The process of construction of knowledge begins with the beginning of life. There is substantial growth in intelligence before language is acquired, and this growth derives from the child's activity rather than from his or her perceptions or observations. From the reflexes and spontaneous movements of the first month after birth, the child progresses to the development of habits, then to the coordination of schemes and means/ends relations, then to the discovery of new means for problem solving, and, finally, to the creation of new combinations of actions never practiced before. These combinations of actions are achieved not through the gropings of trial and error but through what appears to be sudden comprehension.

We have looked at the level of preoperations as both the extension of the sensorimotor period and the basis for the more complex constructions of the concrete-operational level. This stage of development is generally described in terms of what the child is lacking, especially conservation. Our focus has been instead on the positive characteristics of the stage and on the manner in which such characteristics provide the link between the earlier sensorimotor structures and those that will come later.

Two major learning tools that develop during this period are the symbolic and the constituent functions. The symbolic function—the ability to represent internally what is derived from sensorimotor schemes—refers to the child's use of language, gestures, symbolic play, imitation, and any other means of representation. Although Piaget does not underplay the role of language in development, he does argue that language, like other symbolic abilities, is the outgrowth of sensorimotor schemes and not the source of knowledge. In fact, symbolic play (often in combination with language) appears to be children's most active vehicle for structuring reality. The constituent function—the second tool to develop during this period—is based on one-way correspondences (rather than on reversibility) and qualitative (rather than quantitative) identity. Like the symbolic function, the constituent function grows out of sensorimotor action schemes. The mechanism that makes the development of both the symbolic and the constituent functions possible is that of correspondence. Correspondences are instruments of comparison that are basic to the understanding of relations and transformations.

The period of concrete operations is characterized by the child's ability to use operational structures (internalized actions that are reversible). No abrupt change occurs between the stages of preoperations and concrete operations; like all other transitions between stages, development is gradual. At the level of concrete operations, children are able not only to understand and recognize the correspondence between prior and current states but to grasp transformations. Reversibility provides insight into the linkage between states.

The level of formal operations, being the highest level of development described by Piaget, is often thought of as the end point of development. It is not. Rather, it is the level at which form is freed of content and the "opening up of possibilities" reaches its acme. The four transformations—identity, negation, reciprocity, and correlativity—are all integrated, so that operations on operations become possible. There is no end point—in this or any other stage—in the sense that a stable equilibrium is finally attained. Instead, each successive level leads to the ability to reorganize and enrich past understandings. The difference between formal- and concrete-operational thinking lies in the strategies used in problem solving. At the level of formal operations a systematic exploration of all alternatives takes place in accordance with an overall plan; the ability to combine and separate variables enables understanding of their interrelations; and the ability to work within a hypothetical-deductive framework makes it possible for a reasonable possibility to be recognized before any real test is carried out. In short, reversible maneuvering between reality and possibility can now occur.

The examination of various research approaches that have contributed to our understanding of learning brought us to some conclusions—and serious questions—about the types of instructional systems currently popular in English-speaking countries. Many Anglo-American researchers are often puzzled by the purposes and outcomes of Genevan research on learning. Americans stress the acceleration of the acquisition of skills and knowledge and emphasize instructional strategies based on empirical facts. The Genevans don't share these interests. Their studies examine learning as a mechanism of development. They are interested not so much in how empirical facts and skills are acquired but in the way children learn through reflexive abstraction—that is, about the form of knowledge.

Our examination of learning in three types of conflict situations (between predictions and outcome, between subsystems, and between differing views of persons) has indicated that what progress results from any given learning experience is dependent on the child's initial level of competence and that learning in one cognitive area, such as class inclusion, facilitates learning in another, such as conservation. Although the child's own activity is the major impetus for growth, the environment plays a key role in learning by promoting interest and conflict. Furthermore, the Genevans have demonstrated that a child's performance of an activity is not an indication that he understands what he is doing. Learning occurs from the periphery—that is, from the accommodation to objects—to the center—that is, to the ability to use past experience to anticipate results. Knowledge, then, is attained through successive approximations but not in the behavioral sense. The gap between physical and mental coordinations is reduced by *successive wholes*. The ability to anticipate (internal regulation) constitutes the crucial link between practical activity and conceptualization.

What relevance does all of this have for education? There is no one-to-one correspondence between the principles described by Piaget and Inhelder and instructional strategies. Tasks and stage descriptions do not constitute the aspects of Piaget's theory that are most important for educators. This book has consistently emphasized that seeking ways to facilitate reflexive abstraction is the key to fostering growth. The mechanisms of growth depend on contradiction to spark the child's rethinking and reorganization. An adaptation of the method of critical exploration has proven useful in stimulating such a rethinking and reorganization. Only when teachers understand the child's thinking can they engage in the kinds of intense interpersonal dialogues that can lead the child to higher levels of functioning.

But dialogue is not enough. Children must generate hypotheses, test them, and reformulate them when the hypotheses are disconfirmed; then, children must construct generalizations based on the results of their activity. While some hypothesis-testing methods have been used with normal and gifted children, these techniques have seldom been advocated for handicapped children. Yet, since handicapped children proceed through the same stages of development as do normals, with only variations in rate and quality of within-stage performance, there appears to be ample evidence to suggest that special children make effective use of inductive strategies in their spontaneous development. Teaching strategies have simply failed to take advantage of these abilities and have focused instead on the perceptual and/or representational aspects of learning.

It is clear that earlier attempts to apply Piagetian theory to education have been clouded by misinterpretations of the theory as well as by a too-direct transference of stage and task variables from epistemological theory to the realm of educational practice. Whether the future holds brighter prospects is uncertain. More and more frequently teachers express concern about children for whom the traditional curricula are inappropriate, about children who have difficulty "behaving" properly because schooling appears to have little relevance for them, and about children who forget one day what they have learned the day before.

When these concerns were first voiced, the initial response was an openness to new curricula and new instructional strategies. But for most teachers and many children the "new math" and the "new social studies" didn't work out. These instructional strategies often entailed rigorous programs of training in logical deduction that had little appeal for the teachers and even less for the children, whose ways of thinking had little in common with such programs. In short, a whole new set of problems was created. Rather than evaluate these new programs for what was good in them, try to improve them, and learn from previous mistakes, the educational establishment (backed by local and national legislatures) has now retreated "back to basics" and for many children that means back to skills and drills. The educational climate, therefore, may not be conducive to the implementation of our message.

But, although educators may lull themselves into temporary complacency by concentrating on behavioral objectives that define particles of behavior that we are certain we can "teach," the old questions of appropriateness, relevance, and forgetting are likely to rear their heads again and again until teachers stop concentrating on programs and packages and begin concentrating on children. As professionals intimately concerned with the application of psychology to education, and perhaps also as incurable optimists, we are hopeful that continued disturbances will lead to a reorganization of thinking among educators and that at least some educators will find direction in the learning theory of Piaget and Inhelder.

Equilibration

Although Piaget has argued that equilibration constitutes the central concept of his theory, it was not until 1975 that he published *L'Équilibration des structures cognitives,* a book devoted entirely to an explanation of that concept. As Gallagher (1977) notes in her description of the biological, logical, and cybernetic roots of the concept of equilibration, North-Americans have tended to ignore equilibration (dismissing it as "frustrating," "useless," and "misleading") and to emphasize instead the concept of stages. What these psychologists failed to grasp is that equilibration "is not a cumbersome fourth factor [of development] but *the* regulator or prime instrument without which knowledge acquisition is impossible" (p. 29; italics in original).

This primacy accounts both for our focusing so heavily on the concept of equilibration in our discussion of learning and for our decision to provide a more extensive, formal description of the models of equilibration for our advanced readers. The purpose of this appendix is threefold: (1) to illustrate the formal models as Piaget has recently described them, (2) to discuss the relationship among the models, and (3) to describe Piaget's earlier formulation of equilibration in order to draw comparisons between the earlier and the more recent models. The diagrams are all reprinted with the permission of Viking Penguin, Inc., from the English translation of the text on equilibration entitled *The development of thought: Equilibrium of cognitive structures* (Piaget, 1977b).

The Models of Equilibration

Illustrations used in the less formal description of the models presented in Chapter Three will be reintroduced here using Piaget's system of notation. One caveat is in order before the models are described: the use of a formal notational system should not be construed as indicating that these are functions of formal logic or mathematics. As Piaget notes (1970b, p. 723),

> When a psychologist computes the variance of a sample, . . . it does not mean his field has become statistics. . . . To analyze structures, . . . since we are not dealing with quantities, we . . . resort to more general mathematical instruments. . . . But they are only instruments which allow us to reach genuinely psychological entities.

The formal notational system is, then, simply a convenience for the description of psychological functions—that is, interiorized actions or coordinations of actions.

Model IA

Recall that this elementary level of equilibration occurs when children observe the results of their own activity in a situation in which they are interacting with objects. In the example of a child rolling a ball, the formal notational system is the following: Ms refers to the child's movement—the activity of striking or pushing the ball (see Figure A-1).

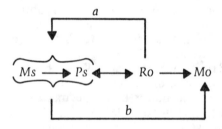

Figure A-1. Model IA. (From *The Development of Thought: Equilibrium of Cognitive Structures*, by J. Piaget. Copyright © 1977 by Viking Penguin, Inc. Reprinted by permission of Viking Penguin, Inc.)

Ps refers to the intensity of that thrust. On the other side of the "equation" are descriptors relating to the object. Ro refers to the resistance of the object—in this case the weight of the ball being pushed—which acts as a kind of filtering system to regulate the actual distance the ball will roll (Mo or movement of the object).

In such a simple activity two covariations may be observed. The first, denoted a, indicates that the intensity of the thrust is dependent on the anticipated magnitude of the resistance the object will offer. One would certainly exert greater effort in attempting to roll a bowling ball than a ping-pong ball for the same distance. Finally, the covariation b describes the relation between the magnitude of the thrust and the actual distance the ball will travel. Simply put, regardless of the size of the ball, it takes a harder push to make it go further. By observing both their own activity and the movement of the ball, children can discover that the distance the ball travels is related to the intensity of the thrust and that it takes a harder push to move a bigger ball. No inferences are necessary. The logico-mathematical structures the child has already achieved enable him or her to observe those facts.

Model IB

In contrast to the first model described, Model IB is not related to the type of situation in which children cause objects to react. In the IB model there is no expenditure of energy. Instead, children operate on objects by attributing logico-mathematical forms to them. If we take one of the examples given in Chapter Three—that of a child grouping "objects to write with"—*As* refers to the child's activity or operation—for example, classification. *Fs* is the actual form the child attempts to apply—in this case the class of "things to write with" (see Figure A-2). The second side of

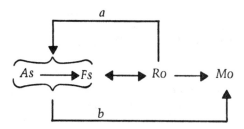

Figure A-2. Model IB. (From *The Development of Thought: Equilibrium of Cognitive Structures*, by J. Piaget. Copyright © 1977 by Viking Penguin, Inc. Reprinted by permission of Viking Penguin, Inc.)

the "equation" remains the same as in the IA model. In this case, however, the resistance of the object refers to the object's "submission" or "refusal" to being placed into such a group. A fork, for example, would not fit well into such a category. In the case of the IB model, *Mo*, instead of being actual movement, refers to the enrichment of the objects by being so classified. The covariations also remain the same as in the IA model. The class being attributed is, of course, based on the perception of the submission of the objects to being classified. The enrichment of the objects is dependent on the classification selected.

What differentiates the IA and IB models is that in the IA model there is an expenditure of energy that is lost to the child. In the IB model there is no necessary expenditure of energy; nothing is lost to the child. There is instead the development of a correspondence (or morphism) between the child's operation and the objects. In effect, both sides of the equation become "things to write with." Once again, however, there is no need to make inferences. The child already has the logico-mathematical knowledge that enables him or her to "read" those observables.

Model IIA

The level-II models refer to situations in which inferences are necessary. Children not only observe their actions but make inferences about how and why these actions have the effects they have. In Chapter Three we gave the example of children attempting to release a ball from a sling, so that it lands in a designated target (a box). The *Obs. S* in the formal notational system refers to what is observable about the child's activity—both the *M*s and the *P*s of the IA model (see Figure A-3). The

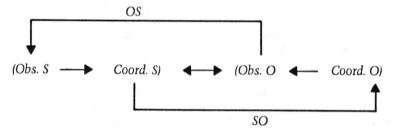

Figure A-3. Model IIA. (From *The Development of Thought: Equilibrium of Cognitive Structures*, by J. Piaget. Copyright © 1977 by Viking Penguin, Inc. Reprinted by permission of Viking Penguin, Inc.)

child is able to observe both his or her activity and its intensity—both the swinging of the sling and the releasing of the ball. *Obs. O* refers to what is observable about the objects—that is, the position of the box and the movement and place of landing of the ball. *OS* refers to the covariations (*a* and *b*) that can be observed between the child's actions and the resultant behavior of the ball. Although *OS* can be thought of as indicating a mutual influence between the actions of the child and the response of the objects, the *Obs. O* to *Obs. S* is the dominant direction. That is because the only way that children can learn about their own actions is to observe their effect on objects. As we noted in the discussion of the research on becoming conscious of the elements of a problem, awareness takes place from the periphery to the center. That means that the observation of what happens to objects is what makes the inferential coordinations possible.

What is new in the level-II models is the introduction of inferential coordinations. These are referred to as *Coord. S*, the inferential coordinations children make about their own actions, and *Coord. O*, the inferences they make about why and how objects respond as they do. The development of these coordinations is generally quite gradual and consists of the reconstruction on a conceptual level of what was previously carried out on a practical level. The reader will recognize that process as reflexive abstraction. Recall that the children propelling a ball into a target with a sling were able to succeed at a very early age. They moved the target to one side or the other where they anticipated the ball to be falling, or they moved their bodies to compensate for the trajectory of the ball. On a practical level, they had solved the problem. But when they were asked to explain what they had done, it became clear that a practical solution was not enough to enable them to understand why moving to one side or the other, moving the box, or releasing the ball at a different point in the rotation worked. Most of the children were able to observe their own actions and the effects that they had on the objects. But only the older children succeeded in explaining the problem. By making hypotheses and checking them and rechecking them and then reformulating new hypotheses and retesting, they had constructed on a conceptual level what they had previously mastered only practically.

The process *SO* in the model expresses the fact that the child can understand causal relationships only through the intermediary of his or her own operations (or preoperations). Children who have achieved reversibility, for example, will interpret the observables differently than do children limited to constituent functions (see Chapter Four for a discussion of constituent functions). As operational competence increases, the nature of the observables—that is, what the child is able to read as facts, characteristics, and so on—actually changes. One child may "see" that the ball makes a sharp turn to enter the target (see Figure 7-3 in Chapter Seven). Others "see" the trajectory as a long smooth curve. Still others "see" the ball continue from the point of release in a straight line. What is observed is dependent on what is already known. Conversely, what is observed enables the child to construct increasingly more accurate concepts.

There are then local feedback arrangements (anticipations and retroactions), which allow the content (or exogenous knowledge) to interact with forms (the endogenous construction). Because causal relations extend beyond what is actually observable, inferences are always necessary for their understanding. The level-I models are artificial and constitute only a special case of the level-II models. The interactions of level-II models are the constituents of a sequential process of equilibration that leads to progressively more advanced states, although it should be noted that errors and regressions do occur. It is this *progressive* movement from lesser to more advanced states that Piaget (1977b) has called *équilibration majorante*—a process that is continuously augmentative and ever heightening.

Model IIB

Model IIB has the same form as model IIA above but refers to the application of operations rather than causal explanations. Type-IIB equilibration involves the application and coordination of operations where inferences are necessary to understand the logic of an interaction. The research done with the Hanoi Tower illustrates equilibration of this type (Piaget, 1976b). Here, the children move different-sized discs from one peg to another without violating the rule that a larger disc can never be placed on a smaller one. The development of a plan to transfer the discs from peg to peg (*Obs. S*) is facilitated by observations of what happens when the discs are actually moved (*Obs. O*) (see Figure A-4). *Obs. O* then serves as a check on *Obs. S.* Verification (comparing the transfer plan with the results of implementation) enables children to make inferential coordinations related to their own actions (*Coord. S*). The level of the children's anticipatory scheme will determine their degree of reliance on *Obs. O* and the accuracy of their inferences.

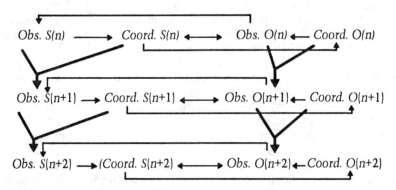

Figure A-4. Equilibration majorante. (From *The Development of Thought: Equilibrium of Cognitive Structures,* by J. Piaget. Copyright © 1977 by Viking Penguin, Inc. Reprinted by permission of Viking Penguin, Inc.)

As each new coordination results from the action of previous coordinations, the augmentative nature of the equilibrations becomes clear (see Figure A-4). Each trial of moving the discs represents a construction at one level that provides support for reconstruction at higher levels. Because the objects (in this case, discs) do not operate independently of the child as with a causal interaction, a correspondence must be developed between the object coordinations (*Coord. O*) and the child's operations (*Coord. S*).

Model IIC

The final model of equilibration is relevant to situations in which causal interactions occur among or between objects. The role of the child is to *understand* the causal relationship and not to intervene in it. The example we presented in Chapter Three is one used by Piaget himself— the interaction between an astronomer and the movement of the heavenly bodies. The difference between this model and the IIA and IIB models is that: (1) *Obs. S* is deleted, since the child performs no actions, and (2) *Obs. S* and *Obs. O* are replaced by *Obs. X* and *Obs. Y,* the observation of two objects—for the purpose of illustration, let's say the moon and a planet (see Figure A-5). Furthermore, the *OS* covariation is replaced by a *YX* relation that indicates that what is observed as the

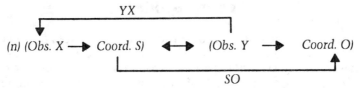

Figure A-5. Model IIC. (From *The Development of Thought: Equilibrium of Cognitive Structures*, by J. Piaget. Copyright © 1977 by Viking Penguin, Inc. Reprinted by permission of Viking Penguin, Inc.)

movement of the moon is a function of the movement of the other celestial bodies. Since the child must interpret the movement of the heavenly bodies in terms of his or her own operations (or preoperations), *Coord. S* remains. Similarly, because it is the coordination of inferences about the behavior of the objects that enables the causal relation to be attributed, *Coord. O* is equally appropriate. If the causal relation that is attributed is in agreement with what actually occurs, the child experiences equilibrium. If not, the contradiction will lead to attempts to revise the explanations until better systems are constructed. Again, the augmentative nature of the equilibration is apparent (see Figure A-4).

Relations among the Models

One common error of interpretation that is made regarding the five models of equilibration is that there is some hierarchical relation among them. This is not the case. The level-I models are not true models of equilibration, because there is never an instance in which the reading of observables is not dependent on prior knowledge. Endogenous under-standings always control what is observed. That is why observables are subjective rather than objective phenomena. We all assimilate objects and events into our own structures. The level-I models, therefore, are simply a special case of the level-II models.

By assuming that a person is at a given level of development and that previous operational achievements enable a direct reading of an object or event, Piaget was able to use the level-I models as a means of simplifying aspects of the very complex interactions he labels as *level II*. The level-II models describe interactions in which the children acquire knowledge about (1) the causal effects of their own actions, (2) the attribution of operational systems, and (3) the causal effects of objects on each other. These levels, therefore, cannot be interpreted in the same way that levels IA, IB, IIA, IIB, and so forth can be interpreted in the analysis of stages of functioning on experimental tasks. They are instead descriptions of different kinds of interactions.

Contrasts between the Earlier and the More Recent Models

Perhaps the best way to clarify the major differences between the older and the more recent models of equilibration is to use the conservation-of-substance experiment as an illustration. Previously, Piaget (1957, 1970b, pp. 725–726) had described the development of conservation in the following way: because the probability of considering only one dimension is greater, the child at first notices only that the ball of clay is longer after it has been changed into a sausage. If the sausage is very long or if the child tires of giving the same argument in the face of repeated questioning, the probability of her noticing the second dimension is increased. She will then alternate between the two. Once the two dimensions are noticed, the probability of noticing a correlation between them is increased. Noticing the correlation enables the child to focus on transformations rather than on static states. Once transformations are taken into account, the probability that she will notice that the transformation can be reversed is increased. Operational reversibility is achieved when the two transformations of widening and lengthening are seen as exactly compensatory. Equilibration was then described by Piaget as a process based on *increasing, sequential probabilities.*

In his more recent description of the development of conservation (described at length in Chapter Five of this book), Piaget takes into account the relationship between affirmations and negations. First, children concentrate on affirmations—the positive, present, observable characteristics of objects and events. They notice that the clay ball has become longer. Negations refer to what the children must construct—in this case, the reduction of thickness. As in the early explanation, the covariation between the lengthening and the thinning must be observed before an exact compensation between the affirmations and the negations can be achieved. Although the model is still to some extent one of sequential probabilities, it is primarily explained as the progressive substitution of endogenous (the negations) for exogenous (the affirmations) knowledge. Although accommodations are often the result of interactions with objects, people, and events, they are controlled by a "reaction norm" (see Chapter Two for a full discussion of this point). It is, then, the child's activity and not chance environmental events that control development and therefore learning.

Piaget (1977b) lists five additional advantages of the elaborated description of equilibration. First, the more recent description applies to causality as well as to the development of the child's operations. Piaget had previously restricted his discussions of equilibration to an explanation of the development of logico-mathematical knowledge. Second, the elaborated models can account for any number of observables and coordinations. Third, each temporary state of equilibrium includes a balance not only between the subject and the object but also between the observables and the coordinations. Fourth, Piaget has now described two potential outcomes of equilibration. One possibility is the stabilization of the equilibrium, either through an accurate response or through error. The second is disequilibrium (again, either through improved conceptualization or through error), which would motivate the search for a better state of equilibrium. Finally, and most importantly, the elaborated models demonstrate quite clearly that there is an interaction between the observables (empirical abstractions) and the coordinations (reflexive abstractions) from the outset.

Speeches by Piaget and Inhelder

Genetic Epistemology and Developmental Psychology

Bärbel Inhelder

Department of Psychology
University of Geneva

The genesis of knowledge, the productivity of the human mind, and its ceaseless inventions and discoveries have always been the central theme of Piaget's theoretical and experimental work in epistemology and psychology. His conceptual approach to these great problems has led to a highly consistent system, which nevertheless is in constant evolution. Growth in the biological sense, with both conservation and transformation of structures, is also the main characteristic of the human mind, and figures prominently in Piaget's theory. Piaget himself seems to have wanted to make this perfectly clear: the subject he chose for this year's research at the International Center for Genetic Epistemology is how the child comes to envisage an ever-wider range of possibilities while simultaneously building up a concept of what is logically necessary.

Although Piaget's publications are widely disseminated, many psychologists find his work difficult to understand. This is partly due, I believe, to the interdisciplinary character of most of Piaget's research; he sets out to solve epistemological problems experimentally by combining

From "The Roots of American Psychology: Historical Influences and Implications for the Future," edited by R. W. Rieber and K. Salzinger, *Annals* of the New York Academy of Sciences, 1977. Reprinted by permission.

the developmental approach with critical studies of the history of science and by using models based on logic, mathematics, and biological cybernetics. This multidimensional approach leads to a remarkably broad perspective of the laws and mechanisms of cognitive development; yet psychology proper has for Piaget always been a by-product of his genetic epistemology, as was stressed by the American Psychology Association when its annual award went to Jean Piaget.

Early Works and Influences

Since this symposium is concerned with the historical background of contemporary psychology, I should like first of all to sketch the initial steps that gradually led Piaget forward; he himself, by the way, maintains that he has never tried to build up a system, but has merely attempted to coordinate the results and interpretations of his many pieces of research, to explain certain key notions, to discern their epistemological significance, and to open up new directions for research.

Piaget took a Ph.D. in zoology and, as he is wont to remark, his only degrees in psychology are honorary. His first steps in psychology and epistemology were undoubtedly influenced by Immanuel Kant and, more directly, by Leon Brunschvicz, James Marc Baldwin, and Pierre Janet, who, like Freud, was a pupil of Charcot. "The children studied by Piaget are young Immanuel Kants and Piaget himself is a young Immanuel Kant grown old," as the Swiss philosopher Jean-Claude Piguet remarked. Writing many volumes on the development of the categories of space, time, and causality, and on number and logic, Piaget chose his problems outside the traditional fields of experimental psychology. He does not use an *a priori* interpretative framework: in line with the biological methods and concepts of his malacological studies, he reaches a kind of dynamic, one might say biological, Kantism, and sees the mechanisms by which knowledge is constructed in an epigenetic perspective; the structures inherent in the subject are considered to be the result of progressive constructions due to the interaction of endogenous regulatory mechanisms and the impact of variations in the environment.

Brunschvicg's influence on Piaget was exerted principally through the former's critical relativism and his historicocritical method of analysis of the laws of evolution and revolution that characterize the progress of mathematics and physics. Since every scientist is first a child who has to discover once more the fundamental concepts of reason, Piaget studied the origins of knowledge in children. Yet, his aim was not to establish a direct parallel between cognitive development and the course of scientific thought, but to look for common mechanisms. Despite the structural differences between the elementary stages of child thought and the higher levels of human reason, many common functional mechanisms have been brought to light.

A number of Piaget's ideas and interests have sprung from Baldwin's work. Baldwin's theoretical project of founding a "genetic logic" has, in a sense, found experimental actualization in Piaget's research. Moreover,

Baldwin's insistence on the social factor in the construction of reason is reflected in Piaget's early work, where the notion of progressive decentration starting from a lack of differentiation between the young child's own point of view and that of others is elaborated, and in which the role of cooperation with their peers in the constitution of logical norms and autonomous morality is stressed. Even in his recent botanical work, in which he is concerned with organic selection, Piaget's findings are once again in agreement with the "Baldwin effect."

The constructivist hypothesis that is gradually refined and enriched in many of Piaget's works finds its clearest expression in the notion of stages in cognitive development. The concept of stages can be traced back to Janet's influence. Janet, while studying what he called "illness of belief" (hysteria and psychasthenia), which he considered to be a disintegration of the synthesis of mental energy, conceived a system of hierarchical stages in mental development. His frequent discussions with his friend Baldwin may well have roused Janet's interest in the development of intelligence in children, the origins of which he placed before the beginning of language.

At first, the concept of stages was used by Piaget as a useful heuristic with which to account for the successive, qualitatively different forms of a construction process; later, the developmental stages define equilibrium states in a continuous process of cognitive structurations whose formation is ordered so that each construction having attained a state of relative equilibrium opens up new possibilities, each step in the process being necessary for the subsequent one.

This conception of stages—which in essence is biological— paralleled embryological and epigenetic processes that have been variously accounted for by concepts such as competence, chreodes, homeorhesis, and so on.

Sensorimotor Development

Piaget's[1, 2] studies on the sensorimotor origins of intelligence were a first example of a synthesis between epistemology and constructivist psychology with biological foundations. Some thirty years later, this first approach was further developed within the framework of modern biology in his work "Biology and Knowledge."[3] Recently, Piaget published a new volume on the same subject, "Adaptation vitale et psychologie de l'intelligence,"[26] which aims to show the existence of a functional continuity between organic and psychological structures, the latter being considered as a special case of biological adaptation; psychological structures show the same kind of reciprocal relationship between assimilation and accommodation as organic structures do, but go further since they can generate new structures.

During the preverbal, sensorimotor period, a certain logic of actions, but without any extension, is built up and lays the foundations for later development of logic and of knowledge of reality. The infant who perceives and manipulates objects does not simply establish associations: because the objects are integrated into his actions, the infant recognizes them and can generalize from one action-situation to another. The fundamental psychological fact is, in this view, assimilation: assimilation between action schemes and objects, but also between different action-schemes that become coordinated and thus prepare what later will be logical operations.[5] The infant establishes correspondences; from the point of view of "putting into," a small box and a little ball are equivalent, since they can both be put into a large box, and he will repeatedly carry out this action, first with the small box, then with the little ball; the infant also notes differences in properties—the same little box and small ball are different, since he can put his finger inside the one but not inside the other, and he will repeatedly poke his finger into the ball and then put it inside the box. Primitive "intersections" are discovered: certain objects (a ball, a round pencil) can be pushed so that they roll along by themselves; others (a small ruler, a spoon) can be stuck into a lump of clay: and, surprise, the pencil can be both an object to be rolled and an object to be a stuck into something else.

Reciprocal assimilations of such nascent systems of action introduce a certain consistency into the immediate concrete universe of the child and lead to the more complex constructions that presage the culmination of the sensorimotor period, such as the capacity of spatial orientation (for the one-year-old, within his immediate environment) according to a system that Poincaré called the "group of displacements" and that, according to him, plays a part in all effective actions. Piaget has shown how this capacity is constructed during the first year or so of the baby's life, in close connection with the construction of the first cognitive invariant, object-permanency, and with the development of sensorimotor intelligence. Thus, the first fundamental forms of knowledge are constructed before the appearance of language and Piaget showed the important part played by the interaction between the infant and his environment. This research, which was published as early as 1936 and 1937, aroused great interest among Freudians such as David Rapaport, Peter Wolff, Thérèse Gouin Decarie, and Sybille Escalona.

From Sensorimotor Intelligence to the Operations of Thought

At some time during the second year of life, this first logic of actions with its principle of invariants and structures of movement in space is fully constructed and a new stage begins. The growth of the child's representational capacities—the symbolic function—makes for a restructuration of what has been acquired at the level of effective actions. Progressively, the child acquires concepts of conservation of numerical and physical quantities,[6] and the development of these concepts goes together with that of concrete operations. Operations are defined as interiorized actions that are reversible, so that any transformation can be either cancelled by its inverse or compensated reciprocal transformation.

Following the sensorimotor period and before the first operator equilibrium is reached, the child's way of reasoning assumes a form that Piaget[7] called "semilogical" or "half-logical," and whose one-way mappings will be transformed by reversibility. The one-way mappings conserve the directional property of the real actions out of which they grew; they are an important step toward concrete operations, but the inverse correspondences have to be established before the first level of equilibrium of thought can be attained. In the well-known problem of the quantity of clay* contained in a lump of play-dough before and after its shape has been altered, the younger child already has mentally established one correspondence: when one rolls out the dough, it becomes longer. He also establishes the inverse relation: when one compresses the dough and rolls it into a ball, it becomes shorter. However, these two correspondences (or functions, as Piaget calls them) remain at first separate; only later does each correspondence become completed by a covariance: when the dough is rolled into a sausage, it becomes thinner; when it is rolled back into a ball, it becomes fatter. As long as the child's thought remains unidirectional, conservation of quantity has no logical necessity. Once the operatory system is functioning, covariations become compensations, and conservation, instead of being only qualitative, becomes quantitative. Qualitative properties are, indeed,[8] in a sense conserved much earlier; the child distinguishes between permanent and nonpermanent qualities of objects, but, though he asserts that "it's still the same play-dough," this does not mean that its quantity did not change.

At each level of organization there is thus harmony between the various systems (action-logic, semilogic, and operatory logic) and their invariant properties (object permanency, qualitative identity, and quantitative conservation). These systems have been formalized by Piaget, and such a structural analysis generates hypotheses about and suggests parallels between behavior patterns that at first might appear to be totally independent. The research on learning,[9] for example, was based on such hypotheses and demonstrated reciprocal interaction between operatory systems by showing that training in conservation concepts greatly improved concepts of class inclusion and vice versa.

Causality

The studies just mentioned are mainly concerned with the way the child constructs a certain consistency in his own thoughts, a development we may consider as being fundamentally logicomathematical. But simultaneously the child also constructs a coherence between what he thinks and what actually happens in reality, and this development provides the bases for his causal explanatory thought.

Piaget[10] devoted one of his early works to the child's concept of causality, and since then causality has been investigated in numerous

*The conservation principle was first discussed by Piaget at the Tercentenary Celebration of Harvard University in 1936.[25]

experimental studies at the Center of Genetic Epistemology.[11] Recurring themes of these studies are the child's understanding of mechanical links when movement is transmitted from one object to another.[12] In general, the results of the experiments point to a parallelism between logicomathematical operations and the understanding of causal phenomena in that the subject "attributes" to the behavior of the objects the operations he elaborates in his logical thinking. Before the child understands transmission, he describes what he seems to observe in the following way: the marble that's rolling down hits the first marble, then skips in and out of the others and continues its trajectory. This is the only explanation he can find for the fact that three marbles remain motionless and only the first one is propelled. Such transmission of movement is understood at the same time that the concept of transitivity is reached in logicomathematical problems. This "attribution" (in mathematical terms) to the objects of the subject's own operations means that objects themselves become operators. From this point of view, the concept of causality, like the operations themselves, involves a compensatory relationship between transformations and conservations.

Nevertheless, the development of the capacity of causal explanation is not simply a repetition of what happens during the construction of logicomathematical operations: the latter are the result of free constructions by the subject, whereas the former depend on the properties of objects and their interactions. These object properties, and the fact that they may resist whatever the child wants to do with them, call for a very different mental effort, which is the main source of the child's discoveries about the physical world.

Other studies were concerned with the child's understanding of probability and chance (or randomness), time and space, measurement, and so on. The experimental situations were mostly chosen because of their epistemological meaning; in all of them it was possible to follow the way the child gradually builds up a coherent system of structures that permit him to deal with many problems of different kinds.

Reflexive Abstraction and Constructive Generalization

How does the child build up these structures, and, especially, how, around the age of 11 or 12, does he attain a logical structure that goes beyond that of classes and relations, beyond the double-entry matrices of the concrete operations period? Piaget[13] calls the mechanism by which this is achieved "reflexive abstraction." Such abstraction takes place when the subject derives from his actions and operations certain principles that lead to a new organization when he is confronted with a new problem. For example, at the level of concrete operations, the child is already capable of substituting one criterion for another (shifting), and of conserving the whole in whatever way it has been divided into parts (Inhelder & Piaget, 1964). This is a manifestation of what has been called "vicariance." Subsequently, by reflexive abstraction, this concept leads to the idea of a division of one and the same totality into all its possible parts. Through this abstraction, which is accompanied by a constructive generalization, the subject reaches the logicomathematical concept of the set of all subsets. The different links between the parts form a combinatory system, one of the most fundamental structures of formal operations.[14]

We have said that reflexive abstraction is always accompanied by constructive generalizations. Just as we have to distinguish two kinds of abstraction, empirical abstraction bearing on objects and their properties and reflexive abstraction bearing on the actions of the subject, two kinds of generalizations have also to be distinguished. One simply extends an already existing concept and involves no more than a verification of the transition from some to all, whereas the other can indeed be called constructive, since it introduces new combinations or operations on operations (such as combinatory systems and the set of all subsets).

At a lower level an example of constructive generalization[13] is the following. The child is given ten sticks of different lengths correctly seriated, and is asked: "How many sticks are there that are bigger than this tiny one?" The child easily shows the smallest stick and correctly counts the others. Then the experimenter shows the biggest stick and asks, "And how many are smaller than this one?" The 5- to 6-year-old will then count the sticks again, whereas one or two years later he will laugh and immediately answer, "Nine also, of course." Such constructive generalization is the main mechanism of progress in mathematics, and it is striking that it should already be present in the child.

The relationship between reflexive abstraction and constructive generalization is necessarily a very close one; each abstraction leads sooner or later to constructive generalizations, and each generalization is based on reflexive abstractions.

Equilibration

Piaget's quest for a model to account for the continuity between biological and psychological adaptation goes back to his very first research, when he was still an adolescent, and may be thought of as the "red thread" that runs through his entire work, reappearing with particular clarity each time he discusses his equilibrium theory. His latest thoughts on equilibrium[4] can be summed up as follows.

Three forms of equilibration can be distinguished. The simplest form, the first to appear during development, is that between assimilation and accommodation. Already in the sensorimotor period, an action scheme applied to new objects becomes differentiated as a function of the object's properties. An equilibrium is reached so that the action scheme is conserved and at the same time adapted to the object's properties. If these properties are unexpected and interesting, the equilibration can lead to the formation of a subscheme, or even of a new scheme, which in turn needs to be equilibrated. These functional mechanisms are at work at all levels.

A second form of equilibration takes place between the subsystems of the system of operations the subject is elaborating, for example, between numerical and spatial measurement systems in problems of quantification where both these subsystems play a part. Since such subsystems generally develop at different rates, conflicts may appear, and equilibration will necessitate a distinction between what is common to both subsystems on the one hand and their specific properties on the other. In one of the learning situations,[9] for example, the children had to build what we called "roads" out of bits of wood, so that their "road" was of the same length as the experimenter's. The child was given bits of wood that were five-sevenths of the length of the bits the experimenter worked with, a fact that they could and did indeed observe in one of the situations where the experimenter put five bits into a straight line and the child was asked to construct his road directly underneath. This problem raises no difficulties. When, however, the experimenter built his road (of five bits of wood) in a zig-zag, and the children were asked to build theirs immediately below, they made the end-points coincide with those of the experimenter's road, thus building a line that was far shorter than the model. When they were asked to build a road of equal length to the zig-zag model not directly below, but somewhere on the other side of the table, they no longer used the "not-going-beyond principle," but used a numerical equivalence idea; they counted the experimenter's bits of wood, five, and used five of their own bits. Going back to the proximity situation, in which four bits of wood constitute a line that does not go beyond the experimenter's, a conflict appears: five is the answer based on numerical evaluation, four is the answer based on the topological correspondence (the "not-going-beyond principle"). The awareness of this conflict often led to curious compromise solutions, such as breaking one piece into two pieces without bypassing the endpoints of the configuration, and later on to correct solutions after a certain number of training sessions.

Piaget distinguishes further that a third form of equilibration is based on the second, but leads to the construction of a new total system; the process of differentiation of new subsystems demands a procedure that allows their integration into a new totality and thus constitutes a third form of equilibration.

Superficially, it would seem that equilibration implies a simple balance between opposing forces: the differentiation that threatens the unity of the whole and the integration that endangers the necessary distinctions. But more profoundly, the particularity of cognitive equilibrium is to ensure that the total structure is continuously enriched by the differentiations and that, reciprocally, these differentiations increase with the variations of the intrinsic properties of the total structure.

In other words, cognitive equilibration has the characteristic of being what Piaget calls "majorante," that is to say, augmentative; in other words, the various disequilibria do not lead to a simple reequilibration in the sense of a return to a former equilibrium state, but to a new and more powerful form of equilibrium that incorporates more numerous internal dependencies and logical implications. From this point of view, disequilibria acquire a functional importance, which is best exemplified by Piaget's work on contradiction.

Contradiction

For Piaget, the periods of disequilibrium should not be explained by pointing to contradictions the subject feels in his logical reasoning; rather, the subject's inconsistencies and contradictions should point to a psychological source of such disequilibria. The problem of contradiction[15, 16] is closely related to another question: why are there so many initial disequilibria, since it might have been expected that subjects at any level of development, however elementary, are capable, without contradictions, of mastering problems that do not go beyond an appropriate level of complexity? It turns out that the psychological source of many inconsistencies and contradictions is to be sought in a simple and general phenomenon: the difficulty of compensating affirmations (or positive factors) by negations (or negative factors). The young child is essentially focused on the effect he wants to achieve through his actions, and is likely to lose sight of the situation he started from. In number conservation situations, for example, the young child feels that something has somehow been added at the end of the transformation, but he does not understand that what has been added must in some way have been subtracted from the initial state.[17] In all mathematical and logical problems, the child "succumbs" to this primacy of positive factors over negative ones, which accounts for the lack of reversibility of thought in these areas. The same phenomenon appears also in different situations: for example, the young child understands quickly what is meant by a full glass, or an almost full or a half-full glass, but has much more difficulty with expressions such as half-empty, almost empty, and so on. Very young children will not accept that a glass can at the same time be half full and half empty; for them, this is a contradictory statement. The fact is doubly instructive for the psychologist. On the one hand, it reaffirms the hypothesis of the primacy of positive factors over negative ones, and on the other hand it shows the importance of what for the adult are pseudocontradictions, such as are encountered in seriation tasks, where for children of a certain level, if B is bigger than A, B cannot at the same time be smaller than C.

Epistemology

Piaget's psychology cannot be separated from his epistemology. His epistemological theory may be called constructivist (and Piaget[18, 19] himself qualifies it thus) in the sense that knowledge is neither preformed in the object (empiricism) nor in the subject (nativism), but results from progressive construction. The two main considerations that lead to the rejection of empiricism are the following.

1. Acts of knowledge are never simply based on associations, but

always on assimilation—i.e., on the integration of present data into already existing structures.

2. If the first point is conceded, development can no longer be an accumulation of pieces of learning, and learning must depend on the laws of development and the competence of the subject, according to his cognitive level, as has been shown in our research on learning and the development of cognition.[9] In other words, knowledge is never a simple copy of reality, but always results from a restructuration of reality through the activities of the subject (on this point Piaget agrees with von Foerster's position concerning the cognitive relationships between subject and object).

To say that knowledge depends on the activities of the subject does not mean that knowledge is innate, since it is precisely the activities of the subject that constantly create new structures and new forms of organization. If knowledge were innate, logical necessity should be present before, rather than after, the subject masters certain constructions. This appears not to be the case. The simplest example is that of the concept of transitivity ($A < C$ if $A < B$ and $B < C$), which is reached at the end of the operatory construction of seriation and is not understood at the level of empirical success in seriating sticks of different lengths.

T. Bower[20] and others, it is true, have shown the existence of certain innate reactions, such as perceptive constancies. But between this early behavior and analogous behavior patterns that arise some months later, there is a necessary reconstruction and no direct continuity as would be supposed by a generalized nativism. Each new stage in cognitive development is characterized by new creations that, in turn, open up new possibilities. When the structure is comparatively weak, the new possibilities are comparatively few, but the more powerful the structure, the greater the number of new possibilities. This principle is illustrated not only by the child's cognitive development, but also by the history of mathematics and physics. Piaget[21] is at present working with the physicist and historian of science Rolando Garcia in order to elucidate the mechanisms that account for both the psychogenetic structuration of intelligence and the historical development of scientific thought.

The constructivist aspect of cognitive development is also manifest in the mechanisms of how subjects become aware of their own action or thought patterns. For most authors, and particularly for Freud, awareness does not go beyond the uncovering of realities that already existed in the subject's unconscious. According to Piaget,[22] awareness always implies a conceptualization and therefore supposes a reconstruction that transforms whatever remained unconscious in action into new realities of a conceptual nature.

Piaget's work in genetic epistemology revealed a striking parallelism between the psychogenesis of concepts and the development of theories in mathematics and physics. The levels of abstraction as well as the types of concepts are obviously quite different among children and among scientists. Yet one finds surprising analogies between children's ways of explaining natural phenomena and the thinking about mechanics in antiquity and the Middle Ages, especially when comparing the answers of children concerning the "explanations" with specific passages in Buridan or Oresme, the great masters of the 14th century. These analogies, however, may be considered as bearing on content of knowledge rather than on mechanisms of concept building. Parallels concerning mechanisms of progress are far more important. These mechanisms characterize not only the *stages* of development, but furthermore—and this is perhaps more important—the transition from one stage to the next.

For example, in the history of geometry before our century, one may consider three stages characterized by (a) the geometry of the Greeks and its evolution up to the end of the 18th century; (b) the projective geometry (Poncelet, Chasles); (c) the "global" conception of geometry introduced by Klein. The development of descriptive geometry by Descartes and Fermat, and of calculus, provided the instruments for the transition from (a) to (b); and group theory for the transition from (b) to (c). Here one finds a similarity with the stages described by Piaget in children as "intrafigural," "interfigural," and "transfigural." The epistemological analysis of these differences shows profound reasons for this parallelism and has demonstrated, beyond expectation, the fertility of psychogenetic research for understanding the evolution of science.

This epistemological theory opened up many new directions in research. In Geneva, colleagues drew upon Piaget's work in pursuing studies in related fields—psycholinguistics, cybernetics, psychopathology of thought, and other fields—as well as in extending the scope of developmental psychology itself.

Until recently, studies in cognitive psychology were mainly concerned with the structural aspects of knowledge and the different modes of apprehending reality, and aimed at an analysis of the subject's cognitive potentialities at different periods of development. Research on learning led toward the study of the dynamic processes that make for the transition from one level of thought to the next. A better understanding of these processes drew attention to the important role played by the different strategies by which the subjects seek to generalize their newly acquired reasoning patterns. The latest research in Geneva[23] is thus concerned with these processes of strategies in children: how does the child come to invent procedures that he thinks will help him to solve a problem, and what kind of relationship exists between his inventions and his "theories in action" or his implicit system of dealing with reality[24] (Karmiloff & Inhelder, 1975)? These are among the fundamental questions we are dealing with at the moment.

For Piaget, psychology may be a mere by-product of his work in epistemology, especially of his constructivist theory of knowledge; but for his colleagues, collaborators, and admirers this by-product constitutes an extraordinarily rich source of inspiration.

Acknowledgement

I wish to express my gratitude to M. and H. Sinclair for their generous help in translating the manuscript.

References
1. PIAGET, J. 1952. *The Origins of Intelligence in Children*. International University Press. New York, N.Y. (First French edition, 1936.)
2. PIAGET, J. 1954. *The Child's Construction of Reality*. Basic Books. New York, N.Y. (First French edition, 1937.)
3. PIAGET, J. 1971. *Biology and Knowledge (An Essay on the Relations between Organic Regulations and Cognitive processes)*. Edinburgh University Press. Edinburgh, Scotland. (First French edition, 1967.)
4. PIAGET, J. 1975. *L'équilibration des structures cognitives (problème central du développement)*. Etudes d'Epistémologie génétique. Vol. XXXIII. PUF. Paris, France.
5. MORENO, L., N. RAYNA, H. SINCLAIR, M. STAMBAK, & M. VERBA, 1976. *Les bébés et la logique*. Les Cahiers du CRESAS no. 14. Paris.
6. PIAGET, J. & B. INHELDER. 1974. *The Child's Constructions of Quantities (Conservation and Atomism)*. Routledge and Kegan Paul. London, England. (First French edition, 1941.)
7. PIAGET, J. *et al.* 1968. *Epistémologie et psychologie de la fonction*. Etudes d'Epistémologie génétique. Vol. XXIII. PUF. Paris, France.
8. PIAGET, J. *et al.* 1968. *On the Development of Memory and Identity*. Heinz Werner Lectures, Series 2. Clark University Press. Worcester, Mass.
9. INHELDER, B., H. SINCLAIR, & M. BOVET. 1974. *Learning and the Development of Cognition*. Harvard University Press. Cambridge, Mass. (French edition, 1974.)
10. PIAGET, J. 1930. *The Child's Conception of Physical Causality*. Harcourt Brace. New York, N.Y. (First French edition, 1927.)
11. PIAGET, J. & R. GARCIA. 1974. *Understanding Causality*. Norton. New York, N.Y. (French edition, 1971.)
12. PIAGET, J., A. SZEMINSKA, & E. FERREIRO. 1972. La transmission médiate du mouvement. In *La Transmission des Mouvements*. Piaget *et al.* Etudes d'Epistémologie génétique. Vol. XXVII. PUF. Paris, France.
13. PIAGET, J. *et al.* *Recherches sur l'abstraction réfléchissante (1 Relations logicoarithmétiques)*. Etudes d'Epistémologie génétique. Vol. XXXIV. PUF. Paris, France. In press.
14. INHELDER, B. & J. PIAGET. 1964. *The Early Growth of Logic in the Child (Classification and Seriation)*. Harper. New York, N.Y. (First French edition, 1959.)
15. PIAGET, J. 1974. *Recherches sur la contradiction. I. Les différentes formes de la contradiction*. Etudes d'Epistémologie génétique. Vol. XXXI. PUF. Paris, France.
16. PIAGET, J. 1974. *Recherches sur la contradiction. 2. Les relations entre affirmations et négations*. Etudes d'Epistémologie génétique. Vol. XXXII. PUF. Paris, France.
17. INHELDER, B. *et al.* 1975. *Relations entre les conservations d'ensembles d'éléments discrets et celles de quantités continues*. Année Psychol. 75: 23-60.
18. PIAGET, J. 1970. *Genetic Epistemology*. Woodbridges Lectures no. 9. Columbia University Press. New York, N.Y.
19. PIAGET, J. 1972. *The Principle of Genetic Epistemology*. Routledge and Kegan Paul. London, England.
20. BOWER, T. 1974. *Development in Infancy*. Freeman. San Francisco, Calif.
21. PIAGET, J. & R. GARCIA. *Mécanismes communs entre la psychogenèse et l'histoire des sciences*. In preparation.
22. PIAGET, J. *et al.* 1976. *The Grasp of Consciousness*. Harvard University Press. Cambridge, Mass. (First French edition, 1974.)

23. INHELDER, B. *et al.* 1976. *Des structures cognitives aux procédures de découverte.* Arch. Psychologie (Geneva) XLIV. (171): 57-22.
24. KARMILOFF, A. & B. INHELDER. 1975. "If you want to get ahead, get a theory." *Cognition* 3(3): 195-212.
25. PIAGET, J. 1937. Principal factors determining intellectual evolution from childhood to adult life. In *Factors Determining Human Behavior.* Cambridge, Mass. Harvard University Press. Cambridge, Mass. Harvard tercentenary publications 32-48.
26. PIAGET, J. 1974. *Adaptation vitale et psychologie de l'intelligence (sélection organique et phénocopie).* Hermann. Paris, France.

The Theory of Stages in Cognitive Development

Jean Piaget

University of Geneva

Ladies and Gentlemen:

I should first like to thank the organizers of this small conference on the role of ordinal scales in the problem of development for having invited both my collaborator and friend, Bärbel Inhelder, and me to participate in your meeting. To be quite honest, I am not an expert in ordinal scales. Since you do me the honor of inviting me to address you, however, I feel that the problem of stages is one that should serve as an introduction to the discussions to be held on ordinal scales.

There are two reasons for this. First, a theoretical one: If ordinal scales do indeed have some basis in reality, then a succession of stages must exist in some form or another. And second, as you all know full well, no general agreement has as yet been reached about the existence of these stages. Our own hypotheses about the existence and the necessary sequence of these stages are not accepted by everybody. Consequently, I feel that it might be useful for Bärbel Inhelder and me if I were to discuss the question of stages with you and thus come to know your criticism, objections, and the problems involved. Generally speaking, however, I feel that it is this working group, whose objective is to study ordinal scales, that will eventually solve the problem of stages. Today, therefore, I shall merely outline the problem and make a few brief comments.

From *Measurement and Piaget*, edited by D. R. Green, M. P. Ford, and G. B. Flamer. Copyright © 1971 by McGraw-Hill, Inc. Reprinted by permission.
Translation by Sylvia Opper, Cornell University.

Each time that a specific problem is studied, as for instance that of causality which is currently receiving our attention, the analysis of the responses and reactions of children of different ages seems to point to the existence of relatively well-defined stages in this limited area. The important point, however, is to discover whether there are any general overall stages in development, and whether the different stages found in these more limited and specific areas contain any elements in common. In other words, is it possible to detect broad periods in development with characteristics that can be applied in a general manner to all the events of these periods? This is the hypothesis that we are trying to investigate.

We postulate four major periods in development. First there is a sensorimotor period which occurs before the advent of language. This period is characterized by what we call "sensorimotor intelligence," which is a type of intelligence resulting in a certain number of performances, such as the organization of spatial relationships, the organization of objects and a notion of their permanence, the organization of causal relationships, etc. After the sensorimotor period, at around the age of 2 years, comes another period which starts with the symbolic or semiotic function. This is called the period of "preoperational thought" since the child is now capable of having representational thought by means of the symbolic function. At this stage, though, the child cannot perform operations in the way that I define this term. In my terminology "operations" are internalized actions which are reversible; that is, they can be performed in opposite directions. Finally, they are coordinated into overall structures, and these structures give rise to a feeling of intrinsic necessity.

The third major period starts at around the age of 7 or 8 years and is characterized by the inception of operations. Initially these operations are concrete; that is, they are used directly on objects in order to manipulate these objects. For instance, the child can classify concrete objects, or order them, or establish correspondences between them, or use numerical operations on them, or measure them from a spatial point of view. The operations remain concrete until the child is about 11 or 12 years of age. Then, at approximately this age, the fourth major period begins. This period can be characterized by formal or propositional operations. This means that the operations are no longer applied solely to the manipulation of concrete objects, but now cover hypotheses and propositions that the child can use as abstract hypotheses and from which he can reach deductions by formal or logical means.

If these four major periods do indeed exist, then we should be able to characterize them in a precise manner. What we have tried to do in the past, and what we are still trying to do, is to describe the characteristics of these stages in terms of general overall structures which become integrated. With development, the more elementary structures become incorporated into higher level structures, and these in turn are incorporated into structures of an even higher level.

Not everyone believes that it is necessary to characterize stages in terms of overall structures. For example, Freud's stages of emotional development are characterized by their dominant traits. There is the oral stage, or the anal stage, or the narcissistic or primary stage, and so forth. The different characteristics exist at all the stages, but at any particular moment one of the characteristics predominates. Freud's stages can therefore be described in terms of dominant characteristics.

Such a characterization is not, I believe, adequate for the cognitive functions. In this area we should attempt to go beyond this. If we were to remain satisfied with the notion of dominant characteristics for the cognitive functions, it would always be somewhat arbitrary as to what exactly is dominant and what is not. This is why we are trying to discover the overall structures in cognition rather than specify the dominant characteristics. This means that we are looking for total structures or systems with their own laws, systems which incorporate all their elements and whose laws cover the entire set of elements in the system. It would be these structures which become integrated with development. I shall stop here, but before ending I should like to repeat that this is an important problem, because there is no consensus as to the existence of such structures. I shall therefore try to support my views in the remainder of my address.

The existence of these overall structures raises a problem: do they in fact really exist in the mind of the subject being studied, or are they merely an invention of the psychologist who studies children or adults? The notion of overall structures presents two difficulties. First, the subject is not conscious of the existence of his cognitive structures. For example, he does not know what a seriation is, or a classification, or a relationship of correspondence. He himself has never given a thought to the nature of these overall structures. He acts, he operates, he behaves. And from this behavior we, the psychologists, detect the structures. But the structures are unconscious. They are expressed in regular forms of responses that we believe we are discovering in the subject's behavior. We also feel that if the underlying structures did not exist, we would not be able to explain such behavior. But the subject himself is not aware of these structures. He is neither a professor of psychology nor a professor of logic. He does not reflect upon the structures that he uses. He simply uses them. This, then, is the first difficulty: do the structures really exist in the subject's mind, or have we perhaps invented them?

The second difficulty is this: if we are to be convinced of the existence of these structures, we should be able to formalize them in logical terms. We then try to adapt this formalization to what we are able to observe in the child. But we can never be sure whether we have invented the formalization or whether it really is an expression of what is to be found in the mind of the child. So you see I am very much aware of the various problems involved in the notion of overall structures. Let me, however, deal with some of them by means of a simple example.

I refer here to the example of seriation. Seriation consists of the ordering of a series of sticks from the smallest one to the tallest. Bärbel Inhelder, Mimi Sinclair, and I have once again returned to this problem of seriation in our recent studies on memory, and our findings confirm the stages discovered in our earlier work. For instance, we found that during the initial stage, which we may call stage A, the youngest subjects maintain that all the sticks are of equal length. During the next stage (stage B), the subjects divide the sticks into two categories, large and small, with no ordering of the elements. At stage C, the children talk of the large ones, the middle-sized ones and the small ones. At stage D, the child constructs a series in an empirical fashion, by trial and error, but he is not able to produce immediately a faultless construction. And finally, at stage E, the child discovers a method: he chooses the largest of all the sticks and he sets this on the table, then he takes the largest of all the remaining sticks and places this beside the first stick, then the largest of the remaining ones, until he has placed all the sticks on the table. At this stage, he constructs a correct ordering without any hesitation, and this construction presupposes a reversible relation. That is to say, an element *a* is both smaller than the ones which have gone before it and larger than the ones to follow. This is a good example of what I mean by a structure.

But let us see what the logicians have to say about this problem. What is a seriation from the formal point of view? Can we discover any relationship between the logician's formalization of a seriation and the child's structure of the same notion? For the logician, a seriation is a chaining of asymmetrical, connex, and transitive relations. As far as asymmetry is concerned, this seems obvious in the present example. This means that one element is larger than another. As for connectivity, this means that all the elements are different and that there are no two alike. And lastly, there is the transitivity relationship. This means that if *A* is larger than *B* and *B* larger than *C*, then *A* is automatically larger than *C*. In the above-mentioned seriation problem, we did not see any evidence of transitivity. Is it part of the structure? Does it exist? Here we can do some separate experiments on the problem by taking three sticks of unequal length. We compare the first with the second, and then hide the first under the table. Then we compare the second with the third, and we say to the child, "You saw beforehand that the first was larger than the second, and now you can see that the second is larger than the third. What is the one under the table like compared to the third one? Is it larger, smaller, or just the same?" Experience has shown that very young children are not able to use the deductive method and are thus unable to solve the problem of transitivity. They reply, "I don't know. I haven't seen them next to each other. I need to see all three together at the same time before I can answer your question."

For the older children, however, who use the deductive method, transitivity is evident. Not only is it evident, but it also is necessary. And here we touch upon the real problem of overall structures: the problem of the appearance at a particular point in development of the feeling of necessity. Until this point, a certain occurrence was either absent or simply probable; now it becomes necessary. How can one explain the apparition of necessity from the psychological point of view? This, I feel, is the real problem of overall structures. How is it that a phenomenon which until then had been merely noted empirically, or else had been felt to be simply probable, now becomes logically necessary from the subject's point of view?

One first reply could be to say that it is an illusion. Hume, in his studies on the notion of causality, maintained that the necessary cause-effect relationship was in fact not necessary at all, but simply due to our associations of ideas or to our habits. So one could say that this feeling of necessity is simply a habit. However, the striking thing here is that the child reaches this feeling of necessity as soon as he has understood the phenomenon in question. One can sometimes witness the precise moment when he discovers this necessity. At the beginning of his reasoning, he is not at all sure of what he is stating. Then suddenly he says, "But it's obvious." In another experiment where Bärbel Inhelder was questioning a child on a problem which is not that of seriation but of recurrent reasoning, but which also involves the feeling of necessity, the child was at first very uncertain. Then suddenly he said, "Once one knows, one knows forever and ever." In other words, at one point the child automatically acquires this feeling of necessity. Where does this necessity come from?

My personal feeling is that there is only one acceptable psychological explanation: this feeling of necessity comes from the closure or completion of a structure. One could, of course, also maintain that necessity is simply an awareness of an idea which was predetermined in the mind, an innate or a prior idea. But this is not a true psychological solution, for it defies verification. Also, if this were indeed true, the feeling of necessity would appear much earlier than it actually does.

This is why I believe that the feeling of necessity is neither a subjective illusion nor an innate or a priori idea. It is an idea which is constructed at the same time as the overall structures. As soon as a structure is sufficiently complete for closure to occur or, in other words, once the internal compositions of the structure become interdependent and independent of external elements and are sufficiently numerous to allow for all types of arrangements, then the feeling of necessity manifests itself. I believe that it is this feeling of necessity which constitutes evidence of the existence of the overall structures which characterize our stages.

I do not want to describe here all the overall structures that can be found. They naturally vary according to the four major stages mentioned earlier. At the sensorimotor level we find composite actions which are performed in a step-by-step or contiguous manner, since the child is not capable of representation which would allow for more complex relationships. His compositions are simply actions which are chained to one another but which nevertheless still form some kind of structure. We find, for instance, in the organization of space, an organization of movements and of positions which mathematicians call the group of displacements. This is one example of a structure, with its characteristic of necessity. That is to say, it is possible to return to the point of departure, and this is a necessary return. Also it is possible to reach one point by a variety of different routes, and these are called detour behaviors. So already in these two types of behavior, return and detour, we see the characteristic of necessity and the existence of overall structures.

At the level of preoperational thought we find other overall structures. These are not yet operational structures in the sense that I described earlier; that is, they are not yet reversible, but they are nonetheless structures with their own laws. Take for example the notion of a function. As an example, we have a piece of string, B, which can be pulled over a spring. If you tie a weight to a segment called A, the segment A' will become shorter. When A becomes shorter, A' becomes longer; when A' becomes shorter, A becomes longer. So the lengthening of A is a function of the shortening of A'. At this point of development the child has not yet acquired conservation. If we were to ask the child if the whole string (B) were equal to the sum of the two parts (A and A'), that is, $B = A + A'$, in both cases (when the string has been pulled down with the weight or not), the child would not give the correct answer because he cannot conserve. This is an example of a function but without reversibility.

In other experiments we also find functions, as for instance in the many-to-one relationship, but this is not accompanied by the reverse relationship of one-to-many. In the one-to-many relationship, or the many-to-one, the child reaches only a partial logic; he has not yet acquired the other half of logic which would be reversibility. Other examples of structures at this level are those of qualitative identity. For example, if one pours liquid from one glass to another as in the well-known experiments on conservation, the child at this stage does not accept the conservation of quantity, but he already admits to the qualitative identity. He will say that it is the same water in both cases, but not the same quantity. Qualitative identity is far easier to achieve. All the child needs to do is to isolate the qualities, whereas for conservation the child must construct the quantities, and this is another matter.

I do not need to remind you that at the level of the concrete operations we find a great many overall structures which are much richer than those of the preoperational level and which we have called groupings. Examples are the notion of seriation mentioned previously, classification, one-to-one correspondence, and many-to-one or one-to-many correspondences. At this level quantification becomes possible as a result of the overall structures, and consequently so, too, do the notions of conservation which were lacking at the preoperational level. Even identity changes and becomes operational and additive. For example, in the conservation problem, the child will say, "It's the same quantity, because you haven't added anything or taken anything away." Nothing has been added and nothing taken away; this is an additive identity and therefore a quantitative one, and no longer simply qualitative identity as when the child says, "It's the same water. It's the same color," etc.

There is no need for me to remind you that at the level of formal or propositional operations we also find even richer structures which are a synthesis of the previous ones. For instance, we have the group of four transformations which combines into a single system the structures of inversion ($A - A = 0$) and the structures of reciprocity ($A = B$ therefore $B = A$). These formal structures incorporate the preceding ones and constitute the termination of the construction of overall structures which has been going on throughout the entire period of childhood. The stages are therefore characterized by successive structures which do not replace each other, but which are integrated into one another. The simplest ones become incorporated into later, more complex ones. For example, the preoperational functions, or identities, are integrated into the concrete operations; then later, these concrete operational structures become incorporated into the formal operational structures.

At this point of our study I should like to note that these two notions of stages and overall structures, which I believe are necessarily closely bound together, have a meaning which is not only a logical and formal one. Despite their formalization, these structures have essentially a biological meaning, in the sense that the order of the stages is constant and sequential. Each stage is necessary for the following one. If this were not the case, one would be in no position to talk of stages. Naturally, the ages at which different children reach the stages may vary. In some social environments the stages are accelerated, whereas in others they are more or less systematically retarded. This differential development shows that stages are not purely a question of the maturation of the nervous system but are dependent upon interaction with the social environment and with experience in general. The order, however, remains constant.

Furthermore, the accelerations or retardations raise one problem which has not yet been studied sufficiently but which will have to be considered in the future. This is the problem of the optimal speed of development. What advantages are to be gained from speeding up the stages? I am often asked the following question in this country: "Can one accelerate the stages indefinitely?" My reply is to ask: "Is there any advantage to be derived from such acceleration?" Take experiments like those of Gruber where he finds that kittens acquire the requisite reactions towards the permanent object by the age of 4 months; that is, they search for objects hidden under a screen. It takes the human baby 9 months to reach this self-same point of development. One can consequently ask whether it would be advantageous for the human baby to reach this point at 4 instead of 9 months. I do not think so, because the kitten does not go very much further. Once it reaches a certain level, it scarcely progresses beyond this point. The human baby, on the other hand, develops more slowly, but in the long run he goes much further. One must remember that the higher the zoological species the longer is its period of infancy. There is a reason for this, and it may be that there is an optimal speed of development for each species. So we return to biology.

Our stages are very similar to those described by Waddington when he speaks of necessary courses which lead to a certain result. He calls these necessary courses or channels "creodes." He also describes certain forms of equilibrium which occur when there is a deviation from the creode due to unforeseen circumstances. In this case some force acts to bring the development back to its normal course. Waddington calls this "homeorhesis." It is a dynamic equilibrium, as opposed to homeostasis which is static. And finally, Waddington stresses what he calls the "time tally." This particular notion of a time tally raises the problem of the optimal speed of the stages of development. One last point is that the stages in embryology have a sequential ordering, with each stage being necessary for the following one. It is not possible to miss a stage in development.

If this were true of psychology, then there would be a relationship or a very close analogy with embryological development. I repeat that this does not mean that everything is genetically or internally determined within a hereditary program, since accelerations or retardations can occur in mental development which appear to be of an even greater magnitude than in embryology.

The present basic problem in the question of stages is that of the passage from one stage to the next. What mechanisms are responsible for this passage? Bärbel Inhelder and her collaborators have been dealing with this specific problem in their study of the possibility of certain forms of learning. These are not the types of learning that take place as a result of repetition or of the external reinforcements as in habit learning. Rather, she has been studying the type of learning which consists of isolating the factors which we believe are active in normal development in order to show how variations in these factors can produce accelerations in certain areas of development, and, more particularly, can result in certain correlations between the various learning experiences.

But I do not wish to discuss this problem here since it is currently in the process of investigation and the results will shortly be published in a book by Inhelder and her collaborators. What I would like to do is to raise the general problem of the passage from one stage to the next. I should like to approach this problem in the following manner. Three models can be used to describe this passage from one stage to the next. First, one could maintain that the successive acquisitions which characterize the stages mentioned earlier are acquisitions which are purely and simply due to environmental pressures, to experience, or to more or less random encounters with certain aspects of the daily social and physical environment. In this case, the succession of the stages would no longer be necessary. It might be a regular succession, with some regularities being more or less emphasized or attenuated depending upon the environment, but there would be no necessary succession.

The second possibility would be that the stages are internally determined; that is, they are predetermined. The succession of stages would be somehow preformed in the hereditary equipment of each individual. This approach is a return to the conception of innate ideas, and this notion, which was not very popular some years ago, has now become fashionable again. I refer in particular to the work being carried out in psycholinguistics by Chomsky, and to work done by certain psychologists who maintain that they are able to find notions of conservation very early in life, and that these notions then deteriorate—I am not quite sure how—only to reappear eventually at a later stage in development. I would classify this second solution as one of predetermination.

And then there is a third approach which is the one to which we subscribe. This solution is difficult to prove. It is even difficult to express or to explain. But once one has understood it, it seems that it is a compelling one, although it still remains to be proved. This third solution is that the stages result in a certain number of overall structures which become necessary with development, but are not so at the beginning of life. For example, the formal structures become necessary once the child possesses the concrete operations. As soon as he can perform the concrete operations, sooner or later he will begin to coordinate reversibility by inversion with reversibility by reciprocity and hence construct the group of four transformations. Similarly, once he is able to manipulate the classifications, sooner or later he will construct a classification of all the classifications, and thus he will end up by producing the combinatorial, which is a necessary form of formal thought.

Thus stages are characterized by overall structures which become necessary but which are not so initially. Formal structures become necessary when the concrete structures are complete; concrete structures become necessary when the structures of identity, of functions, etc., are complete; and these in turn become necessary when the sensorimotor functions are complete. But nothing is given in an a priori or innate fashion; nothing is preformed or predetermined in the activity of the baby. For instance, we could search far and wide in the behavior of the baby without finding even the rudiments of the group of four transformations, or of the combinatorial. These are all constructed and the construction—this I find to be the great mystery of the stages— becomes more and more necessary with time. The necessity is at the end of development, not at the point of departure. This, then, is the model upon which we are trying to base our work and our experiments.

There are still two more remarks that I should like to add before closing. First, that the stages which I have just discussed are those of intelligence, of the development of intelligence, and more particularly of the development of the logicomathematical operations. They refer to those operations of which the subject is, in a way, the master or the director and which he can apply at will, in such a manner as he deems suitable, to a particular group of objects. When we study other cognitive functions, things naturally become more complex and the stages may be far less evident. In the field of perception, for example, we find hardly any stages as far as the primary or field effects are concerned. We do find some semistages in the perceptual activities, but these are not nearly as well defined as the stages of intelligence.

With mental imagery, we find essentially two periods. There is one preceding the concrete operations when mental images are mainly reproductory and static. During this period children have great difficulty in representing or imagining transformations or movements. The anticipatory images which are necessary for the representation of transformations only make their appearance at the level of the concrete operations. So here we find the beginnings of a stage, but again far less evident than in the field of intelligence.

In our recent research into memory, we find three distinctions. These are: recognitive memory, which is by far the earliest type of memory to appear and which is found right at the beginning of the sensorimotor level; evocative memory, which only appears with the semiotic function from the age of two or three years onwards; and then, between the two, there is a level of reconstructive memory which is still bound up with movement, with action, but which is more than simple recognition. These are very elementary distinctions which don't go very far in the differentiation of stages.

Even in the area of intelligence, as I mentioned before, the stages which I have just described are those of the logico-mathematical operations. Because here the subject does what he wants, in a manner of speaking. For the notion of causality, on the other hand, which we are studying at present, knowledge is physical and no longer logico-mathematical, and so the resistances of the object present all sorts of new problems. Consequently the stages are far less clear. At first, we had the impression that there were very few stages in the development of the notion of causality. Now we are slowly finding some. However, we are not yet at the point of being able to describe these stages in terms of the characteristics of overall structures such as described earlier. This is the first of my two concluding remarks.

Finally, a fairly important problem for the theory of stages is that of time lags. At certain ages the child is able to solve problems in quite specific areas. But if one changes to another material or to another situation, even with a problem which seems to be closely related, lags of several months are noted, and in some cases even of 1 or 2 years. Let us take one example, the problem of inclusion. The child is given a bunch of flowers, some of which are primroses, while others are tulips, daisies, or any other flowers. If you were to ask the child, "Are all the primroses flowers?" he will reply, "Of course." If you then ask, "Are there more flowers or more primroses in this bunch?" the child, instead of comparing the primroses with all the flowers, will compare them with all the flowers which are not primroses. And he will answer, "There are more," or "There are less," or "There are the same number," depending upon the result of this comparison, as if he were not able to include the part in the whole. This is the problem of class inclusion.

This problem is solved at approximately the age of 8 years for the flowers. But Bärbel Inhelder and I have noted that if one uses animals, for example, the problem becomes more complicated. If one asks the child, "Are all sea gulls birds?" he will reply, "Of course." If you ask, "Are all the birds sea gulls?" he will reply, "Of course not. There are also blackbirds, sparrows, etc." Then if you ask, "If you look out of the window, can you tell me whether there are more sea gulls or more birds in Geneva?" the child finds this more difficult to answer than for the flowers. Why is this? Is it because one cannot make a bunch with the sea gulls as with the flowers? I do not know. But this is one example of the problem. It is possibly a poorly chosen one, but there are any number of these problems of time lags between the solution of a problem with a certain material and the solution of the same problem with another material.

I have often been reproached for not having produced a sufficiently precise theory of these time lags in the same way as one can try to produce a theory of the overall structures or of the positive characteristics of stages. But time lags are a negative characteristic which form an obstacle to the construction of the overall structures. My reply to such a reproach is merely the following: time lags are always due to an interaction between the person's structures on the one hand, and the resistances of the object on the other. The object may be flowers, which offer little resistance; one places them on the table, and one makes a bunch of them. But there are other objects which offer more resistance, as for instance the birds. One cannot put them on the table. Some resistances of objects are unpredictable. When one encounters them, one can explain them, but always after the event. It is not possible to have a general theory of these resistances.

And so, in concluding, I should like to find some sort of an excuse for this failure by a comparison with physics. Physics is a much more advanced science than psychology, a more exact science which permits mathematical theories in almost all areas. But there is one area where physicists have not yet managed to produce a general theory. This is the problem of friction. Friction is the resistance of an object when you make it move along a surface. Physicists explain the role of friction in such and such a situation, but they have not yet come up with a general theory for this phenomenon. Time lags are somewhat analogous; they are comparable to all the concrete situations where friction is involved. Some areas are manipulated with ease; others offer all sorts of resistances. This problem still remains to be solved.

As you see, I have tried to be honest in my address by pointing out the various problems and difficulties which still remain. But I repeat, I am counting especially on the work that you are going to do here in your meeting on ordinal scales to shed some light on the difficult question of stages.

Problems of Equilibration

The title "Equilibration" refers to one factor that I think is essential in cognitive development. In order to understand the role of this factor, we must relate it to the classical factors that have always been understood to be pertinent in cognitive development. There are three such classical factors: the influences of the physical environment, the external experience of objects; innateness, the hereditary program; and social transmission, the effects of social influences. It is clear that all three are important in cognitive development. I will begin by discussing them separately. But as we discuss them, I think we will see that no one of the three is sufficient in itself. Each one of them implies a fundamental factor of equilibration, upon which I shall place special emphasis.

I will start by discussing the role of physical experience. It is clear that this is indispensable in cognitive development. There can be no development without contact with physical objects—that is, contact with the physical environment. In terms of classical empiricism, the role of acquired experience simply amounts to perceptions that we draw from objects and associations among perceptions. As I see it, there never can be pure association in the classical sense in which the empiricists mean it. The manner of linkage that always intervenes in the whirlpool of associations is in reality an assimilation in the biological sense of the term, an integration of external data into the structures of the subject.

Any action on the part of a subject gives rise to schemes of assimilation. That is, an object can be taken into certain schemes through the actions that are carried out on it; each of these schemes of assimilation goes hand in hand and with an aspect of accommodation of the schemes to the situation. Thus, when a subject takes cognizance of or relates to an object, there is a pair of processes going on. It is not just straight association. There is a bipolarity, in which the subject is assimilating the object into his schemes and at the same time accommodating his schemes to the special characteristics of the object. And in this bipolarity and sharing of processes, there is already a factor of equilibration between assimilation and accommodation.

Assimilation is a form of integration. It presupposes an instrument by which the data can be assimilated into the structures of the subject. An excellent example of assimilation as integration is the notion of horizontality of the level of water. Children see water in various forms every day. They see water in glasses from which they drink; they see water in bottles that they tip. Moreover, they see water running in bathtubs and lakes and rivers. In all cases, the water is horizontal. So the notion that water is horizontal should be a basic permanent notion. It even seems to assert itself in a more primitive manner as the child's own body is bound to positions where horizontality or verticality intervene. He can tell whether he is standing up or whether he is lying down; he is aware of the sensoritonic attitudes. You would expect this postural awareness to give him the understanding necessary to realize that water is always horizontal.

In some research we did many years ago, we asked the child to predict what would happen to the water inside a bottle if we tipped it. The child was unable to see the water inside the bottle because it was covered. He was asked to draw a picture of the water inside the bottle when it was tipped. The average age at which children could answer this correctly and draw a horizontal line was about 9 years of age. I say average age because, of course, some children advance more rapidly than others. Moreover, the populations we studied were from an impoverished area of Geneva, and it is possible that in more highly civilized regions the age is younger. However, in Geneva the average child is 9–10 years of age before he can predict where the water will be in the covered container when it is tipped. Before that, he always draws the line parallel to the bottom of the bottle as it is when the bottle is upright. Then there are various intermediary stages between drawing a parallel and drawing a horizontal line. This seems to be quite strong evidence of the fact that seeing is not enough, because children have been seeing this phenomenon all their lives. But within the experiment, we even gave the children a chance to see by taking the cover off the bottle. If the child had drawn the water parallel to the bottom of the bottle, when we uncovered and tipped the bottle and the child compared the bottle with his drawing, he would say, "Yes, that's just the way I drew it. Just like my drawing." He doesn't even seem to be able to see that the line is horizontal.

Why is the child unable to see that the line of water is horizontal?

The reason for this is that he does not possess the necessary instruments of assimilation. He hasn't yet developed the system of coordinates that will enable him to put the water into a frame of reference with points outside the bottle, such as the table top or the floor. As adults, we operate with a coordinate spatial system of verticality and horizontality at all times. The child doesn't have the framework that enables him to make the extrafigural comparison needed to go outside the framework of the bottle. He reasons only by an intrafigural frame of reference until about the age of 9, when these systems of coordinates are being built. He remains inside the framework of the bottle; his only points of reference are the base of the bottle, which results in his drawing the water parallel to the base or sometimes to the corners of the bottle. He may draw a line from one corner to another that is slightly tipped, but it is still not considered horizontal. His frame of reference remains the bottle itself.

This seems to me a very striking example of the complexity of the act of assimilation, which always supposes instruments of integration. A well-developed structure within the subject is needed in order for him to take in the data that are outside. Assimilation is clearly not a matter of passively registering what is going on around us. This leads to the critical examination of the famous stimulus-response scheme, the classical model of behaviorism.

It is true, of course, that stimuli give rise to responses. However, this only raises much more basic, more preliminary questions. Why does a given stimulus give rise to a certain response? When is an organism sensitive to a particular stimulus? The very same organism may at one time not be sensitive to a particular stimulus and not give any response to it and then later be sensitive to the stimulus and respond to certain stimuli, whereas other organisms may not. Therefore, the fundamental question is: What makes an organism respond to a certain stimulus?

The organism is sensitive to a given stimulus only when it possesses a certain competence. I am borrowing this word from embryology in the sense in which Waddington has used it. He has referred to the influence of an inductor. Waddington has shown that an inductor that modifies the structure of the embryo does not act in the same way at all levels of development. If the inductor is present before the embryo has the competence to respond to it, the inductor has no effect at all; thus, it does not modify the structure. The embryo must be at a point of being competent to respond to the inductor before the inductor can have its effect.

The phenomenon is the same in cognition. Stimulus-response is not a one-way road, a unilateral scheme. A subject is sensitive to a stimulus only when he possesses a scheme that permits the capacity for response, and this capacity for response supposes a scheme of assimilation. We again have to create an equilibrium between assimilation, on the one hand, and accommodation to a given or an external stimulus, on the other hand. The stimulus-response scheme must be understood as reciprocal. The stimulus unleashes the response, and the possibility of the response is necessary for the sensitivity to the stimulus. The relationship can also be described as circular, which again poses the problem of equilibrium, an equilibrium between external information serving as the stimulus and the subject's schemes or the internal structure of his activities.

I would like to make two final points concerning the role of the physical environment. I will first discuss the development of the notion of conservation. As you know, if one transforms a ball of clay into a sausage shape, the young child will tell you that there is more clay in the sausage than in the ball because the sausage is longer. Second, even though no clay was added and no clay was taken away, the child believes that the sausage shape and the ball will weigh differently. The child will also say that one would displace more water in a vessel than the other, indicating different volumes in the ball and the sausage shapes. These notions of conservation are acquired in a certain order: first, the conservation of the substance, that is the quantity of material; next, with quite a notable time-lag, the conservation of weight; finally, the conservation of volume, in the sense one can evaluate volume by the displacement of the level of water. What strikes me as very interesting is that the conservation of the amount of clay—the conservation of the substance—is the first concept of conservation that a child attains. But it is clear that conservation of substance—that is, the amount of clay—is not observable. The child can observe the size of the clay, perceive its volume, and lift it to sense its weight, yet he believes they have changed. And yet somehow he believes that the amount of clay has remained the same even though it is not observable or clearly measurable.

It is, it seems to me, very important that conservation of substance can only be the product of reasoning. It is not a product of perception. The child has simply become aware that something must be conserved when things are transformed in order to make the process of rational thought at all possible. So the scheme of the conservation of the amount of clay imposes itself on the child for rational rather than for perceptual reasons.

Finally, I would like to distinguish between two kinds of experience in connection with the factor of external experience. Classical empiricists assume there is only physical experience. In physical experience, information is drawn from the objects themselves. For example, you can have various objects and see that they differ in weight. But there is a different kind of experience that plays a necessary role at the preoperational level. I will call this *logicomathematical experience*. In logicomathematical experience, the information is drawn not from the object but from the subject's actions and from the subject's coordination of his own actions, that is, the operations that the subject effects on the objects.

There is a very banal example of logicomathematical experience that I have often quoted. One of my friends who is a great mathematician described to me an experience that he had as a child. While counting some pebbles, he arranged them in a line, counted them from left to right, and found that there were ten. He then decided to count them from right to left and found there were still ten. He was surprised and delighted, so he changed the shape again. He put them in a circle, counted around the circle, and found there were still ten. With mounting enthusiasm, he counted around from the other direction and there were still ten. It was a great intellectual experience for him. He had discovered that the sum ten is independent of the order of counting. But unlike their weight, neither the sum nor the order is a property of the pebbles. The sum and the order come from the actions of the subject himself. It was he who introduced the order and it was he who did the counting. So logicomathematical experience is experience in which the information comes from the subject's own actions and from the coordinations among his actions. This coordination of actions naturally poses a problem of equilibrium much more than a problem of action from external experience.

Finally, as for the role of experience, it is clear that there is an undeniable role played by experience in cognitive development; however, the influence of experience has not resulted in a conception of knowledge as a simple copy of outside reality. In external experience, knowledge is always the product of the interaction between assimilation and accommodation, that is, an equilibrium between the subject and the objects on which the knowledge rests.

The second factor I would like to discuss is that of the innateness or hereditary programming of development. It is, of course, obvious that the factor of innateness plays as fundamental a role as the maturation of the nervous system and is a condition of cognitive development. But it is a condition that only opens up possibilities. The problem is how these possibilities are realized, that is, how they are actualized. In sensorimotor development, it is easier to see how hereditary transmissions play a central role. For instance, at the sensorimotor level, the coordination between grasping and vision seems to be clearly the result of the myelinization of certain new nerve paths in the pyramidal tract, as physiologists have shown. This myelinization seems to be the result of hereditary programming. However, in the domain of higher, representative, and especially operational cognitive structures, these structures are not innate. Logical transitivity, for example, imposes a necessity on the subject with an obviousness internal to the subject. Yet this necessity is not a proof of innateness.

We have conducted a very simple experiment to test the notion of transitivity. We asked children first to compare the length of two pencils. Children see that A is smaller than B. We then hide A and show B and C; C is very obviously longer than B. We then ask the child, "Do you think that C is longer than the first one you saw, smaller than the first one you saw, or about the same length?" The little children will say, "I can't tell. I didn't see them together." The child does not make the inference we would make from the information that allows for transitivity. It seems to impose itself on us with a feeling of necessity that C must be longer than A. But small children do not have that same feeling of necessity. This feeling of necessity is tied to the operational structure I have been calling *seriation* or *serial ordering*.

As you know, if children are asked to put ten sticks in order of length from shortest to longest, their ability to do so develops through very varied stages, in which they experience some laborious trial and error.

Small children are likely to make pairs of short and long sticks but fail to coordinate the pairs among themselves. They have recognized that some sticks are short and some are long, but not much more than that. Older children make trios—the repetition of a pattern of short, medium, and long—but do not coordinate the trios among themselves. Slightly older children are able to produce an incomplete empirical series, that is, with errors, gropings, and corrections. Finally, at about 7 years of age, children have developed a method, a method that I call *operational*. They first look for the shortest of all the elements and place it on the table, then look for the smallest of those remaining and place it next to the shortest, and then look for the next shortest and place it. I refer to this method as *operational* because it implies a certain reversibility. It implies the comprehension of the fact that any element—say, element E—is at once bigger than all those preceding it and smaller than those that remain. There is a coordination that permits a construction of the seriation without errors. When this system is followed, once you know that objects A, B, and C were the shortest on the table, it is not necessary to compare object D with objects A, B, and C. You know that it must be longer than them and that it must be shorter than the others.

The notion of transitivity is, thus, tied to the operational structuration of the series. Transitivity feels necessary to us and imposes itself upon us because of the nature of the closed operational structure; it is a result of the closing of this structure. And this, of course, means equilibrium. The structure, until it is closed, is not in a state of equilibrium. Once it is closed, we again find equilibrium to be an important factor.

The notion of the influence of innate factors in development is gaining new acceptance these days. Two of its leading proponents are Chomsky, the linguist, and Lorenz, the ethologist. Chomsky, of course, has done very great work in his development of the notion of transformational grammar, work that I admire greatly. He has hypothesized that from the beginning of these transformations, there is a fixed innate core that contains the most general forms of language, for example, the relationship between subject and predicate. This innate core contains both the possibility of construction of language and a rational structure, which consequently would be innate.

It seems to me that this hypothesis is not necessary. As we all know, language develops during the second year of childhood and not from birth. As we also know, it develops at the end of the period of sensorimotor development, with all the numerous stages of construction involved in this form of intelligence. It seems to me that sensorimotor intelligence, once achieved, contains all that is necessary to furnish Chomsky's innate fixed core without having need to appeal to a hereditary structure.

Konrad Lorenz, the great ethologist, agrees with Kant: the important forms of our thinking, the important categories, are present in us before any experience; that is, they are innate. He goes as far as to say that the general ideas of the mind are preformed in the embryo before the individual has the need for them, just as the horses' hooves or fishes' fins are preformed in the embryo before they are needed by the adult. However, Lorenz, as a biologist, recognizes the limitations of such an explanation. Each animal species has its own heredity. Then, if one brings the ideas of intelligence or reason back to innate structures, that means that heredity can vary from one species to another following the hereditary patrimony of the species. Realizing this difficulty, Lorenz follows through very logically by concluding that these innate notions are not necessary, as they might be if the hereditary programs were constant across all species. Since hereditary programs vary from species to species and there is nothing necessary about them, these innate ideas must be only innate working hypotheses. Thus, this means that innate ideas have lost their aspect of necessity. This does not mean that essential categories are not *a priori* and cannot exist before any experience, but it does mean that they cannot be accounted for by their intrinsic necessity.

I would conclude in discussing the role of biology as a factor of development that what is important for us to take from biology is not the notion of hereditary programming, since it is variable and it cannot lead to the kind of necessity that we feel. We should take the much more general notion of self-regulating mechanisms. Self-regulating mechanisms are important throughout every level of biological development. One finds regulation at the level of the genome, where self-regulatory mechanisms are an essential condition of functioning. There are regulations in the course of embryological development that Waddington calls *homeorhesis*. At the physiological level, homeostasis is a self-regulating mechanism; similarly, in the nervous system, the reflex arc is a homeostat. On the level of human conduct and even at the level of logical operational thinking, there are similar self-regulatory mechanisms. It seems to me that this notion of self-regulation, which consequently is one of equilibration, is much more fundamental and much more general than the more narrow notion of variable hereditary programming. It is, then, self-regulation that is the important idea for us to take from biology.

I now come to the third classical factor of development: the social factor, the role of education and language in development. I will try to be very brief so that I can get on to equilibration. The role of education and language is clearly fundamental, but once again it is subordinated to assimilation. There can be no effect of social or linguistic experience unless the child is ready to assimilate and integrate this experience into his own structures.

The special problem of the relationship between language and logic is one that I would like to discuss at some greater length. Many people are of the opinion that an individual's grasp of logic is dependent upon the syntax and the logical relationships embedded in the language in which people are speaking to him. Logic develops out of the language. This is the position of the logical positivists.

In Geneva, one of our colleagues, Hermine Sinclair, has done some work on the problem of the relationship between logic and language.

Sinclair was a linguist before she came to Geneva to go into experimental psychology. In her research, she first identified two groups of children. One group were nonconservers, in the sense that they thought that a change in shape would entail a change in the amount of substance. The other group were conservers, in that they knew that the change in shape did not alter the amount of the substance. Then, she looked at the language of these two groups of children in different situations. For example, the children were asked to compare short, long, fat, and thin pencils. She found that the children who were nonconservers did not use comparative terms in describing the pencils and did not contrast two dimensions. They would just say that one pencil is big and that one pencil is fat. The children who were conservers, however, used comparisons. They talked in sentences that contrasted variables, such as saying that one is fatter but shorter, the other thinner but longer.

Sinclair then trained the nonconservers to learn the verbal expressions of the other, more advanced group. This language training was not easy, but it was possible. After the nonconservers had mastered the language expressions of the conservers, she readministered the conservation experiment to see whether the training increased their ability to conserve.

Progress was only minimal; nine-tenths of the children made no progress toward conservation, although they had mastered the more sophisticated language. One-tenth of the children made very slight progress. This would lead us to believe they would have made this progress normally in that period of time. We have been pursuing other research in Geneva since Sinclair's study; it all supports the general conclusion that linguistic progress is not responsible for logical or operational progress. It is rather the other way around. The logical or operational level is likely to be responsible for a more sophisticated language level.

I am now discussing the role of equilibration, that is, the fourth factor in psychological and cognitive development. It seems to me that there are two reasons for having to call in this fourth factor. The first is that since we already have three other factors, there must be some coordination among them. This coordination is a kind of equilibration. Secondly, in the construction of any operational or preoperational structure, a subject goes through much trial and error and many regulations that in a large part involve self-regulations. Self-regulations are the very nature of equilibration. These self-regulations come into play at all levels of cognition, including the very lowest level of perception.

I will begin with an example at the level of perception. We have studied a number of optical illusions, by asking subjects to make perceptual judgments of an optical illusion. For example, we have often used the Müller-Lyer illusion, an illusion of the diagonal of the lozenge, which is always underestimated. One can present the subject with a successive series of judgments to make between the standard and the variable. The variable varies between presentations but the standard is a constant. The subject has to judge whether the variable is shorter than, longer than, or equal to the standard. I have always admired the patience of children under 7 years of age who will sit through 20 or 30 or 40 presentations at a time.

In children under 7 years of age, we find no notable transformations, that is, at the end of 30 or 40 trials, they make the same errors that they did at the beginning. With adults, on the contrary, the repetition of the judgment results in a very clear diminishing of the illusion. Some are able to eliminate the effect of the illusion altogether. Among children from 7 years (the beginning of cognitive operations) to adulthood, one can observe a progressive diminishing of errors. It is important to note that the subject does not know the results of his judgments. There was no external reinforcement, yet the perceptual mechanism seems to have its own regulations, so that after 20 or 30 or 40 trials, an adult subject can eliminate the effect of the illusion altogether.

At the representational level, in both preoperational and operational structures, we can distinguish three kinds of equilibrium. The first one is the relationship between assimilation and accommodation, of which I previously spoke. There is an equilibrium between the structures of the subject and the objects; its structures accommodate to the new object being presented and the object is assimilated into the structures. It is this first fundamental form of equilibration that was exemplified by the horizontality of water and the notion of conservation. I will not repeat these examples here.

The second kind of equilibrium is an equilibrium among the subsystems of the subject's schemes. In reality, the schemes of assimilation are coordinated into partial systems, referred to as *subsystems* in relation to the totality of the subject's knowledge. These subsystems can present conflicts themselves. In general terms, I will say that, for example, it is possible to have conflicts between a subsystem dealing with logicomathematical operations (such as classifications, seriation, and number construction) and another subsystem dealing with spatial operations (such as length and area). For example, when a child is judging the quantity of a number of sticks, there may be in one collection a small number of long sticks laid out. In another collection, a larger number of shorter sticks may be laid out. If he is basing his judgment on number, he would make one judgment of quantity. If he is basing his judgment on length, he would make a different judgment of quantity. These two systems can evolve at different speeds. Of course, as they evolve, there is a constant need for coordination of the two, that is, an equilibration of subsystems.

The third kind of equilibrium in cognitive development appears to be fundamental. Little by little, there has to be a constant equilibrium established between the parts of the subject's knowledge and the totality of his knowledge at any given moment. There is a constant differentiation of the totality of knowledge into the parts and an integration of the parts back into the whole. This equilibrium between differentiation and integration plays a fundamental biological role.

At the level of cognitive functions, there is a fundamental form of equilibrium because integration, as a function of differentiation, poses new problems. These new problems lead to the construction of new actions upon the previous actions, or new operations upon the previous operations. The construction of operations upon operations is probably the secret of development and of the transition from one stage to the next.

I would like to point out that the notion of operation itself involves self-regulatory mechanisms. They are—in Ashby's sense, in his cybernetic terminology—the perfect regulations in that the outcome is anticipated before the act is actually carried out. The feedback, which at lower levels has incomplete reversibility, now becomes a feedback with perfect reversibility in the sense of inversion or reciprocity. This is an example of perfect compensation—otherwise said, attained equilibrium.

I would like to explain the reasons for the role of equilibrium. All operational subject structures, on the one hand, and all causal structures in the domain of physical experience, on the other hand, suppose a combination of production and conservation. There is always some production—that is, some kind of transformation—taking place. Similarly, there is always some conservation, something that remains unchanged throughout the transformation. These two are absolutely inseparable. Without any transformation, we have only static identity. The world becomes rigid and unchanging in the sense that Parmenides (c. 539 B.C.) conceived it. Without any conservation, we have only constant transformation. There is total change; the world is always new and it becomes unintelligible. It becomes like the world of Heraclitus with its river in which one was never able to bathe twice. In reality, there are always both conservation and production.

Conservation demands compensations and, consequently, equilibration. If something is changed, something else must change to compensate for it, so that a conservation results. Even in physics, all the transformations that take place involve compensations that lead to a conservation. These compensations are organized in group structures, in the mathematical sense of the term. Furthermore, there is no conservation without production, and production with conservation results in a constant demand for new construction.

Where I speak of equilibrium, it is not at all in the sense of a definitive state that cognitive functioning would be able to attain. Attained equilibrium is limited and restrained, and there is a tendency to go beyond it to a better equilibrium. I would speak of the law of optimalization, if this term did not have technical meanings too precise for its psychological use. So, simply stated, there is a continual search for a better equilibrium. In other words, equilibration is the search for a better and better equilibrium in the sense of an extended field, in the sense of an increase in the number of possible compositions, and in the sense of a growth in coherence.

I would now like to point out the fundamental difference between biological or cognitive equilibrium and physical equilibrium. In physics, equilibrium is a question of a balance of forces. Take, for example, a balance with two weights, one on each side. Between the two are the level and the fulcrum, which are only organs of transmission. They are passive mediators permitting the action from one side to the other.

In another example, the Le Châtelier-Braun experiment, a piston presses down on a container that is full of gas. The gas is compressed while the force of the piston increases the pressure. The force of the piston heats the gas, making it agitate. This makes the gas hit back with pressure on the sides of the container and eventually back onto the piston. It compensates for the initial force that was pressing down on the piston and presses the piston back up again. Le Châtelier referred to this as the moderation of the original cause. Here again, the container plays the role of the transmitter, a passive mediator that receives and sends back the shocks.

In biological or cognitive equilibrium, on the other hand, we have a system in which all parts are interdependent. It is a system that should be represented in the form of a cycle. A has its influence on B, which has its influence on C, which has its influence on D, which again influences A. It is a cycle of interactions among the different elements. It also has a special feature of being open to influences from the outside. Each of the elements can interact with external objects. For instance, the cycle can take in A' and B'.

In the case of biological or cognitive equilibrium, the links are not passive; they are the very sources of action. The totality presents a cohesive force that is specific and that is precisely the source of the assimilation of new elements of which we have been speaking since the beginning of this talk. The system forms a totality in order to assimilate the outside elements. This equilibrium between the integration and the differentiation of the parts in the whole has no equivalent in physics. It is found only in biological and cognitive equilibrium.

In closing, I would just like to cite two references on the matter of the cohesive force of the totality, the source of equilibrium in biological and cognitive structures. The first is from Paul Weiss, the great biologist, who in his work on cells pointed out that the structure of the totality of the cell is more stable than the activity of its elements. Inside the cell the elements are in constant activity, but the total structure of the cell itself has a much more continuing stability.

My second reference is in the cognitive domain. I would like to speak of the works of Presburger, cited by Tarski, which point out the existence of systems that as totalities are closed on themselves and are completely coherent. All aspects are decidable, in the logical sense of the term, within the total system, while the subsystems are not so closed and every aspect is not entirely decidable. This seems to me a very fine example of the kind of equilibrium about which I am talking; the totality has its own cohesion and equilibrium by integrating and differentiating the parts at the same time.

Creativity

Jean Piaget

University of Geneva

There are two problems involved in a discussion of creativity. One is the problem of the origins or causes of creativity. The second is the problem of the mechanism: how does it take place, what is the process of a creative act, how does one build something new, how can something new come out of what was not there before?

I would first like to say a few words about the source or causes. It is very clear that this is wrapped in mystery; indeed some individuals are clearly more creative than others. Other individuals are much less creative, but it is certainly not just a matter of genius.

Nonetheless, even if it is present in all of us, the source remains mysterious. It is some sort of inborn aptitude. It is fashionable now among some psychologists, when they are confronted with something that is difficult to explain, to call it innate or hereditary, as if that were an explanation. But it is no explanation at all, for it only places the problem in the field of biology.

And in biology we are very far from being able to explain any sort of mental aptitude, let alone creativity. Creativity is not always a matter of precocity among those individuals who develop to be very creative. It is not that they are always precocious. Mozart of course is one of the best examples of a precocious, creative soul. But many others have become

Given as a talk in the 1972 Eisenhower Symposium "Creativity: Moving Force of Society," Johns Hopkins University, Baltimore, Maryland, 1972. Reprinted by permission of Johns Hopkins University and Jean Piaget.
Translated by Eleanor Duckworth; edited by J. Gallagher.

creative very late in their lives; it was very late that they came upon their most original ideas.

The best example of this is Kant. For many, many years Kant was not a Kantian. Most of his life he spent as a disciple of Wolf, and it was just in his later years that his own originality blossomed. So the source, the origin of creativity, to me remains a mystery and it is not explicable. But as I said a moment ago, every individual who does any work has some new ideas, however modest they may be, and creates them in the course of his efforts.

A few more words on the source or origin of creativity. In the course of my life, it has happened that I have come upon one or two little ideas, and when I reflect upon the origin of these, I find there are three conditions. The first condition is to work alone, to ignore everybody else, and to mistrust every influence from the outside.

When I was a student, I had a professor of physics who said: "Every time you start to work on a new problem, do not read anything. Instead, go as far as you can go on your own. After you have gone as far as you can on your own and you come to your solution, then read what has been said about it and take that into account and make any corrections that you might think justified." I am afraid I may have followed this precept too completely; that is, I may have read too little. But to console myself or to take away any feelings of guilt I may have had, I like to think of Freud's dictum that the greatest punishment that divinity sends to him who writes is to have to read the works of others.

The second condition that I think is necessary is to read a great deal in other disciplines, not in one's own discipline. For a psychologist, for instance, it is important to read in biology, epistemology, and logic, so as to develop an interdisciplinary outlook. Reading a lot in the related and surrounding fields, but not in one's own precise field, is necessary.

And a third aspect I think in my case has been that I have always had in my head an adversary—that is, a school of thought whose ideas one considers to be wrong. Maybe one will do them injustice and deform them by taking them as adversary. But nonetheless, one's own ideas are always there as a contrast.

My own personal whipping boy is the logical positivists or empiricists in general. This has been my adversary all through my life. For instance, the activity of the subject, the knowing subject, is minimized in logical positivism, whereas in my own thinking the activity of the subject is at the very center of the development of intelligence.

Knowledge in my view is a structuration of reality and not just a copy. The development of intelligence is not just a matter of empirical associations, but it is a construction on the part of the subject. So throughout all my work, the adversary has been empiricism, logical positivism. As I say, I may not always be just to my adversary, but it serves a useful role for me.

And now I would like to go on to the second aspect of the topic—that is, the mechanism of creativity. I think that it is the study of the psychology of intelligence that can teach us the most about this question. The development of intelligence is a continuous creation. Each stage in the development produces something radically new, totally different from what was there before. And the whole development is characterized by these appearances of totally new structures.

Intelligence is not a copy of reality; it is not performed in the objects. It is a construction on the part of the subject that enriches the external objects. The subject adds this dimension to the external objects rather than drawing this dimension from the external objects.

Consider the notion of number, for instance, or the notion of group. These frameworks enable us to understand objects in different ways, but they are not drawn from the objects; they are added to the objects. Intelligence is really an act of assimilation in a really biological sense. The outside is incorporated into the structures of the knowing subject; that is, it is in terms of the subject's structures that the outside world is understood. This creation of novelty happens of course in each generation—it happens in each individual. Each child reconstructs the same kind of intelligence and the same kind of knowledge for himself.

For instance, counting or reciting the names of the numbers certainly comes to him from the outside. The notion of number is something quite different from learning how to recite the names of the numbers. And the notion of number is constructed by the child as a creative act, as a matter of fact, as a multitude of creative acts.

I would like to give one example of this kind of creation, with the kind of thinking mathematicians call *recurrence* or *iteration*. We have two glasses and we ask the child to drop beads into the glasses; that is, he puts one bead in each glass over and over again. One of the glasses is hidden from his view so he can't see that they keep looking the same behind the screen. If you ask them at some point whether there is the same number in each of the glasses, children, even when they are very young, will say yes, there is the same amount in each glass: "I put in the same amount every time."

But then if you ask "Well now, if you keep doing that, you keep doing that all day long, all night, and you kept going and going, would you still have the same, or could you know?" And then the very little children say "Oh well, gee, I couldn't know that now, I'd have to see. So far as I can see, no. But if I kept going and going, I couldn't tell."

Whereas when they are a little older, at 5 or 6 years of age, they can know that, by virtue of repeating this action, it is guaranteed that they are all putting the same number of beads in each pile. It is expressed very beautifully by one 5½-year-old who said "When you know that once, you know it forever." That was not anything that he had learned, that anybody had ever sat him down and taught him, or that objects had taught him. It was created by himself at that moment to explain for himself this particular situation.

If, as we have said, intelligence is not something that is drawn from objects but is rather something that is added to them, then perhaps you could make another hypothesis—namely, that it is innate, that the structures are a property of the subjective part of our biological heredity. But I do not believe this to be the case either, because we do not see the emergence of something that was there already; we see its construction.

For instance, consider the very seemingly basic notion of transitivity: if *A* equals *B*, and *B* equals *C*, *A* must equal *C*. That is not an innate notion, for something as simple and basic as that is not innate. We can see the process of its construction in every child up through the age of 6 or 7. Younger than that, the notion is not as evident as it is for adults and not necessary at all.

But then of course one could say that it might be maturation. Not everything that is inherited is obvious at birth. Some things develop according to a fixed maturation schedule. But I do not think this is the case either, because there is always a fixed time scale to maturational development. Puberty for instance comes at a rather confined time scale, whereas in the development of intellectual stages there are very great variations. The work that we have done in Geneva has been done in a great variety of other countries where children were in school or not in school, in the cities or in the country.

For instance, in Iran a study was made comparing children in the country with those living in the city of Teheran. We find in all these cases that the stages are the same, which does suggest that there is a biological aspect. However, the ages are not at all the same, so there are great variations in the speed of the development.

So this seems to me to say that the structures are not preformed, for it is not just a matter of unfolding according to an internal clock. There really is a construction for each individual, for it is a matter of his creation of something new. This is a psychological problem, and that is the one I would like to look at now by looking at its mechanism.

The hypothesis that I am proposing for the discussion which will follow these remarks is that the creation of novelty is due to a process of reflexive abstraction. There are two kinds of mental abstraction. One is empirical abstraction, the kind that is most commonly referred to, in Aristotle's sense, when information is drawn from objects. You have two objects and you find a difference in weight between them. You compare colors by looking at them, so you can abstract from the objects the notion of weight and the notion of color. These notions are drawn from your own perceptions; that is, they are empirical.

There is another kind of abstraction, reflexive abstraction, where you abstract not from objects but from your own actions. What is important is the coordination of actions with the source in the subject's own actions.

In very young children, it often seems as if this kind of reflexive abstraction were confused with empirical abstraction, for it is hard to tell them apart. It seems as if a child were paying attention to properties of objects, but this is an illusion. What he is really abstracting is from his own actions.

Consider an example of reflexive abstraction at work even when there are objects involved. I have a mathematician friend who says that his career as a mathematician stemmed from the day when he was a child counting pebbles out in the yard. He had a collection of pebbles which he laid out in a line, and he counted them: one, two, three, four, five, six, seven, eight, nine, ten. He thought "That's fine." And then he counted back in the other direction, and to his great astonishment he got ten again! So, he put them in a circle and he counted them again and he got ten. He counted them in the other direction of the circle and there were still ten. And he was just full of enthusiasm, because he was discovering it was turning out to be always ten, that the sum of objects is independent of their order.

But I ask you, what does this act of abstraction consist of? The order was not a property of the pebbles, for they were in total disorder. He introduced the order into them. The sum was not a property of the pebbles either. The pebbles are there but they do not have a sum. You have to put them into one-to-one correspondence with something—your ten fingers or the numerals from 1 to 10, if you will—in order for the pebbles to have a sum. So here are the two notions, the sum and the order, and the relation between them that were drawn from his own actions rather than from any kind of empirical abstraction.

So I am proposing that all actions, all acts of intellectual creativity, are processes of reflexive abstraction. And I would like to go on now to try to analyze why.

Why is it that this process of reflexive abstraction would be the source of novelty and the source of creative intellectual acts? There are two aspects to this which are distinct but inseparable nonetheless. There are two senses of the word reflection. The first is a physical sense. There is a physical reflection taking place here in the sense of reflection in a mirror. There is a transposition, simply like a mirror reflection, from a lower level of intellectual construction to a high level of intellectual construction.

For instance, consider when you are moving from action to the representation of the action—that is, from just being able to do something to thinking about the doing of that thing. In this sense, the moment of becoming conscious of your action is the movement from one level to a higher one. In that sense there is a reflection from the action level to the representational level.

The other kind of reflection that is involved, however, is in the sense of mental reflection—that is, when one reflects. In this sense one is not just reflecting onto a higher level, but one is reconstructing on a higher level what existed already on a lower level. Now, the higher level is always a wider, more all-embracing field, so that when one reflects onto a higher level, it is incumbent upon one to enrich it with new elements. So you have to enlarge it as well as to transpose it on the second level.

I would like to give the example of the group of displacements in space. For small children, 1 year or so, at the sensorimotor level, their intelligence is all in their actions, for they are not representing their thoughts to themselves. For instance, they can be outdoors in the garden or in their house and can coordinate their displacements in space. They can come back to the same point they were at before. They can get to a different point through a number of different routes and know where to go next in order to get to that other point. But these are all at the level of action. It is all moving from one moment to the next, using indicators that are there at the present moment. These children do not go back to put together everything that they have done in the past. It is a moment-to-moment kind of being able to find oneself in space.

At the next level, the ability to move oneself about and know where one is in space is reflected at the representational level. But now there are new elements in that it is not just a matter of going from one spot to the next and from one moment to the next, but one can have an image of the whole face, the whole garden, and where all the points are in that garden. One can also consider where they are when they are in another given point. So, this representation gives the possibility for reversibility, since there is a wholeness involved, and it gives the possibility for compositions that give a reason to the relationships which on the earlier level were simply lived and not reasoned.

I would like to give another example of a notion that is drawn from—that is, reflected up onto a higher level. The example is the notion of order. One might think that the notion of order was drawn from objects. Think, for example, of the bars of a crib or a set of fence posts that a child might be walking by. They are both laid out in systematic order. It does seem that the order is there in the objects themselves.

When Hemholtz was analyzing the genesis of numbers, he considered that the ordinal aspect was more primitive than the cardinal aspect because it is given in experience. One can simply perceive the ordering.

In reality, any time that one wants to apprehend order, even when it is there already, it is a different case from that of the mathematician who introduced the order into the pebbles. In this case there is a systematic regularity that is visible, but in order to apprehend that regularity you need to have ordered actions. You have to have a regular, systematic look at the bars, or you have to touch the fence posts in an ordered, systematic way in order to apprehend the order and system that is already there. Otherwise, it goes unperceived.

Hemholtz also made the case that memory is ordered and that it is again inherent and simple, but that is not at all the case. Memory is a difficult job of reconstruction, and there is a lot of deduction that is involved in deciding whether a certain act came before or after another act.

So, a number of years ago, the behaviorist Daniel Berlyne spent a year with us in Geneva. He was looking at the problem of the genesis of the idea of order. He looked at it in a number of different ways, but he found that he could not account for it in his behavioral terms as just a perceptive reading of ordered events. In order to account for it, he had to attribute to the apprehending subject an internal counter. And for me that is precisely what is the ordering action. That's fine with me if he has to add that to his behaviorism!

The ordering action is not a property of the objects. It is the creation of reflexive abstraction. It is a reflection on your ordered acts that allows you to apprehend order in the world. And this is the case for order right up to the highest levels of mathematical thinking.

I would like to take an example of reflexive abstraction in the creative act from outside the realm of psychology. This one comes from mathematics, the queen of sciences itself. The body of mathematics is a model of creativity, and it also rests on a process of reflexive abstraction. Therefore, it is of special interest.

When I say that mathematics is a model of creativity, I am again contrasting my position with the logical positivists who would say mathematics is only language, and tautological language at that. But in point of fact, mathematics is much more than that. It is not tautological at all, but, as any system of transformations must be, it is a construction. All of the history of mathematics is a history of reflexive abstraction. And I would like to outline three main periods to make that point.

The first period was the Greek period, where there was a great amount of mathematical creativity. In that period, mathematical beings were beings outside the subject and in the objects. For Pythagoras, numbers were in the objects; for Euclid, geometric figures were real figures, ways of describing real figures. For Plato, mathematical beings were not in objects, but they were ideal beings, they were still quite external to the knowing subject. The Greeks of course had to use operations in their mathematical thinking, but they were not conscious of it. For instance, anything that touched algebra, where perhaps their own operations became somewhat more visible, they did not allow into the field of mathematics. Algebra was just some sort of recipe dealing with a subject's reasoning; it was not part of mathematics.

I think that this very realistic vision of mathematics has limits. This is what can explain the decadence of Greek mathematics at its end in the Alexandrian Period. The creativity wore out, I think, and it seems to me that was because of the absence of any cognizance or any conscious awareness of one's own activity in mathematics.

The second period was the beginning of this conscious awareness of the subject's own contribution to mathematics. This came in the 17th century, with the development of algebra. The Arabs had done some development of algebra before, but in this tradition it was Viète and Descartes who worked on algebra.

Another example is Descartes' outlining the operations in such a way as to make a general statement that brings together what is in common in the two fields of algebra and geometry. Finally, Newton generalized the operations to infinity with the creation of calculus.

So these were all examples of becoming consciously aware of the operations that are involved in doing mathematics. And yet in this period, mathematicians were still not aware of structures. For them, each operation was a free product of the mathematician's will. They were not yet aware that operations were tied to one another in structured groups.

So the third major period in the history of mathematics I am proposing started in the 19th century with the discovery of the group by Galois. Then it went through a generalization into all areas of mathematics, and it is in full bloom in the 20th century with various structures, such as group structures and lattices and so forth, throughout the area of mathematics.

I find these three stages very interesting; they are all creative. But the first one, the ignoring of the role of the mathematician himself in creating a mathematics, seems sterile and leads to its own sterilization. The second stage was discovering the subject's role in the operations, and the third stage was putting operations together into structures. Each time the progress was a progress in reflecting—that is, a reflexive abstraction—on the advances that had been made at the previous stage.

I would like to give one more example from the area of child psychology. You are probably familiar with the conservation experiments that we have done in Geneva, where two equal quantities, such as water, are presented to a child. Then one of them is poured into a container of a different shape, and the child tends to think that in this new container, since the water goes up higher, there is more. Thus, for the child, there is no longer the same amount of water as there was before.

Or changing the shape of one of two balls of clay makes the child think, at the age of 4 or 5 or 6 or so, that there is now more clay in one ball because it is longer. And then, at the age of 7 or 8, the questions are not difficult and the child thinks you are rather idiotic to be asking him.

But, how does he discover this conservation event? A number of people throughout the world have been doing these experiments again and coming up with different explanations. Bruner sees it as a kind of generalization of the identity of that piece of clay or that body of water. The Soviet psychologists see it as a product of experience.

I have been looking at conservation experiments again, from the point of view of this reflexive abstraction, and it seems to me that it turns out to be a good example. In conservation—let's say, the example of the clay—there is always a positive element; you are adding some clay onto one end. But the clay that is being added onto one end of the ball is taken away from the side, and the amount of the clay in the ball has not changed. What was added onto one end has been taken away from another part of the ball of clay. (And that is still true, despite any baby's protests.[1])

The child however, as a nonconserver, is focusing only on the positive aspect. There is more clay being added there, and he is totally forgetting the fact that there is some being taken away from somewhere else. He is not at all conscious of the entirety—the totality of the act.

So when he discovers conservation, what he is discovering is the totality of the whole action, that what is added onto one part of the ball of clay is part and parcel of what was taken away from the other part. He is becoming consciously aware, he is reflecting upon his whole action. And when he can tie it all together and see that there is a negative element as well as the positive element, the taking away as well as the adding to, this is what leads to conservation.

Ladies and gentlemen, I notice that I have been speaking for too long, so I would like to conclude. I have taken many of my examples from childhood because that is the maximum creative time in the life of a human being. The sensorimotor period, for instance, before the

---

[1]An infant in the audience cried loudly at this point in the lecture, so Piaget added a humorous element (Editor's note).

development of language, is incredible in its amount of invention and discovery. I have also taken some examples from mathematics. I could just as well have taken them from physics—in the area, for instance, of the construction of physical models.

I would just like to close by repeating the words of a physicist who works with us in Geneva, doing experiments with children on their thinking in this area. What he said was what distinguishes creative physicists from run-of-the-mill physicists—that the creative physicist, in spite of his knowledge, succeeds in staying in part a child, with the curiosity and the candor of invention that characterize most children until they are deformed by adult society.

Glossary

Accommodation The process that accounts for modifications in the assimilation schemes. Whenever a child applies an assimilation scheme, that scheme is adjusted to ensure its appropriateness for any given situation. It is through these active adjustments that the assimilation schemes become differentiated and new schemes gradually emerge.

Affirmation A positive characteristic of an object. Affirmations are observed perceptually and are primary characteristics (such as the obvious longer length of a ball of clay when changed into a sausage). Therefore, the subject need not actively verify, infer, or make a labored construction as in negation.

Alpha behavior Attempts to compensate for a disturbance or perturbation by ignoring or canceling it. For example, a child may know that, when ball *A* hits ball *B*, the latter will go off in a straight trajectory. However, when ball *B* is deflected when hit on the side, the child may try to cancel this unexpected result by using more force in a straight-forward motion.

Assimilation The process through which experiential data are incorporated into existing structures. It involves both empirical and reflexive abstractions. Of critical importance is the fact that assimilations do not occur as the result of any external pressure. Humans (as well as other biological organisms) are naturally active; therefore, it is in their nature to seek assimilable material from their environments. (See also **Assimilation by generalization, Reciprocal assimilation,** and **Recognitory assimilation.**)

Assimilation by generalization At the sensorimotor level, the extension of a scheme to an ever-increasing number of objects—for example, extending the scheme of sucking to a variety of objects.

Beta behavior Attempts to compensate for a disturbance or perturbation by taking that disturbance into account and integrating it into the existing level of understanding. For example, if the child observes that ball *B* is deflected by ball *A*, he or she tries to change positions in order to learn the variations of the deflection.

Class inclusion An operation of classification that implies the grouping of objects according to their similarities. Specifically, the operation is centered on the child's ability to construct the negation of the nonclass (flowers minus tulips equals nontulips—all flowers that are not tulips).

Compensation Actions aimed at neutralizing or canceling a disturbance. They constitute an important aspect of construction.

Concrete-operational stage First stage of operational intelligence (approximately 7 to 12 years) related to the concrete. Each of the operations of this stage, such as classification and seriation, is achieved by a gradual equilibration between disturbances and compensating reactions—that is, by the gradual balancing of affirmations and negations.

Conservation The understanding (construction) that certain aspects of a situation or object are invariant, even though they are transformed. For example, children conserve quantity when they understand that the amount of water does not change if poured from a low, wide container into a tall, thin container. True conservation is an empirical indicator of operational reversibility, a mental phenomenon. The revised explanation for conservation is based on commutability (the whole is conserved even though parts are rearranged) and the balancing of affirmations and negations.

Constituent function The elementary function of the preoperational period expressing the interdependency of the covariations of objects' properties. For example, when a string is pulled through a pulley, there is an interdependency between the length of the segment being pulled and the length of the remaining segment. The relationship is understood as not necessarily reversible, for it implies a one-way logic or semilogic of an elementary function.

Contradiction The lack of balance in an equilibrating system. Contradictions constitute the driving force of development, because they lead to compensations and, hence, reequilibrations. They are not inherent in thought but arise because thought is elaborated only gradually. Whereas the human mind tends to concentrate spontaneously on affirmations, the negations are constructed only gradually. Unless an exact compensation between affirmations and negations exists, contradictions result.

Coordination Inference, or a construction deemed necessary to understand relations between objects or events—for example, the logical necessity that the water line in a tilted jar be parallel to the table rather than to the bottom of the jar. Coordination implies a "bringing into relationship"—that is, a construction of new relations that goes beyond what is observed. (See also **Observables**.)

Correspondences Instruments, or the means of comparisons that aid in the retention of what may be repeated in a relationship. No transformation is needed. The comparisons involved may be simple (one-to-one correspondence) or complex (discovery of the covariance or dependency between functions, such as the relationship between the lengthening of segment *A* and the shortening of segment *B* when a string is pulled).

Development The general, spontaneous process of growth (both biological and psychological). It is the result of the interplay of four factors: physiological maturation, physical knowledge, social knowledge, and equilibration. In discussions of learning, the Genevans differentiate between development (learning in the broad sense) and learning in the strict sense.

Disequilibrium A state of nonbalance in cognitive development that may be due to perturbations (connected with a lack of balance between assimilations and accommodations) or to the dominance of affirmations over negations (as in contradiction). For example, an infant may be able to pull a small toy through the bars of the playpen but may be perturbed when he or she meets failure with a larger toy. The necessary accommodation of turning or reaching over the top has not been made. A higher equilibrium is reached when the accommodation is made; thus, disequilibrium forces a person to go beyond a present level of understanding to seek a new equilibrium.

Empirical abstraction The process of acquiring physical knowledge. Whatever we observe about objects or events is *selected,* in the sense that we choose (consciously or unconsciously) what to notice and what to ignore. The term is used by Piaget to highlight the *activity* of the child as he or she learns about the physical properties of the world. Empirical abstraction relates only to the observable features of objects, so it is always dependent on logico-mathematical structures.

Endogenous knowledge Logico-mathematical knowledge. It originates in the internal coordination of the actions or operations of the subject. For example, in the understanding of transitivity, it is necessary to coordinate that *A* is smaller than *C if A* is smaller than *B* and *B* is smaller than *C.* The distinctive characteristic of endogenous knowledge is *necessity.*

Equilibration The self-regulatory process whose mechanisms are assimilation and accommodation. It enables external experience to be incorporated into internal structures in such a way that existing structures are conserved and enriched (through the integration and differentiation of assimilation schemes). Piaget also uses the term to refer to the coordination among equivalent schemes and to the maintenance of the hierarchical organization between the organism as a whole and its parts.

Equilibrium A balance or level of understanding reached in cognitive development. The balance may be between assimilation and accommodation or between affirmations and negations. Equilibrium is a state; equilibration is the process. However, equilibrium as a state is fleeting. It is dynamic and opens up new possibilities for growth in understanding.

Exogenous knowledge Knowledge that originates in what is observed—that is, knowledge based on experience with, or actions of the subject on, external objects. Lifting two objects and observing that one is lighter than the other represents an example of exogenous knowledge.

Formal-operational stage Second and final stage of operational intelligence (beginning in preadolescence and continuing into adulthood), characterized by the understanding of the real as one among other possibilities and by the ability to separate the form of an argument from its content. It is a period of reflected abstraction, in which the subject is more likely to state a general, verbal rule after solving a problem.

Gamma behavior Behavior in which an unexpected result is not considered to be a disturbance or perturbation, since that result is understood as an integral part of the system. For example, the possible deflection that occurs when one ball hits another ball is understood by the subject and can be predicted. Gamma behavior is another term for the replacement of exogenous knowledge by an endogenous reconstruction in cognitive development. (See also **Phenocopy.**)

Genetic epistemology Piaget's scientific discipline centered on *constructivism*—that is, the interaction or active relationship between the knowing subject and the object to be known. (Since *genetic* is sometimes misinterpreted as relating to maturation, *developmental* or *constructivist epistemology* is the preferred term.)

Genotype Traditionally, the fundamental hereditary makeup of an organism. Piaget prefers the term *genome,* defined as the hereditary material functioning as a whole or as a controlling system made up of interacting genes. (See also **Phenotype.**)

INRC group A mathematical structure used by Piaget for the stage of formal operations as a model for problem solving, which involves double systems of reference and proportions. For example, if an object is capable of moving in two different directions on a board that is moving in two different directions, four movements and two systems of reference are involved. The INRC group is a structure that builds on previous operations that a person possesses but of which that person is unaware.

Learning In its strict sense, the acquisition of some specific information from the environment; in its broad sense, information acquired through experience as well as equilibration. It is through the process of equilibration that new information is incorporated into previously existing knowledge and simultaneously effects modifications in the way prior knowledge has been organized.

Logical necessity The conviction that certain generalizations are necessary once a certain result is observed. For example, if it is understood that A is smaller than B and B is smaller than C, of necessity A is smaller than C.

Logico-mathematical knowledge Knowledge derived from thinking about one's experiences with objects and events. It comprises the framework into which physical knowledge is integrated and therefore given meaning, and it includes structures for organizing, constructing, and transforming empirical data.

Negation A characteristic of an object or action that must be slowly constructed by the subject (such as the loss in width of a ball of clay elongated into a sausage). During the early stages of cognitive development, the positive characteristics dominate; with balancing of affirmations and negations, higher levels of understanding are reached through the mechanisms of equilibration.

Observables Whatever the child is able to identify during the reading of events or objects. The nature of observables undergoes changes as negations are constructed. A child, for example, who "sees" that one clay ball has become longer than another because it was rolled into a sausage will, after constructing the negation that the ball has simultaneously become thinner, "see" that the two balls still contain the same amount of clay. What was observable during the first reading has been considerably altered by the construction of the negation, and a new observable has emerged.

Operation An action that can be internalized or thought about and that is mentally reversible—namely, that it can take place in one direction or in the opposite direction. An operation always implies conservation and the relation to a system of operations, or total structure. For Piaget, operations are the *result*, not the *source*, of growth in intelligence.

Phenocopy Replacement of an initial phenotype by a genotype representing the same distinctive characteristics. The cognitive equivalent of the biological concept of phenocopy is the replacement of exogenous (originating in the observables) by endogenous (logico-mathematical) reconstructions.

Phenotype Adapted response of the genetic pool to environmental tensions. For Piaget, this adapted response means that the organism is not merely dependent on the environment, for often the organism chooses its environment and also modifies it. Therefore, by definition, phenotype is the product of a continuous interaction between the hereditary material and environmental influences.

Physical knowledge Knowledge of the physical properties of the external world. Physical knowledge is abstracted directly from objects and events and can be interpreted only within a logico-mathematical framework. Examples of physical knowledge include color, size, weight, height, texture, and intensity.

Preoperational (representational) stage The period of intellectual development (approximately 2 to 6 or 7 years) between sensorimotor intelligence and concrete operations. With language, symbolic play, and mental images, the child is able to internalize, or mentally represent, actions. It is the period in which the semilogic of constituent functions emerges. For example, the child understands that, when a string is pulled, an increase in segment *A* is accompanied by a decrease in segment *B*.

Primary circular reaction The infant's active reproduction of a result first obtained by chance. It pertains to a learning phenomenon centered on the infant's own body, such as bringing the hand in front of the face and repeatedly opening and closing it. These reactions are elementary with compensation of type-alpha constructions.

Qualitative identity The type of identity characteristic of the child who is able to state that it is "the same clay" when a ball of clay is elongated into a sausage. The properties of the object are observed directly without an understanding that the quantity is conserved. In qualitative identity, the semilogical system of one-way dependencies is brought into play.

Quantitative identity The type of identity characteristic of the child who is able to state that a ball of clay that has been changed into a sausage is the same as the unchanged ball of clay. The arguments used are based on a system of operations: logical identity, reversibility by cancellation of the change, and compensation based on reciprocity (balancing of affirmations and negations, in that every increase in length implies a decrease in width).

Reciprocal assimilation The coordination of two schemes previously acquired and maintained as circular reactions. At first, a child may temporarily stop sucking a toy and stare at it simply because of visual interest. When a reciprocal assimilation occurs, the infant will repeatedly move the toy while staring at it, so that he will continually keep the toy in view. Thus, the scheme for looking at the toy and the scheme for moving it are assimilated into each other.

Recognitory assimilation The beginning of differentiation or discrimination in the application of a scheme. For example, when a child is nursing, she will express disappointment and start to cry if she mistakenly sucks her blanket instead of the nipple. Her reaction reveals her awareness of the distinguishing characteristics of an object she desires and anticipates but fails to attain. Thus, the child's general reflex of sucking has been elaborated to recognize significant sensory patterns in the world of objects.

Reflexive abstraction The process through which one derives information from one's own actions and from the coordination of actions (putting them into correspondence, linking them, ordering them, and so forth). It provides the links between and among experiences and can be detected even in the very earliest and most elementary behaviors of infants. Reflexive abstraction has two aspects: a projection from a lower to a higher level—for example, from the sensorimotor level to the level of thought—and a reorganization or reconstruction of knowledge at the higher level.

Regulation (regulatory mechanisms) Part of the equilibration model. Whenever the results of an action, through feedback, cause modifications in future replications of that action, such regulatory mechanisms are said to be operating. All regulations are reactions to disturbances, but not all disturbances lead to regulations.

Reversibility The essential aspect of an operational structure; mental activity having identical paths to and from an end point. True reversibility is manifested when children have a mental understanding that, when a clay ball is rolled into a sausage, its increased length is compensated by a loss in width. If, in order to determine whether the amount of clay is the same regardless of the change in shape, the child needs to change the sausage back into a ball, the term *pseudoreversibility (renversabilité)* applies.

Scheme A term often used for structure at the sensorimotor level; an action that can be generalized to analogous situations—for example, when the action of sucking the nipple is generalized to sucking toys. (The term *schema,* used in early Piagetian writings, means the perceptual aspects of an action.)

Secondary circular reaction A learning phenomenon in which the infant becomes interested in the continuation of a result such as the repeated striking of a swinging object that was first struck by chance. Differs from primary circular reaction in that the interest is centered on the external result and not on activity as such.

Sensorimotor stage The stage characterized by the form of intelligence that precedes language (approximately 0 to 18 months). It is a period of direct actions, without mental representation of the actions. Disturbances to be regulated by compensations are noticed at this level through sensorimotor channels.

Seriation The operation of ordering of objects according to their differences. At the basis of the understanding of seriation is the ability to apply the transitivity argument: if A is smaller than B and B is smaller than C, then, of necessity, A is smaller than C.

Spiral of Knowing An inverted cone-shaped model used by Piaget to demonstrate the meaning of equilibration in relation to the development of intelligence (constructivist epistemology). The model provides for the internal regulations that react to external disturbances.

Structure As a mathematical concept, a system with a set of laws that apply to the system as a whole and not only to its elements (for example, the series of whole numbers). Psychologically, the term refers to the sum total of what a child's mind is able to do. If a child is able to seriate a set of uneven sticks, we infer that the structure of asymmetric relationships exists for that child.

Symbolic function Means by which the child in the preoperational stage represents the world; it includes language, imitation, symbolic play, mental imagery, pictures, and gestures. The stress is on the interiorization of imitation.

Tertiary circular reaction A learning phenomenon in which the infant does not just repeat an interesting result (as in secondary circular reaction) but invents new movements intentionally in order to observe what happens. For example, a 1-year-old may press on all sides of a new box, after first pressing on one place, so as to observe the resulting various positions of the box. Beta behavior (compensating for a disturbance by taking it into account) is first noticed at the level of tertiary circular reactions.

References

Adams, M. J., & Collins, A. *A schema-theoretic view of reading* (Technical Report No. 32). Chicago: University of Illinois Center for the Study of Reading, April 1977.

Adler, M. J. Some implications of the theories of Jean Piaget and J. S. Bruner for education. *Canadian Education and Research Digest*, 1964, 4, 291–305.

Ajuriaguerra, J. de, Jaeggi, F., Guignard, F., Kocher, F., Maquard, M., Paunier, A., Quinodoz, D., & Siotis, E. Organisation psychologique et troubles de développement du langage (Etude d'un groupe d'enfants dysphasiques). *Problèmes de psycholinguistique.* Paris: Presses Universitaires de France, 1963, 109–140.

Allen, V. L., & Feldman, R. S. Learning through tutoring: Low-achieving children as tutors. *Journal of Experimental Education*, 1973, 42, 1–5.

Allport, D. A. The state of cognitive psychology. *Quarterly Journal of Experimental Psychology*, 1975, 27, 141–152.

Anderson, R. C., Spiro, R. J., & Montague, W. E. *Schooling and the acquisition of knowledge.* Hillsdale, N.J.: Erlbaum, 1977.

Beilin, H. Learning and operational convergence in logical thought development. *Journal of Experimental Child Psychology*, 1965, 2, 317–339.

Beth, E. W., & Piaget, J. *Mathematical epistemology and psychology.* Dordrecht, Holland: Reidel, 1966.

Bovet, M. Etudes interculturelles du développement intellectuel et processus d'apprentissage. *Revue Suisse de Psychologie Pure et Appliquée*, 1968, 27, 189–199.

Bovet, M. *Etude interculturelle des processus de raisonnement. Notions de quantités physiques et relations spatio-temporelles chez des enfants et des adultes non-scolarisés.* Thesis, University of Geneva, 1971.

Bovet, M. Piaget's theory of cognitive development and individual differences. In B. Inhelder & H. E. Chipman (Eds.), *Piaget and his school.* New York: Springer-Verlag, 1976.

Bradfield, R. H. Precision teaching: A useful technology for special education teachers. In H. Bradfield (Ed.), *Behavior modification of learning disabilities.* San Rafael, Calif.: Academic Therapy Publications, 1971.

237

Braine, M. D. S., & Shanks, B. L. The development of conservation of size. *Journal of Verbal Learning and Verbal Behavior*, 1965, 4, 227–242.

Brainerd, C. J. Judgments and explanations as criteria for the presence of cognitive structures. *Psychological Bulletin*, 1973, 79, 172–179.

Brainerd, C. J. Postmortem on judgments, explanations, and Piagetian cognitive structures. *Psychological Bulletin*, 1974, 81, 70–71.

Brainerd, C. J. Feedback, rule knowledge, and conservation learning. *Child Development*, 1977, 48, 404–411.

Brainerd, C. J. Recent developments in neo-Piagetian learning research. *The Genetic Epistemologist*, 1978, 7, 1–2.

Brainerd, C. J., & Allen, T. W. Experimental inductions of the conservation of "first-order" quantitative invariants. *Psychological Bulletin*, 1971, 75, 128–144.

Brill, M., Weiserbs, B., & Reid, D. K. *The relations among seriation, class inclusion, conservation, and academic achievement in emotionally disturbed and learning disabled children*. Paper presented at the 8th Annual Symposium of The Jean Piaget Society, Philadelphia, May 1978.

Brison, D. W. Acceleration of conservation of substance. *Journal of Genetic Psychology*, 1966, 109, 311–322.

Brogle, J. F. Performance of normals and retardates of Piaget's conservation tasks. *Dissertation Abstracts*, 1971, 31, 6870-6871B.

Brown, A. L. Conservation of number and continuous quantity in normal, bright, and retarded children. *Child Development*, 1973, 44, 375–379.

Brun, J. *Education mathématique et développement intellectuel*. Thesis, University of Lyon, 1975.

Bruner, J. The course of cognitive growth. *American Psychologist*, 1964, 19, 1–15.

Bruner, J. *Beyond the information given*. New York: Norton, 1973.

Bruner, J. Fie on methodological quarrels (Comment on Kuhn's review of *Learning and the development of cognition*, by B. Inhelder, H. Sinclair, & M. Bovet). *Contemporary Psychology*, 1976, 21, 226–227.

Bruner, J., Olver, R. R., & Greenfield, P. M. (Eds.). *Studies in cognitive growth*. New York: Wiley, 1966.

Carlson, J. S. *Cross-cultural Piagetian studies: What can they tell us?* Paper presented at the meeting of the International Society for the Study of Behavioral Development, University of Michigan, Ann Arbor, 1973.

Carlson, J. S., & Michelson, L. H. Methodological study of conservation in retarded adolescents. *American Journal of Mental Deficiency*, 1973, 78, 348–353.

Carpenter, T. E. A pilot study for a quantitative investigation of Jean Piaget's original work on concept formation. *Educational Review*, 1955, 7, 142–149.

Claparède, E. *Experimental pedagogy and the psychology of the child*. New York: Arno Press, 1975. (Originally published, 1911.)

Cohen, G. M. Conservation of quantity in children: The effect of vocabulary and participation. *Quarterly Journal of Experimental Psychology*, 1967, 19, 150–154.

Cole, M., Gay, J., Glick, J., & Sharp, D. Linguistic structure and transposition. *Science*, 1969, 164, 90–91.

Cole, M., Gay, J., Glick, J., & Sharp, D. *The cultural context of learning and thinking*. London: Methuen, 1971.

Cromer, R. F. Conservation by the congenitally blind. *British Journal of Psychology*, 1973, 64, 241–250.

Cross, G. R. *The psychology of learning: An introduction for students of education*. New York: Pergamon, 1974.

Dasen, P. R. Cross-cultural Piagetian research: A summary. *Journal of Cross-Cultural Psychology*, 1972, 3, 23–40.

Dasen, P. R. *Piagetian psychology: Cross-cultural contributions*. New York: Gardner, 1977.

Davis, R. B. The structure of mathematics and the structure of cognitive development. *Journal of Children's Mathematical Behavior*, 1971–1972, *1*(1), 71–97.

Denis-Prinzhorn, M., & Grize, J. B. La méthode clinique en pédagogie. In F. Bresson & M. de Montmollin (Eds.), *Psychologie et épistémologie génétiques: Thèmes Piagétiens*. Paris: Dunod, 1966.

Denis-Prinzhorn, M., Kamii, C., & Mounoud, P. Pedagogical applications of Piaget's theory. In L. Glogau (Ed.), *Inside Piaget: Practical considerations for the classroom*. South Orange, N.J.: Pragmatix, 1975.

Deshler, D. D. Introducing Public Law 94–142: The Education for All Handicapped Children Act of 1975. *DCLD Newsletter*, 1976, *2*, 10–24.

DeVries, R. *The two intelligences of bright, average and retarded children*. Paper presented at the Meeting of The Society for Research in Child Development, Philadelphia, May 1973.

DeVries, R. Theory in educational practice. In R. Colvin & E. Zaffiro (Eds.), *Preschool education: A handbook for the training of early childhood educators*. New York: Springer, 1974.

DeVries, R. Early education: Applications versus implications. In J. M. Gallagher & J. A. Easley (Eds.), *Knowledge and development. Vol. 2: Piaget and education*. New York: Plenum, 1978.

Ditisheim, M. *Quelques reflexions psychopédagogiques sur la valeur de l'erreur*. Unpublished paper, University of Geneva, 1975.

Doise, W., Mugny, G., & Perret-Clermont, A. N. Social interaction and the development of cognitive operations. *European Journal of Social Psychology*, 1975, *5*, 367–383.

Doise, W., & Perret-Clermont, A. N. Social interaction and the development of cognitive operations. *European Journal of Social Psychology*, 1975, *5*, 18–29.

Duckworth, E. Piaget rediscovered. In R. E. Ripple & V. N. Rockcastle (Eds.), *Piaget rediscovered: A report of the Conference on Cognitive Studies and Curriculum Development*. Ithaca, N.Y.: Department of Education, Cornell University, 1964.

Duckworth, E. The having of wonderful ideas. In M. Schwebel & J. Raph (Eds.), *Piaget in the classroom*. New York: Basic Books, 1973.

Duckworth, E. Either we're too early and they can't learn it or we're too late and they know it already: The dilemma of "applying Piaget." *Harvard Educational Review*, 1979, *49*, 297–312.

Easley, J. A. The structural paradigm in protocol analysis. *Journal of Research in Science Teaching*, 1974, *11*, 281–290.

Easley, J. A. On clinical studies in mathematics education. *Mathematics Education Information Report*. ERIC Science, Mathematics and Environmental Education Clearing House in cooperation with the Center for Science and Mathematics Education, Ohio State University, 1977.

Easley, J. A. Four decades of conservation research—What do they mean for mathematics education? In J. M. Gallagher & J. A. Easley (Eds.), *Knowledge and development. Vol. 2: Piaget and education*. New York: Plenum, 1978.

Endler, N. S., Boulter, L. R., & Osser, H. (Eds.). *Contemporary issues in developmental psychology* (2nd ed.). New York: Holt, Rinehart & Winston, 1976.

Engelmann, S. Does the Piagetian approach imply instruction? In D. Green, M. Ford, & G. Flamer (Eds.), *Measurement and Piaget*. New York: McGraw-Hill, 1971.

Engelmann, S., & Bruner, E. *Distar Reading I and II*. Chicago: Science Research Associates, 1969.

Erlwanger, S. H. Benny's conception of rules and answers in IPI mathematics. *Journal of Children's Mathematical Behavior*, 1973, *1*, 7–26.

Erlwanger, S. H. *Case studies of children's conceptions of mathematics.* Doctoral dissertation, University of Illinois at Urbana-Champaign, 1974.

Erlwanger, S. H. Case studies of children's conceptions of mathematics (Pt. 1). *Journal of Children's Mathematical Behavior*, 1975, *1*, 157–283.

Falmagne, R. J. *Reasoning: Representation and process.* Hillsdale, N.J.: Erlbaum, 1975.

Feigenbaum, J., & Sulkin, H. Piaget's problem of conservation of discontinuous quantities: A teaching experience. *Journal of Genetic Psychology*, 1964, *105*, 91–97.

Filer, A. A. Piagetian cognitive development in normal and in emotionally disturbed children. *Dissertation Abstracts International*, 1972, *33*, 2342.

Flavell, J. H. *Cognitive development.* Englewood Cliffs, N.J.: Prentice-Hall, 1977.

Fowles, B. R., & Voyat, G. Piaget meets Big Bird: Is TV a passive teacher? *Urban Review*, 1974, *7*, 69–80.

Friedland, S. J., & Meisels, S. J. An application of the Piagetian model to perceptual handicaps. *Journal of Learning Disabilities*, 1975, *8*, 20–24.

Friedman, J., & Pasnak, R. Attainment of classification and seriation concepts by blind and sighted children. *Education of the Handicapped*, 1973, *5*, 55–62.

Frostig, M., & Maslow, P. Reading, developmental abilities, and the problem of the match. *Journal of Learning Disabilities*, 1969, *2*, 571–574.

Furth, H. G. *Thinking without language: Psychological implications of deafness.* New York: Free Press, 1966.

Furth, H. G. *Piaget and knowledge.* Englewood Cliffs, N.J.: Prentice-Hall, 1969.

Furth, H. G. *Piaget for teachers.* Englewood Cliffs, N.J.: Prentice-Hall, 1970.

Furth, H. G. Linguistic deficiency and thinking: Research with deaf subjects 1964–1969. *Psychological Bulletin*, 1971, *76*, 58–72.

Furth, H. G. *Deafness and learning: A psychosocial approach.* Monterey, Calif.: Brooks/Cole, 1973.

Furth, H. G. Comments on the problems of equilibration. In M. H. Appel & L. S. Goldberg (Eds.), *Topics in cognitive development. Vol. 1: Theory, research, and application.* New York: Plenum, 1977.

Furth, H. G., & Wachs, H. *Thinking goes to school.* New York: Oxford University Press, 1974.

Gallagher, J. M. Cognitive development and learning in the adolescent. In J. Adams (Ed.), *Understanding adolescence* (2nd ed.). Boston: Allyn & Bacon, 1973.

Gallagher, J. M. *Piaget's developmental epistemology and analogy: A return to philosophical roots.* Paper presented at the annual meeting of the American Psychological Association, Washington, D.C., September 1976.

Gallagher, J. M. Piaget's equilibration theory: Biological, cybernetic, and logical roots. In M. H. Appel & L. S. Goldberg (Eds.), *Topics in cognitive development. Vol. 1: Equilibration: Theory, research, and application.* New York: Plenum, 1977.

Gallagher, J. M. The future of formal thought research: The study of analogy and metaphor. In B. Presseisen, D. Goldstein, & M. Appel (Eds.), *Topics in cognitive development. Vol. 2: Language and operational thought.* New York: Plenum, 1978. (a)

Gallagher, J. M. Reflexive abstraction and education: The meaning of activity in Piaget's theory. In J. M. Gallagher & J. A. Easley (Eds.), *Knowledge and development. Vol. 2: Piaget and education.* New York: Plenum, 1978. (b)

Gallagher, J. M. Equilibration—The central concept of Piaget's theory: An answer to Brainerd's critique of the criteria for stages. *The Behavioral and Brain*

Sciences; An International Journal of Current Research and Theory, 1979, 2 (2), 141.

Gallagher, J. M., & Mansfield, R. J. Cognitive development and learning in the adolescent. In J. Adams (Ed.), *Understanding adolescence* (4th ed.). Boston: Allyn & Bacon, 1980.

Gallagher, J. M., & Noppe, I. C. Cognitive development and learning in the adolescent. In J. Adams (Ed.), *Understanding adolescence* (3rd ed.). Boston: Allyn & Bacon, 1976.

Gallagher, J. M., & Reid, D. K. An empirical test of judgments and explanations in Piagetian-type problems of conservation of continuous quantity. *Perceptual and Motor Skills*, 1978, 46, 363–368.

Gallagher, J. M., & Wright, R. J. Children's solution of verbal analogies: Extension of Piaget's concept of reflexive abstraction. In H. Gardner (Chair), *Thinking with the left hand: Children's understanding of analogy and metaphor.* Symposium presented at the Meeting of The Society for Research in Child Development, New Orleans, March 1977.

Gallagher, J. M., & Wright, R. J. Structure of analogy items: A Piagetian interpretation. In J. Magary (Ed.), *Piagetian theory and the helping professions.* Los Angeles: University of Southern California, 1979.

Gardner, H. *The quest for mind: Piaget, Lévi-Strauss, and the structuralist movement.* New York: Knopf, 1973.

Garonne, G., Guignard, F., Rodriguez, R., Lenoir, J., Kobr, F., & Degailler, L. La débilité mental chez l'enfant. *Psychiatrie de l'Enfant*, 1969, 12, 201–219.

Garrison, M. (Ed.). Cognitive models and development in mental retardation. *American Journal of Mental Deficiency*, 1966, 70 (4). (Monograph)

Gelman, R. Conservation acquisition: A problem of learning to attend to relevant attributes. *Journal of Experimental Child Psychology*, 1969, 7, 167–187.

Gelman, R., & Weinberg, D. H. The relationship between liquid conservation and compensation. *Child Development*, 1972, 43, 371–383.

Getman, G. N. The visuomotor complex in the acquisition of learning skills. In J. Hellmuth (Ed.), *Learning disorders* (Vol. 1). Seattle: Special Child Publications, 1965.

Glick, J. Cognitive development in cross-cultural perspective. In F. D. Horowitz (Ed.), *Review of child development research* (Vol. 4). Chicago: University of Chicago Press, 1975.

Goldschmid, M. L. Different types of conservation and nonconservation and their relation to age, sex, IQ, MA, and vocabulary. *Child Development*, 1967, 38, 1229–1246.

Goldschmid, M. L. The relation of conservation to emotional and environmental aspects of development. *Child Development*, 1968, 39, 579–589. (a)

Goldschmid, M. L. Role of experience in the acquisition of conservation. *Proceedings of the 76th Annual Convention of the American Psychological Association*, 1968, 3, 361–362. (b)

Goldschmid, M. L., & Bentler, P. M. The dimensions and measurement of conservation. *Child Development*, 1968, 39, 787–802.

Goodman, K. S. Reading: A psycholinguistic guessing game. In H. Singer & R. B. Ruddell (Eds.), *Theoretical models and processes of reading* (2nd ed.). Newark, Del.: International Reading Association, 1976.

Goodnow, J. J. A test of milieu differences with some of Piaget's tasks. *Psychological Monographs*, 1962, 76 (36).

Goodnow, J. J., & Bethon, G. Piaget's tasks: The effect of schooling and intelligence. *Child Development*, 1966, 37, 573–582.

Gréco, P., Inhelder, B., Matalon, B., & Piaget, J. La formation des raisonnements récurrentiels. In P. Gréco, B. Inhelder, B. Matalon, & J. Piaget (Eds.), *Etudes* d'épistémologie génétique (Vol. 17). Paris: Presses Universitaires de France, 1963.

Gruen, G. Experiences affecting the development of number concepts in children. Child Development, 1965, 36, 963–979.

Guilford, J. P. The nature of human intelligence. New York: McGraw-Hill, 1967.

Halford, G., & Fullerton, T. A discrimination task which induces conservation of number. Child Development, 1970, 41, 205–213.

Hall, E. A conversation with Jean Piaget and Bärbel Inhelder. Psychology Today, 1970, 3, 25–32; 54–56.

Hammill, D. Training visual perceptual processes. Journal of Learning Disabilities, 1972, 5, 552–562.

Hatwell, Y. Privation sensorielle et intelligence. Paris: Presses Universitaires de France, 1966.

Henderson, E. H. Do we apply what we know about comprehension? In N. B. Smith (Ed.), Current issues in reading. Newark, Del.: International Reading Association, 1969.

Henriques-Christofides, A., & Moreau, A. Quelques données nouvelles sur les opérations combinatoires et la pensée formelle. Cahiers de Psychologie, 1974, 17, 55–64.

Heron, A. Concrete operations, 'g' and achievement in Zambian children: A non-verbal approach. Journal of Cross-Cultural Psychology, 1971, 2, 325–336.

Hood, H. An experimental study of Piaget's theory of development of numbers in children. British Journal of Psychology, 1962, 32, 300–303.

Howell, R. W. Evaluation of cognitive abilities of emotionally disturbed children: An application of Piaget's theories. Dissertation Abstracts International, 1972, 32(9-A), 5027–5033.

Iano, R. Learning deficiency versus developmental conceptions of mental retardation. Exceptional Children, 1971, 38, 301–311.

Inhelder, B. Cognitive development and its contribution to the diagnosis of some phenomena of mental deficiency. Merrill-Palmer Quarterly, 1966, 12, 299–321.

Inhelder, B. The diagnosis of reasoning in the mentally retarded. New York: Day, 1968. (Original French: Le diagnostic du raisonnement chez les débiles mentaux. Thesis, University of Geneva, 1943.)

Inhelder, B. Memory and intelligence in the child. In D. Elkind & J. Flavell (Eds.), Studies in cognitive development. New York: Oxford University Press, 1969.

Inhelder, B. Dies academicus. University of Geneva, 1975, 103–110.

Inhelder, B. Foreword. In S. Modgil & C. Modgil (Eds.), Piagetian research: Compilation and commentary (Vol. 1). Windsor, U.K.: NEER Publishing Company, 1976. (a)

Inhelder, B. Introduction. In B. Inhelder & H. H. Chipman (Eds.), Piaget and his school: A reader in developmental psychology. New York: Springer-Verlag, 1976. (b)

Inhelder, B. Memory and intelligence. In B. Inhelder & H. H. Chipman (Eds.), Piaget and his school: A reader in developmental psychology. New York: Springer-Verlag, 1976. (c)

Inhelder, B. The sensorimotor origins of knowledge. In B. Inhelder & H. H. Chipman (Eds.), Piaget and his school: A reader in developmental psychology. New York: Springer-Verlag, 1976. (d)

Inhelder, B. Genetic epistemology and developmental psychology. In R. W. Rieber & K. Salzinger (Eds.), The roots of American psychology: Historical influences and implications for the future. Annals of the New York Academy of Sciences, 1977, 291, 332–341.

Inhelder, B., Ackermann-Valladao, E., Blanchet, A., Karmiloff-Smith, A., Kilcher-Hagerdorn, H., Montangero, J., & Robert, M. Des structures cognitives aux procédures de découverte: Esquisse de recherches en cours. *Archives de Psychologie,* 1976, *44,* 57-72.

Inhelder, B., Blanchet, A., Sinclair, H., & Piaget, J. Relations entre les conservations d'ensembles d'éléments discrets et celles de quantités continues. *Année Psychologique,* 1975, *75,* 23-60.

Inhelder, B., Bovet, M., & Sinclair, H. Developpement et apprentissage. *Revue Suisse de Psychologie Pure et Appliquée,* 1967, *26,* 1-23.

Inhelder, B., & Chipman, H. H. (Eds.). *Piaget and his school: A reader in developmental psychology.* New York: Springer-Verlag, 1976.

Inhelder, B., & Piaget, J. *The growth of logical thinking from childhood to adolescence.* New York: Basic Books, 1958.

Inhelder, B. & Piaget, J. *The early growth of logic in the child.* London: Routledge & Kegan Paul, 1964.

Inhelder, B., Sinclair, H., & Bovet, M. *Learning and the development of cognition.* Cambridge, Mass.: Harvard University Press, 1974.

Kahn, J. V. Training educable mentally retarded and intellectually average adolescents of low and middle SES for formal thought. *American Journal of Mental Deficiency,* 1974, *79,* 397-403.

Kahn, J. V. Relationship of Piaget's sensorimotor period to language acquisition of profoundly retarded children. *American Journal of Mental Deficiency,* 1975, *79,* 640-643.

Kamara, A., & Easley, J. A. Is the rate of cognitive development uniform across cultures? A methodological critique with new evidence from Themne children. In P. R. Dasen (Ed.), *Piagetian psychology: Cross-cultural contributions.* New York: Gardner, 1977.

Kamii, C. One intelligence indivisible. *Young Children,* 1975, *30,* 228-238.

Kamii, C., & Derman, L. Comments on Engelmann's paper. In D. Green, M. Ford, & G. Flamer (Eds.), *Measurement and Piaget.* New York: McGraw-Hill, 1971.

Kamii, C., & DeVries, R. Piaget for early education. In M. C. Day & R. K. Parker (Eds.), *Preschool in action* (2nd ed.). Boston: Allyn & Bacon, 1977.

Karmiloff-Smith, A., & Inhelder, B. If you want to get ahead, get a theory. *Cognition,* 1975, *3,* 195-212.

Kephart, N. C. *The slow learner in the classroom* (2nd ed.). Columbus, Ohio: Merrill, 1971.

Kershner, J. R. Visual-spatial organization and reading: Support for a cognitive developmental interpretation. *Journal of Learning Disabilities,* 1975, *8,* 30-36.

Kingsley, R., & Hall, V. Training conservation through the use of learning sets. *Child Development,* 1967, *38,* 1111-1126.

Klees, M., & Lebrun, A. Analysis of the figurative and operative processes of thought of 40 dyslexic children. *Journal of Learning Disabilities,* 1972, *5,* 14-21.

Knight-Arest, I., & Reid, D. K. *Peer interaction as a catalyst for conservation acquisition in normal and learning-disabled children.* Paper presented at the 8th Annual Symposium of the Jean Piaget Society, Philadelphia, May 1978.

Knoblock, P. Open education for emotionally disturbed children. *Exceptional Children,* 1973, *39,* 358-365.

Kohlberg, L. Early education: A cognitive-developmental view. *Child Development,* 1968, *39,* 1013-1062.

Kuhn, D. Mechanisms of change in the development of cognitive structures. *Child Development,* 1972, *43,* 833-844.

Kuhn, D. Inducing development experimentally: Comments on a research paradigm. *Developmental Psychology,* 1974, *10,* 590-600.

Lathey, J. Training effects and conservation of volume. *Child Study Center Bulletin,* 1968, *4,* 92-100.

Lemos, M. de, Conceptual development in aboriginal children: Implication for aboriginal education. In S. S. Dunn & C. M. Taty (Eds.), *Aborigines and education.* Melbourne: Sun Books, 1969.

Liben, L. S. The facilitation of long-term memory improvement and operative development. *Developmental Psychology,* 1977, *13,* 501–508. (a)

Liben, L. S. Memory from a cognitive-developmental perspective: A theoretical and empirical review. In W. Overton & J. M. Gallagher (Eds.), *Knowledge and development. Vol. 1: Advances in research and theory.* New York: Plenum, 1977. (b)

Lister, C. The development of a concept of volume conservation in ESN children. *British Journal of Educational Psychology,* 1970, *40,* 55–64.

Lovell, K. Some recent studies in cognitive and language development. *Merrill-Palmer Quarterly,* 1968, *14,* 123–138.

Mahaney, E. J., & Stephens, B. Two-year gains in moral judgment by retarded and nonretarded persons. *American Journal of Mental Deficiency,* 1974, *79,* 134–141.

Marchi, J. Y. Comparison of selected Piagetian tasks with the WISC measures of mental retardation. *Dissertation Abstracts,* 1971, *31,* 6442-A.

McManis, D. L. Conservation of mass, weight, and volume by normal and retarded children. *American Journal of Mental Deficiency,* 1969, *73,* 762–767.

Mermelstein, E., & Meyer, E. Conservation-training techniques and their effects on different populations. *Child Development,* 1969, *40,* 471–490.

Mermelstein, E., & Shulman, L. S. Lack of formal schooling and the acquisition of conservation. *Child Development,* 1967, *38,* 39–52.

Miller, C. K. Conservation in blind children. *Education of the Visually Handicapped,* 1969, *1,* 101–105.

Miller, C. K., Zumoff, J., & Stephens, B. A comparison of reasoning skills and moral judgments in delinquent, retarded, and normal adolescent girls. *Journal of Psychology,* 1974, *86,* 261–268.

Miller, S. A., & Brownell, C. A. *Peers, persuasion, and Piaget: Dyadic interaction between conservers and nonconservers,* Report No. 44, Developmental Program, Department of Psychology, University of Michigan, April 1974.

Mohseni, N. *La comparaison des réactions aux épreuves d'intelligence en Iran et en Europe.* Thesis, University of Paris, 1966.

Moore, G., & Stephens, B. Two-year gains in moral conduct by retarded and nonretarded persons. *American Journal of Mental Deficiency,* 1974, *79,* 147–153.

Moursund, J. P. *Learning and the learner.* Monterey, Calif.: Brooks/Cole, 1976.

Mugny, G., Doise, W., & Perret-Clermont, A. N. Conflict de centrations et progrès cognitif. *Bulletin de Psychologie,* 1976, *29,* 199–204.

Murray, F. B. Cognitive conflict and reversibility training in the acquisition of length conservation. *Journal of Educational Psychology,* 1968, *59,* 82–87.

Murray, F. B. Acquisition of conservation through social interaction. *Developmental Psychology.* 1972, *6,* 1–6.

Murray, F. B., Ames, G. J., & Botvin, G. J. Acquisition of conservation through cognitive dissonance. *Journal of Educational Psychology,* 1977, *69,* 519–527.

National Advisory Committee on Handicapped Children. *Special education for handicapped children* (First annual report). Washington, D.C.: U.S. Department of Health, Education and Welfare, January 31, 1968.

Neale, T. M. Egocentrism in institutionalized and non-institutionalized children. *Child Development,* 1966, *37,* 97–101.

Neimark, E. Intellectual development during adolescence. In E. D. Horowitz (Ed.), *Review of child development research* (Vol. 4). Chicago: University of Chicago Press, 1975.

Nicolich, L. M. Beyond sensorimotor intelligence: Assessment of symbolic maturity through analysis of pretend play. *Merrill-Palmer Quarterly*, 1977, *23*, 39–99.

Oléron, P. *Recherches sur le développement mental des sourds-muets*. Paris: Centre National de la Recherche Scientifique, 1956.

Oléron, P., & Herren, H. L'acquisition des conservations et le langage. *Enfance*, 1961, *14*, 201–219.

Overton, W. General systems, structure and development. In K. F. Riegel & G. C. Rosenwald (Eds.), *Structure and transformation: Development and historical aspects*. New York: Wiley, 1975.

Papalia, D. E. The status of several conservation abilities across the life span. *Human Development*, 1972, *15*, 229–243.

Papert, S. Theory of knowledge and complexity. In G. J. Delenoort (Ed.), *Process models for psychology*. Rotterdam: Rotterdam University Press, 1973.

Pascual-Leone, J. On learning and development, Piagetian style: A reply to Lefebvre-Pinard. *Canadian Psychological Review*, 1976, *17*, 270.

Pascual-Leone, J., Goodman, D., Ammon, P., & Subelman, I. Piagetian theory and neo-Piagetian analysis as psychological guides in education. In J. M. Gallagher & J. A. Easley (Eds.), *Knowledge and development. Vol. 2: Piaget and education*. New York: Plenum, 1978.

Peill, E. J. *Invention and discovery of reality*. New York: Wiley, 1975.

Perret-Clermont, A. N. *L'interaction sociale comme facteur du développement cognitif*. Thesis, University of Geneva, 1976.

Piaget, J. *The child's conception of physical causality*. London: Kegan Paul, 1930. (Original French edition, 1927.)

Piaget, J. *Plays, dreams, and imitation in childhood*. New York: Norton, 1951. (Original French edition, 1945.)

Piaget, J. Autobiography. In E. G. Boring, N. S. Langfeld, H. Werner, & R. M. Yerkes (Eds.), *History of psychology in autobiography* (Vol. 4). Worcester, Mass.: Clark University Press, 1952. (a)

Piaget, J. *The origins of intelligence in children*. New York: International Universities Press, 1952. (Original French edition, 1936.) (b)

Piaget, J. *Logic and psychology*. Manchester, U.K.: Manchester University Press, 1953.

Piaget, J. *The construction of reality in the child*. New York: Basic Books, 1954. (Original French edition, 1937.)

Piaget, J. Logique et équilibre dans les comportements du sujet. In L. Apostel, B. Mandelbrot, & J. Piaget (Eds.), *Etudes d'épistemologie génétique. Vol. 2: Logique et équilibre*. Paris: Presses Universitaires de France, 1957.

Piaget, J. Apprentissage et connaissance (Pt. 1). In P. Gréco & J. Piaget (Eds.), *Etudes d'épistémologie génétique. Vol. 7: Apprentissage et connaissance*. Paris: Presses Universitaires de France, 1959.

Piaget, J. *Etudes sociologiques*. Geneva: Droz, 1965.

Piaget, J. Nécessité et signification des recherches comparatives en psychologie génétique. *International Journal of Psychology*, 1966, *1*, 3–13.

Piaget, J. Language and thought from the genetic point of view. In J. Piaget, *Six psychological studies*. New York: Random House, 1967.

Piaget, J. *On the development of memory and identity*. Barre, Mass.: Barre, 1968.

Piaget, J. *The mechanisms of perception*. London: Routledge & Kegan Paul, 1969. (Original French edition, 1961.)

Piaget, J. *Genetic epistemology*. New York: Columbia University Press, 1970. (a)

Piaget, J. Piaget's theory. In P. H. Mussen (Ed.), *Carmichael's manual of child psychology* (Vol. 1). New York: Wiley, 1970. (b)

Piaget, J. *Science of education and the psychology of the child*. New York: Orion, 1970. (First part originally published, 1935; in its entirety, 1969.) (c)

Piaget, J. *Structuralism*. New York: Basic Books, 1970. (d)

Piaget, J. *The child's conception of movement and speed.* New York: Basic Books, 1970. (Original French edition, 1946.) (e)

Piaget, J. *Biology and knowledge.* Chicago: University of Chicago Press, 1971. (Original French edition, 1967.) (a)

Piaget, J. *Insights and illusions of philosophy.* New York: World Publishing, 1971. (Original French edition, 1965.) (b)

Piaget, J. *Psychology and epistemology.* New York: Grossman, 1971. (Original French edition, 1957.) (c)

Piaget, J. The theory of stages in cognitive development. In D. R. Green, M. P. Ford, & G. B. Flamer (Eds.), *Measurement and Piaget.* New York: McGraw-Hill, 1971. (d)

Piaget, J. Intellectual evolution from adolescence to adulthood. *Human Development,* 1972, 15, 1–12. (a)

Piaget, J. *The principles of genetic epistemology.* New York: Basic Books, 1972. (b)

Piaget, J. Some aspects of operations. In M. W. Piers (Ed.), *Play and development.* New York: Norton, 1972. (c)

Piaget, J. A structural foundation for tomorrow's education. *Prospects,* 1972, 2, 12–27. (d)

Piaget, J. *Main trends in psychology.* London: Allen & Unwin, 1973. (a)

Piaget, J. *To understand is to invent: The future of education.* New York: Grossman, 1973. (b)

Piaget, J. *Adaptation vitale et psychologie de l'intelligence: Sélection organique et phénocopie.* Paris: Hermann, 1974. (a)

Piaget, J. *Recherches sur la contradiction. 1: Les differentes formes de la contradiction. Etudes d'épistémologie génétique* (Vol. 31). Paris: Presses Universitaires de France, 1974. (b)

Piaget, J. *Recherches sur la contradiction. 2: Les relations entre affirmations et négations. Etudes d'épistémologie génétique.* (Vol. 32). Paris: Presses Universitaires de France, 1974. (c)

Piaget, J. Autobiography (1950–1966). In S. Campbell (Ed.), *A Piaget sampler.* New York: Macmillan, 1976. (Original French edition, 1966). (a)

Piaget, J. *The grasp of consciousness: Action and concept in the young child.* Cambridge, Mass.: Harvard University Press, 1976. (b)

Piaget, J. The possible, the impossible, and the necessary. *The Genetic Epistemologist: Quarterly Newsletter of The Jean Piaget Society,* 1976, 6, 1–12. (c)

Piaget, J. Chance and dialectic in biological epistemology: A critical analysis of Jacques Monod's theses. In W. Overton & J. M. Gallagher (Eds.), *Knowledge and development. Vol. 1: Advances in research and theory.* New York: Plenum, 1977. (a)

Piaget, J. *The development of thought: Equilibrium of cognitive structures.* New York: Viking Penguin, 1977. (Original French edition, 1975.) (b)

Piaget, J. Phenocopy in biology and the psychological development of knowledge. In H. W. Gruber & J. J. Voneche (Eds.), *The essential Piaget.* New York: Basic Books, 1977. (c)

Piaget, J. Problems of equilibration. In M. H. Appel & L. S. Goldberg (Eds.), *Topics in cognitive development. Vol. 1: Equilibration: Theory, research, and application.* New York: Plenum, 1977. (Originally published, 1972.) (d)

Piaget, J. *Recherche sur l'abstraction réfléchissante. 1. L'abstraction des relations logico-arithmetiques. Etudes d'épistémologie génétique* (Vol. 34). Paris: Presses Universitaires de France, 1977. (e)

Piaget, J. The role of action in the development of thinking. In W. Overton & J. M. Gallagher (Eds.), *Knowledge and development. Vol. 1: Advances in research and theory.* New York: Plenum, 1977. (f)

Piaget, J. Some recent research and its link with a new theory of groupings and conservations based on commutability. In R. W. Rieber & K. Salzinger (Eds.), *The roots of American psychology: Historical influences and implications for the future. Annals of the New York Academy of Sciences*, 1977, *291*, 350–357. (g)

Piaget, J. *Behavior and evolution.* New York: Pantheon Books, 1978. (a)

Piaget, J. Correspondences and transformations. In F. B. Murray (Ed.), *Impact of Piaget's theory.* Baltimore: University Park Press, 1978. (b)

Piaget, J. (with G. Henriques). *Recherches sur la généralisation. Etudes d'épistémologie et de psychologie génétiques* (Vol. 36). Paris: Presses Universitaires de France, 1978. (c)

Piaget, J. *Success and understanding.* Cambridge, Mass.: Harvard University Press, 1978. (Original French edition, 1974.) (d)

Piaget, J. *Les morphismes* (in press).

Piaget, J., & Garcia, R. *Understanding causality.* New York: Norton, 1974.

Piaget, J., & Inhelder, B. *The child's conception of space.* New York: Norton, 1967. (Original French edition, 1948.)

Piaget, J., & Inhelder, B. *The psychology of the child.* New York: Basic Books, 1969. (Original French edition, 1966.)

Piaget, J., & Inhelder, B. *Mental imagery in the child: A study of the development of imaginal representation.* New York: Basic Books, 1971. (Original French edition, 1966.)

Piaget, J., & Inhelder, B. *Memory and intelligence.* New York: Basic Books, 1973. (Original French edition, 1968.)

Piaget, J., & Inhelder, B. The child's construction of quantities: Conservation and atomism. London: Routledge & Kegan Paul, 1974. (Original French edition: *Le développement des quantités physiques chez l'enfant: Conservation et atomisme.* Neuchâtel: Delachaux et Niestlé, 1942.)

Piaget, J., & Inhelder, B. *The origin of the idea of chance in children.* New York: Norton, 1975. (Original French edition, 1951.)

Piaget, J., & Szeminska, A. The child's conception of number. London: Routledge & Kegan Paul, 1952. (Original French edition, 1941.)

Piaget, J., & Voyat, G. Identité d'un corps en développement. In J. Piaget, J. B. Grize, A. Szeminska, & T. Vinh-Bang (Eds.), *Epistémologie et psychologie de l'identité. Etudes d'épistémologie génétique* (Vol. 24). Paris: Presses Universitaires de France, 1968.

Pinard, A., & Laurendeau, M. "Stage" in Piaget's cognitive developmental theory: Exegesis of a concept. In D. Elkind & J. H. Flavell (Eds.), *Studies in cognitive development.* New York: Oxford University Press, 1969.

Price-Williams, D. R. A study concerning concepts of conservation of quantities among primitive children. *Acta Psychologica*, 1961, *18*, 293–305.

Ranson, J. *Application des épreuves Piaget-Inhelder à un groupe de débilités mentaux.* Lyon: Bosc, 1950.

Rardin, D. R., & Moan, C. E. Peer interaction and cognitive development. *Child Development*, 1971, *42*, 1685–1699.

Reese, H. W., & Schack, M. L. Comment on Brainerd's criteria for cognitive structures. *Psychological Bulletin*, 1974, *81*, 67–69.

Reid, D. K. *The effects of cognitive tempo and the presence of a memory aid on conjunctive concept attainment in educable mentally retarded boys.* Unpublished doctoral dissertation, Temple University, 1974.

Reid, D. K. *Early identification of children with learning disabilities.* New York: Regional Access Project, Region II, New York University, 1977.

Reid, D. K. Genevan theory and the education of exceptional children. In J. M. Gallagher & J. A. Easley (Eds.), *Knowledge and development. Vol. 2: Piaget and education.* New York: Plenum, 1978.

Reid, D. K. Learning and development from a Piagetian perspective: The exceptional child. In I. Sigel, R. M. Golinkoff, & D. Brodzinsky (Eds.), *Piagetian theory and research: New directions and applications.* Hillsdale, N.J.: Erlbaum, in press. (a)

Reid, D. K. Toward an application of developmental epistemology to the education of exceptional children. *Eighth Annual Proceedings of the Conference on Piagetian Theory and the Helping Professions.* Los Angeles: University of Southern California, in press. (b)

Reid, D. K., & Knight-Arest, I. *Cognitive processing in learning disabled and normally achieving children.* Paper presented at the NATO International Conference on Intelligence and Learning, York, England, July 1979.

Reid, D. K., Knight-Arest, I., & Hresko, W. P. Cognitive development in learning disabled children. In J. Gottlieb & S. S. Strichart, (Eds.), *Current research and application in learning disabilities.* Baltimore: University Park Press, in press.

Rosenthal, T. L., & Zimmerman, B. J. Modeling by exemplification and instruction in training conservation. *Developmental Psychology,* 1972, *6,* 392–401.

Rothenburg, B. B., & Orost, J. H. The training of conservation of number in young children. *Child Development,* 1969, *40,* 707–726.

Rubin, A. D. A theoretical taxonomy of the differences between oral and written language. In R. J. Spiro, B. C. Bruce, & W. F. Brewer (Eds.), *Theoretical issues in reading comprehension.* Hillsdale, N.J.: Erlbaum, in press.

Rumelhart, D. E. *Toward an interactive model of reading* (Technical report No. 46). La Jolla, Calif.: Center for Human Information Processing, 1976.

Saarni, C. Cognitive and communicative features of emotional experience—Or do you show what you think you feel? In M. Lewis & L. Rosenblum (Eds.), *Development of affect.* New York: Plenum, in press.

Schmelkin, L., & Reid, D. K. *The effects of verbalization and the presence of a memory aid on conjunctive concept attainment in normal and mentally retarded children* (Final report, Grant G00-75-00359). Washington, D.C.: Bureau of Education of the Handicapped, 1976.

Schmid-Kitsikis, E. *L'examen des opérations de l'intelligence: Psychopathologie de l'enfant.* Neuchâtel: Delachaux et Niestlé, 1969.

Schmid-Kitsikis, E. Exploratory studies in cognitive development. In F. J. Mönks, W. W. Hartup, & J. de Wit (Eds.), *Determinants of behavioral development.* New York: Academic Press, 1972.

Schmid-Kitsikis, E. Piagetian theory and its approach to psychopathology. *American Journal of Mental Deficiency,* 1973, *77,* 694–705.

Schmid-Kitsikis, E. The cognitive mechanisms underlying problem-solving in psychotic and mentally retarded children. In B. Inhelder & H. H. Chipman (Eds.), *Piaget and his school: A reader in developmental psychology.* New York: Springer-Verlag, 1976.

Schmid-Kitsikis, E., & Ajuriaguerra, J. de. Aspects opératoires en psychopathologie infantile. *Revue de Neuropsychiatrie Infantile,* 1973, *21,* 7–21.

Schwebel, M., & Raph, J. (Eds.). *Piaget in the classroom.* New York: Basic Books, 1973.

Sigel, I. E. The Piagetian system and the world of education. In D. Elkind & J. H. Flavell (Eds.), *Studies in cognitive development: Essays in honor of Jean Piaget.* New York: Oxford University Press, 1969.

Sigel, I., Roeper, A., & Hooper, R. A training procedure for Piaget's conservation of quantity: A pilot study and its replication. *British Journal of Educational Psychology,* 1966, *36,* 301–311.

Silverman, I. W., & Geiringer, E. Dyadic interaction and conservation induction: A test of Piaget's equilibration model. *Child Development,* 1973, *44,* 815–820.

Silverman, I. W., & Stone, J. Modifying cognitive functioning through participation in a problem-solving group. *Journal of Educational Psychology,* 1972, 63, 603–608.

Sinclair, H. *Acquisition du langage et développement de la pensée.* Paris: Dunod, 1967. (a)

Sinclair, H. Conduites verbales et deficits operatoires. *Acta Neurologica Psychiatrica Belgica,* 1967, 67, 852–860. (b)

Sinclair, H. Piaget's theory of development: The main stages. In M. F. Rosskopf, L. P. Steffe, & S. Taback (Eds.), *Piagetian cognitive-development research and mathematical education.* Washington, D.C.: National Council of Teachers of Mathematics, 1971. (a)

Sinclair, H. Representation and memory. In M. F. Rosskopf, L. P. Steffe, & S. Taback (Eds.), *Piagetian cognitive-development research and mathematical education.* Washington, D.C.: National Council of Teachers of Mathematics, 1971. (b)

Sinclair, H. Language acquisition and cognitive development. In T. E. Moore (Ed.), *Cognitive development and the acquisition of language.* New York: Academic Press, 1973.

Sinclair, H. Developmental psycholinguistics. In B. Inhelder & H. H. Chipman (Eds.), *Piaget and his school: A reader in developmental psychology.* New York: Springer-Verlag, 1976.

Sinclair, H. Recent developments in genetic epistemology. *The Genetic Epistemologist: Quarterly Newsletter of The Jean Piaget Society,* 1977, 6, 1–3.

Sinclair, H., & Bronckart, J. P. SVO a linguistic universal? A study in developmental psycholinguistics. *Journal of Experimental Child Psychology,* 1972, 14, 329–348.

Skinner, B. F. *Science and human behavior.* New York: Macmillan, 1968.

Smedslund, J. The acquisition of conservation of substance and weight in children. 3: Extinction of conservation of weight acquired "normally" and by means of empirical controls on a balance. *Scandinavian Journal of Psychology,* 1961, 2, 85–87. (a)

Smedslund, J. The acquisition of substance and weight in children. 5: Practice in conflict situations without reinforcement. *Scandinavian Journal of Psychology,* 1961, 2, 156–160. (b)

Smedslund, J. The acquisition of conservation of substance and weight in children. 5: Practice in conflict situations without reinforcement. *Scandinavian Journal of Psychology,* 1961, 2, 156–160. (b)

Smith, F. *Comprehension and learning: A conceptual framework for teachers.* New York: Holt, Rinehart & Winston, 1975.

Smith, F. *Understanding reading: A psycholinguistic analysis of reading and learning to read* (2nd ed.). New York: Holt, Rinehart & Winston, 1978.

Smith, I. The effects of training procedures on the acquisition of conservation of weight. *Child Development,* 1968, 39, 515–526.

Stephens, B. Symposium: Developmental gains in reasoning, moral judgment, and moral conduct of retarded and nonretarded persons. *American Journal of Mental Deficiency,* 1974, 79, 113–115.

Stephens, B. Piagetian theory: Applications for the mentally retarded and the visually handicapped. In J. F. Magary, M. K. Poulsen, P. J. Levinson, & P. A. Taylor (Eds.), *Sixth Annual Proceedings of the Conference on Piagetian Theory and the Helping Professions.* Los Angeles: University of Southern California, 1977.

Stephens, B., & McLaughlin, J. A. Two-year gains in reasoning by retarded and nonretarded persons. *American Journal of Mental Deficiency,* 1974, 79, 116–126.

Strauss, S., & Langer, J. Operational thought inducement. *Child Development,* 1970, *41,* 163–175.

Swize, L. M. The relationship between performance on Piagetian conservation tasks and intelligence and achievement in educable mentally retarded children. *Dissertation Abstracts International,* 1972, *32,* 3806.

Tessier, F. A. The development of young cerebral-palsied children according to Piaget's sensorimotor theory. *Dissertation Abstracts International,* 1970, *20,* 4841.

Tuddenham, R. D. *Psychometricizing Piaget's méthode clinique.* Paper presented at the convention of the American Educational Research Association, Chicago, February 1968.

Tuddenham, R. D. *A "Piagetian" test of cognitive development.* Paper presented at the Symposium on Intelligence, Ontario Institute for Studies in Education, Toronto, May 1969.

Tulving, E., & Donaldson, W. (Eds.). *Organization of memory.* New York: Academic Press, 1972.

Turiel, E. An experimental test of the sequentiality of developmental stages in the child's moral judgments. *Journal of Personality and Social Psychology,* 1966, *3,* 611–618.

Vitello, S. Facilitation of class inclusion among mentally retarded children. *American Journal of Mental Deficiency,* 1973, *78,* 158–162.

Voyat, G. Minimizing the problems of functional illiteracy. *Teachers College Record,* 1970, *72,* 171–186.

Voyat, G. The development of operations: A theoretical and practical matter. In M. Schwebel & J. Raph (Eds.), *Piaget in the classroom.* New York: Basic Books, 1973.

Voyat, G. In tribute to Piaget: A look at his scientific impact in the United States. In R. W. Rieber & K. Salzinger (Eds.), *The roots of American psychology: Historical influences and implications for the future. Annals of the New York Academy of Sciences,* 1977, *291,* 342–349.

Voyat, G. Cognitive and social development: A new perspective. In J. Glick & K. A. Clarke-Stewart (Eds.), *The development of social understanding.* New York: Gardner Press, 1978. (a)

Voyat, G. *Psychosis: A cognitive and psychodynamic perspective.* Paper presented at the 8th Annual Interdisciplinary Conference on Piagetian Theory and the Helping Professions, Los Angeles, February 1978. (b)

Waddell, V. *Some cultural considerations on the development of the concept of conservation.* Unpublished paper presented to a genetic-epistemology seminar, Australian National University, October 1968.

Waddington, C. H. *The nature of life.* London: Allen & Unwin, 1961.

Wallace, G., & Kaufman, J. M. *Teaching children with learning problems* (2nd ed.). Columbus, Ohio: Merrill, 1978.

Wallach, L., & Sprott, R. L. Inducing number conservation in children. *Child Development,* 1964, *35,* 1057–1071.

Wallach, L., Wall, A., & Anderson, L. Number conservation: The roles of reversibility, addition/subtraction, and misleading perceptual cues. *Child Development,* 1967, *38,* 425–442.

Warner, B. J., & Williams, R. Piaget's theory and exceptional children: A bibliography, 1963–1973. *Perceptual and Motor Skills,* 1975, *41,* 255–261.

Wason, P. C. The theory of formal operations: A critique. In B. A. Geber (Ed.), *Piaget and knowing: Studies in genetic epistemology.* London: Routledge & Kegan Paul, 1977.

Webb, R. A. Concrete and formal operations in very bright 6- to 11-year-olds. *Human Development,* 1974, *17,* 292–300.

Weisz, J. R. Studying cognitive development in retarded and nonretarded groups: The role of theory. *American Journal of Mental Deficiency*, 1976, 81, 235-239.

Wermus, H. Les transformations involutives (reciprocités) des propositions logiques. *Archives de Psychologie*, 1972, 162, 153-170.

Wilton, K. M., & Boersma, F. J. Eye movements and conservation development in mildly retarded and nonretarded children. *American Journal of Mental Deficiency*, 1974, 79, 285-291.

Winer, G. Induced set and acquisition of number conservation. *Child Development*, 1968, 39, 195-205.

Woodward, M. The behavior of idiots interpreted by Piaget's theory of sensorimotor development. *British Journal of Psychology*, 1959, 29, 60-71.

Woodward, M. Concepts of number of the mentally retarded subnormal studied by Piaget's method. *Journal of Child Psychology*, 1961, 2, 249-259.

Woodward, M. Concepts of space in the mentally subnormal studied by Piaget's method. *British Journal of Social and Clinical Psychology*, 1962, 1, 25-37.

Zigler, E. Developmental versus difference theories of mental retardation and the problem of motivation. *American Journal of Mental Deficiency*, 1969, 73, 536-556.

Zilkha, P. *Training children to conserve volume: An experimental inducement of development.* Unpublished doctoral dissertation, New York University, April 1976.

Name Index

Subject Index